WOMEN TREATING WOMEN

Case Material From Women Treated by Female Psychoanalysts

WOMEN TREATING WOMEN
Case Material From Women Treated by Female Psychoanalysts

Anne E. Bernstein, M.D.
Gloria Marmar Warner, M.D.

INTERNATIONAL UNIVERSITIES PRESS, INC

New York New York

Library of Congress Cataloging in Publication Data

Bernstein, Anne E.
  Women treating women.

  Bibliography: p.
  Includes index.
  1. Women—Mental health. 2. Women—Psychology.
3. Psychoanalysis. 4. Women psychoanalysts. 5. Psychotherapist and patient.
I. Warner, Gloria Marmar.
II. Title.
RC451.4.W6B47   1984   155.6'33   84-8996
ISBN 0-8236-6863-0

Manufactured in the United States of America

Dedication

For our husbands, Drs. Richard Warner and Richard Bernstein, and for our children, especially Laura, Lynn and Lili, who sensed (or hoped) that we were doing something worthwhile, and who helped each other and the two of us through it.

For all women who work together, to further knowledge about them, and to thus improve their own lives as well as the lives of their sisters and daughters.

Contents

Acknowledgements   xi

Introduction   xiii

CHAPTER 1 A HISTORICAL REVIEW OF FEMALE
            PSYCHOLOGY   1
    Freudian Theory   1
        Summary of Freud's Theories of Feminine
        Psychology   7
    Contributions of Freud's Female Contemporaries[1]   8
        Helene Deutsch   8
        Marie Bonaparte   10
        Karen Horney   11
        Ernest Jones   13
        Clara Thompson   13
        Melanie Klein   14
    Later Contributions from Psychoanalysis   15
        Phyllis Greenacre   16
        Judith Kestenberg   19
        Margaret Mahler   22
        Edith Jacobson   24

CHAPTER 2 CONTEMPORARY CONTRIBUTIONS FROM
            DIRECT OBSERVATION AND RESEARCH   27
    Adult Studies   27
        Alfred Kinsey   27
        William Masters and Virginia Johnson   27
        Mary Jane Sherfey   29
    Child Studies   29
        Eleanor Galenson and Herman Roiphe   30
        Henri Parens   32

[1]One male contemporary is also included for his contributions to the psychology
of women.

Robert Stoller   33
John Money and Anke Erhardt   34
James Kleeman   36
Other Stages of Development Pivotal to Female
    Psychology   39
    Latency: Virginia Clower, Harold Blum   39
    Adolescence: Samuel Ritvo   41

CHAPTER 3 METAPSYCHOLOGICAL
           CONSIDERATIONS TOWARD A NEW THEORY
           OF FEMALE PSYCHOLOGY   45
    Roy Schafer   45
    Laila Karme   49
    Summary and Conclusions   50

CHAPTER 4 WHAT DOES A WOMAN WANT?
           PREOEDIPAL CONSIDERATIONS   53
    Fantasy of the Phallic Mother   55
    Fantasy of the Illusory Phallus   57
    Fantasy of the Vagina Dentata   62
    Fantasy of Maternalization of the Father   65
    Castration Anxiety Related to Fear of Maternal
        Loss   70
    Penis Envy in Preoedipal Fear of Maternal Loss   73

CHAPTER 5 WHAT DOES A WOMAN WANT? OEDIPAL
           CONSIDERATIONS   79
    The Crossroads of Separation-Individuation   79
    Deformation of the Oedipal Complex   80
        Vagueness of Female Genitalia   80
        Severe Trauma   82
        Separation from the Mother   88
        Physical Illness or Disability   94
        The Wish for a Baby   96

CHAPTER 6 WHAT DOES A WOMAN WANT?
           POSTOEDIPAL CONSIDERATIONS   109
    Latency   109
    Adolescence   111
        Pathology of Adolescence   114

Special Postoedipal Issues   116
    Masturbation   116
    Menstruation   136

CHAPTER 7 WHAT DOES A WOMAN WANT? OTHER
UNIQUE OPPORTUNITIES FOR WOMEN TO
REWORK SEPARATION-INDIVIDUATION AND
THE OEDIPAL CONFLICT   143
Pregnancy   143
Motherhood   147
Abortion   152
Stillbirth   155
Menopause   156
Grandmotherhood   158

CHAPTER 8 MUTILATING EXPERIENCES UNIQUE TO
WOMEN   161
Mastectomy   161
Hysterectomy   165

CHAPTER 9 THE PSYCHIC STRUCTURE OF WOMEN   171
The Superego   171
The Ego Ideal   173
Masochism   175
Narcissism   177
The Ego   178
The Symptom-Free Successful Woman   179

CHAPTER 10 TREATMENT OF WOMEN BY WOMEN   181
Problems of Therapist Gender   181
    The Male Analyst   181
    The Female Analyst   183
Case Studies   186
    Case   1: A Woman with Hypochondriasis,
               Depression, Paranoia and Severe
               Penis Envy   186
    Case   2: A Young Woman with Homosexual
               Behavior   196
    Case   3: Misdiagnosis of a Young Woman
               who Appeared Helpless, Depressed
               and Suicidal   204

Case 4: A Woman with a Real Physical
         Disability   212
Case 5: A Male Analyst, Female Supervisory
         Assistance and a Patient with Severe
         Early Trauma and Loss   223
Case 6: Death of the Mother and the Wish
         for a Baby as a Replacement   232
Case 7: Sexual Promiscuity as a Result of the
         Repeated Witnessing of Parental
         Intercourse   238
Case 8: A Patient Whose Father was her
         Maternal Object   250
Case 9: Anorexia Nervosa as a Result of
         Maternal Invasiveness   263
Case 10: The Search for a Baby in an
         Adolescent Girl With a History of
         Maternal Abandonment and Paternal
         Seduction   269

Glossary   277
References   293
Name Index   301
Subject Index   303

ACKNOWLEDGEMENTS

Dr. Gloria Warner and I received the editorial corrections to our rough draft of the manuscript, that has become this book, shortly before her hospitalization for cancer surgery. We worked together through the horrors of her chemotherapy. She so desperately wanted to see "her book" published.

In the aftermath of her untimely death in November of 1983, our families mourned together. I didn't think that I would be capable of further work on the page proofs of the book. I had promised her months before that "Where I go now, I go for us both." Two dear friends came forward volunteering their own time and experience. They are Dr. Susan Commanday, Professor at Rockland Community College, and Dr. Jack Hawkins, President of the Emory Psychoanalytic Alumni Association. Dr. Gloria was a giver all her life she would have expected no less of her friends. I am deeply grateful that these two people joined hands with me and refused to let me falter, or fail to fulfill her dream.

Anne E. Bernstein, M.D.

Introduction

More women than men seek psychoanalysis or psychoan-alytically-oriented psychotherapy. Although many are re-lieved of symptoms and find their lives much improved, others still have residual problems that are unsolved. It is the contention of the authors that the latter is often a result of the traditional theoretical orientation of the analyst about female psychology. The contributions of Freud and many later thinkers are critically reviewed, and a new theory pro-posed that is not incompatible with the body of psychoan-alytic theory. Case material is presented to validate the authors' assumption and to confirm that their theoretical orientation results in a better treatment outcome.

Women, in all walks of life, are no longer willing to accept that their anatomy makes their destiny. They seek answers to why they are considered second-class citizens, or why, if they "make it" in a man's world, it is such an uphill struggle. They are bitter about formulations concern-ing penis envy, inevitable masochism, narcissism, cognitive inferiority and emotionality that allegedly interferes with objective judgment.

The authors show that women are indeed different from men, and that these differences are caused by the varied relationships between the infant girl and her mother.

The major trauma for infants of both sexes is the in-evitable separation from the all-caring, all-protective mother. For girls, this is even more difficult because they have been held physically closer from infancy. In addition to this loss comes the realization that boys have a visible portion of anatomy that girls lack. Boys turn to their penises for pleas-ure and comfort and to maintain a tie to mother. This protects them against depression, unlike girl children who tend to turn inwards to a fantasy life for solace. How serious this depression will be depends on the relationship of the girl child to both parents. In short, the problems of women cannot be solved by providing them with penises, but by understanding and changing the patterns of parenting.

For a long time after Freud's discovery of infantile sexuality, women conceded to the Freudian view, which focused predominantly on the importance of the absence of a phallus for the psychology and sexuality of women. Since then, many authors have expanded and changed Freud's views. But it is only recently that militant feminists have fought against male chauvinism and even questioned the necessity of motherhood, which they now see as a handicap. The authors think that women do not have to shrink or fight, but that they have a viable alternative in the ways in which they raise their young.

We will begin by discussing the contributions of psychoanalysts. We have made this choice because we feel that only these authors have studied females in depth and over an extended period, thus obtaining data that can be compared to our own.

Although we cover all aspects of female development, our primary focus is the overriding importance of the relationship of the preoedipal daughter to her mother, which we feel shapes the future of the daughter's self-image, sexuality and oedipal complex. With this as our basis, we explore the transference and countertransference implications of women treating women. Included here are issues of separation-individuation of the female child from her mother, the double loss of mother and the simultaneous recognition of the absence of a phallus, as well as the universal depression of young girls. In addition, we present a related discussion of the many fantasies that develop in women, like masturbatory fantasies and those of the illusory phallus and the phallic mother.

We also examine the ubiquitous presence of castration anxiety in both girls and women and its importance in relation to the early mother-child relationship. This relationship determines the mode of entry of a female into the oedipal complex, which need *not* be via the discovery of the anatomical difference between the sexes. Rather, it may be related to a primary identification with the mother (e.g., the wish for a baby), or be a way of reuniting the intrapsychic representation of the self and that of the longed-for and only partially separated mother.

The impetus for writing this book has occurred within the current sociocultural climate wherein increasing numbers of women are now seeking treatment by women.

CHAPTER 1

A Historical Review of Female Psychology

FREUDIAN THEORY

Sigmund Freud was born in Freibourg (then part of the Austro-Hungarian Empire) in 1856. As a physician, his initial interest was in the treatment of neurological disorders of organic origin. Later he began to treat "hysterical" patients, mostly female, who exhibited bizarre symptomatology that could not be understood in terms of known neurological pathways. However, they did respond to hypnosis, and through it symptom removal could be effected.

Freud initially used hypnosis with his patients lying on a couch and soon discovered that they would often fall into a trance-like state. Many spoke freely and resisted his attempts to interrupt them. They revealed personal thoughts of a most initimate nature, which they clearly would not have done (even if they could) in their normal state of consciousness. Freud found that the opportunity to verbalize their worry, shame, guilt and nervousness often brought symptom relief, a process later referred to as the "cathartic method." The first case histories are contained in the monograph *Studies in Hysteria* (Breuer and Freud, 1892).

Freud continued to treat patients, asking questions or giving explanations that helped them to make the connection

1

between their troubled thoughts and feelings and the symbolic representation in symptoms. In particular, many of his patients told him stories of childhood sexual experiences and seductions, which he at first took literally. He later realized that these were fantasies, and began to evolve his theory that all symptoms represent the conflict between forbidden wishes and the defenses against their expression.

From the psychoanalysis of adult patients and supervision of the treatment of a phobia in a young child (Freud, 1909), Freud (1905a, 1905b) formulated his then revolutionary theory of infantile sexuality. It said that human beings are sexual creatures from the earliest moments of life and that sexual drives, which center around the body's mucocutaneous junctions and proceed from one primary zone to the next, require discharge. In brief, the oral phase of development occupies the first year of life, when the mouth is the leading zone and sucking is the earliest sexual manifestation. The anal zone is the target of sexualization during the second year of life, at which time sexual excitation focuses on the activities of withholding and letting go of feces, and the third erotogenic zone is the phallus in boys and the clitoris in girls occurring during the third year of life. Freud further believed that the oedipal conflict coincided with this stage in development.

In addition, Freud (1923a, 1924, 1925a) hypothesized that for the female the clitoris was equivalent to a little penis. He noted that the vagina, which he thought was not easily available for inspection, was unknown to the small female child. Therefore, sexuality for both sexes was essentially phallic (Freud, 1905a).

Later Freud (1925b) postulated that the oedipal conflict was intimately related to the discovery of the anatomical difference between the sexes. The little boy, in love with his mother and seeing his father as a rival, developed a fantasy that if a human being was without a penis, he could also lose his. Thus, the fear of castration led to his giving up his mother as a sexual love object and to an identification with his father. The little girl, upon discovering her "inferior genital organ," would invariably experience envy of the penis. She would blame her mother for her castrated state and would angrily reject her. She would thus turn to her father with the fantasy of obtaining his penis and then, of having his baby. Therefore, in the little girl the discovery of the anatomical difference between the sexes would usher in the beginning of the oedipal conflict. Other outcomes, Freud noted, were that the little girl, feeling inadequate, might identify with her father. This would lead to her adoption of his characteristics, namely his masculine aspirations and intellectual abilities, in order to repair her own sense of bodily damage. She might even take his sexual preference, thus becoming homosexual (Freud, 1924).

Freud (1912a) stressed that the female child must change the sex of her object choice, give up masturbation with her inferior organ (clitoris), and eventually shift her erotic interest to her vagina as the primary organ of pleasure and gratification. Later, in puberty and adulthood, the normal female would develop the capacity for vaginal (female) as opposed to clitoral (male) orgasm.

Freud thought that the female child lost interest in masturbation because of the following sequence of events: (1) observation of the anatomical difference between the sexes, (2) castration anxiety, (3) penis envy, and (4) renunciation of pleasure in clitoral stimulation (masculine phallic sexuality) accompanied by feelings of inferiority (Freud, 1925b, 1931, 1933a, 1940). He stated that the operation of the oedipus complex was secondary and that the castration complex preceded it. His formulation for male children was quite the opposite. He said that the boy's oedipal complex was squelched by his observation of the anatomical difference between the sexes and the resultant castration anxiety.

Freud's (1924) formulation about the oedipus complex in girls was that it was simpler than in boys. It consisted only of the fantasied taking of the mother's place and the adoption of the feminine attitude toward the father. He argued that the little girl must suppress her aggressiveness (1933a) and become "passive" and "masochistic." She would then develop secondary narcissistic maneuvers, such as genital exhibitionism (symbolic), shown in dressing up in pretty clothes and jewelry. She also would be committed to reproduction rather than to other social options.

Freud's (1923b) formulation of the vicissitudes of early female development had major consequences for his model of the mind, which was composed of three agencies. The first, the id, was said to be the repository of instinctual demands; the second, the ego, was posited to be a very complex administrative structure mediating between instinctual demands, conflicts and the real world; and the third which he called the superego (or conscience) was seen as the repository for morality and ethical standards. Freud regarded the major motivation for superego formation as castration anxiety. In his view the little girl already was castrated (1925b). She lacked the necessary castration anxiety for formation of a superego which would be autonomous, impersonal and independent of emotion. He stated that women, therefore, have less of a sense of justice than men, are less ready to submit to the necessary deprivations of life, and are influenced in their judgment by their emotions (Freud, 1923b).

Within the ego, Freud (1923b, 1926a) postulated a substructure called the ego ideal, which is what the self would like to be and what the parents wish the child to be. It is also composed of good partial images of parents and other early objects. Since Freud envisioned the little girl as angrily rejecting her mother for not providing her with a penis, he reasoned that she would not incorporate anything positive about her mother into her ego ideal. This, of course, implies an incomplete ego ideal.

In the course of treating patients, Freud (1920b) further became aware of a very intense relationship that they tended to develop towards him. This relationship (transference) he learned, was a repetition of the patient's infantile relationships with his or her parents. Psychoanalytic treatment depends on the development, exploration and analysis of the transference in terms of its genetic roots. In his treatment of women, Freud was primarily aware of their transference to him as the oedipal father.

Freud (1915) defined countertransference as the unconscious response of the analyst to the patient's material, based on the analyst's own unresolved infantile problems. In this regard, we suspect that because of Freud's own unresolved problems in his early relationship to his mother, he failed to observe or analyze the maternal transferences of his female patients. Thus, he could not reconstruct the preoedipal influences on later psychic development of his female patients. We know that Freud alternately defended against and enacted his maternal countertransference feelings. It is well known, for example, that it was not unusual for him to give food to his patients. Moreover, that he continued to smoke even after developing cancer of the mouth, points to some problem in early oral gratification. It is no surprise that Freud did not analyze his own preoedipal configuration since this requires the development of a deep transference neurosis, with the exploration of dependent oral fantasies in the presence of a benign analyst.

Freud's analysis of his oedipal conflict was conducted via his transference relationships with men to whom he wrote and with whom he tried to collaborate. Those women, such as Helene Deutsch and Marie Bonaparte, who were his colleagues, resembled his picture of women as identified with their fathers. It is likely that his heavy emphasis on the oedipal conflict and penis envy, to the exclusion of preoedipal transferences, similarly defended him against the awareness of his female and maternal identifications.

Freud treated many women, and although he was privy to intimate fantasies and details of their sexual lives, they remained a mystery to him. He said, ''We know less about the sexual life of little girls than of boys. But we need not feel ashamed of this distinction; after all, the sexual life of adult women is a 'dark continent' for psychology'' (Freud, 1925b, p. 243).

Yet, he worked well with women and shared the process of theory-building with several female contemporaries as well as with his daughter. He asked Marie Bonaparte, ''What does a woman want?'' However, he was certain that penis envy was the bedrock of female sexuality (Freud, 1937). Freud (1920a) did touch on the long pregenital connectedness between mother and daughter, but did not see it as being pivotal to the female's psychological development.

Freud also neglected the primary femininity arising out of the girl's early identification with her mother. He did not recognize that there are several entrances to the oedipal conflict for both boys and girls. Despite his belief in the multifactorial determination of all fantasies and conflicts, he failed to explore why penis envy should have such a decisive influence on women's psychological development or why it should cause profound narcissistic injury.

In short, there are many areas of feminine sexuality in Freud's writings that are incomplete or even erroneous: He postulated a basic human bisexuality (1905a) despite the fact that he ignored the feminine side of his own nature; he was unaware of the existence of a variety of masturbatory activities in little girls; he did not know about the differences in the ways mothers nurture and relate to their sons and to their daughters; he wrote about homosexuality in women, but only as a manifestation of their identification with their fathers; he did not connect female homosexuality with chil-drearing in the preoedipal years or the yearning for the preoedipal mother. But, if Freud was wrong about the psy-chology of women, totally or in part, he at the very least furnished a conceptual model to be built upon and chal-lenged. In fact, Freud was more generous about objections and corrections to his early theories when they were made by women, with whom he was less competitive (e.g., He-lene Deutsch, Marie Bonaparte, Karen Horney and Clara Thompson). He even stated that the definitive work on fe-male sexuality would have to be done by female analysts (1933a).

Summary of Freud's Theories of Feminine Psychology

As a background for the understanding of a contem-porary psychology of women, the keystones of Freud's the-ory of female psychology are as follows: The little girl, like the little boy, has a primary and masculine (phallic) sex-uality, with her clitoris experienced as a small penis. When the little girl discovers the anatomical distinction between the sexes she experiences penis envy and feels inferior. Thus, she gives up masturbation and becomes passive, masochistic, and narcissistic. The little girl blames her mother for her genital inferiority, rejects her and becomes rivalrous with her. She then turns to her father for reparation, and does not introject a positive image of her mother as part of her ego ideal. Because the little girl sees herself as already having been castrated, she has no castration anxiety; thus, she does not form a firm superego. She wishes for her father's penis and as a consolation prize fantasizes having his baby. Therefore, the wish for pregnancy is seen as a derivative of penis envy, rather than as the result of a firm identification with the mother's role as bearer and primary nurturer.

CONTRIBUTIONS OF FREUD'S FEMALE CONTEMPORARIES[1]

Several of Freud's female contemporaries attempted to expand and change Freud's theory of female sexuality.

Helene Deutsch

In several books and papers published between 1925 and 1945, Helene Deutsch carefully framed her modifications of Freud's hypotheses, while providing further evidence confirming aspects of his theory of female psychology (Deutsch, 1925, 1930, 1944, 1945). For example, she postulated a gradual detachment from the mother, rather than a sudden hateful rejection based on penis envy and devaluation of women. She agreed with Freud that masochism, passivity and narcissism are essentially feminine traits, and she thought that female sexuality involves a submissive wish to be raped by the father.

For Deutsch, masochism had another origin as well—she considered it a normal component of motherhood. She felt that masochism in women was not only the norm, but a necessary prerequisite for a healthy, female maternal adaptation. She assumed that a normal woman should be content with a passive, masochistic position, making the distinction that being sexually receptive and maternally nurturant is not the same as being masochistically submissive.

[1] One male contemporary, Ernest Jones, is also included for his contributions to the psychology of women.

However, she also observed that little girls are more intelligent and gregarious and form more internal object relations than little boys of equal age. According to her studies, empathy and intuition were essentially feminine traits, whereas intellectual activity and exploration were regarded as expressions of aggression and, therefore, primarily masculine traits.

She made an immense contribution to psychoanalysis, albeit believing intellectuality and cognition to be masculine traits paid for with the sacrifice of valuable feminine qualities. At the same time, she challenged Freud's ideas that mothers invariably favor sons, and acknowledged that mothers wish to perpetuate themselves and their relationship to their own mothers through their daughters.

In a 1961 panel, Helene Deutsch reported her findings after forty years of the psychoanalytic study of women (Deutsch, 1925, 1930, 1944, 1945, 1960). Her observations (along with later ones of Therese Benedek (1968) predated direct observational results of Masters and Johnson (1960). Deutsch reported that there were two sexual organs in the female, the clitoris as the sexual organ per se and the vagina as the reproductive organ, and that sexual excitement flowed from the clitoris to the vagina. She surmised that the clitoral role was central in biological destiny, and that it was not merely eroticized because it had been the original organ of masturbation. She listened to her patients describe the rhythmic sucking and relaxing movements of the vagina and concluded that the muscular apparatus of the vagina may or may not be involved in orgastic activity.

As early as 1925 Deutsch had depicted female sexual psychology as the product of both the pregenital and genital maturational sequences. Moreover, it was suggested by Moore (1968) that Deutsch's criteria for successful psychoanalytic treatment of frigidity—intrapsychic changes, lessening of unfavorable pregenital fixations and regressions, resolution of oedipal problems and bisexuality, development of control over the main source of sexual inhibition (feminine masochism) and attainment of a post-ambivalent state of object relationships—be generally accepted.

In summary, Helene Deutsch maintained her early position of agreement with Freud that at first a woman wants a penis and then she wants a baby. She did, however, acknowledge the importance of the pregenital mother-daughter relationship in the determination of female psychology. In addition, she recognized the clitoris as a primary sexual organ, not merely an inferior analog of the penis which a woman must later renounce. Her work was derived directly from the psychoanalytic treatment of women; it was not extrapolated from the analysis of men or from the analysis of the oedipal complex in women. Later formulations based on child observations and on adult sexual responses confirmed what her adult women patients reported and remembered, and what Deutsch had reconstructed in their analyses.

Marie Bonaparte

Marie Bonaparte was another female analyst who corresponded closely with Freud. She was able to contradict Freud's theory of primary clitoral masculine sexuality in women by describing the primary vaginal sensations in girl children (Bonaparte, 1953). However, she believed in the primary role of passivity and masochism in women (Bonaparte, 1963), and also pointed out how these characteristics might contribute to frigidity. She felt that women were more poorly endowed with genital sexual drive than men. Reporting observable masochistic phenomena in women, she said that a mature woman has overcome the infantile fears arising out of a sadomasochistic concept of sexual intercourse and from derivative defensive reactions against the experience of sexuality (Bonaparte, 1963).

Bonaparte, like Deutsch, remained committed to Freud's basic theory of female sexuality. Freud did not reject those contributions of hers which expanded and modified his initial views of the subject. In fact, it was the examination of her work that led him to expect that the major contributions to the further elucidation of female sexuality would come from female analysts.

Karen Horney

Karen Horney, a female analyst who initially agreed with Freud's hypotheses about female sexuality (Horney, 1924), shortly thereafter reversed her thinking and sharply challenged his views (Horney, 1926). She hypothesized that Freud's formulations about penis envy, female masochism and female inferiority represented the wishful fantasies of male children about women, and espoused the view that masculine narcissism was responsible for the emphasis on penis envy as pivotal in female psychology. Specifically, she felt that male castration anxiety and fear of castrated women led them to overvalue the penis. Later, she added her belief that many adult men cling to their infantile fantasies to compensate for their envy of the female breast and the ability to bear children (Horney, 1932). She stated that most men fear and hate sexually active women whom they perceive as a threat, and believed that the roots of these feelings lay in the rage of the little boy at his mother for forbidding him the expression of sexual wishes toward her. In addition, she noted that little boys perceived their penises as much too small for their mothers. They therefore felt rejected and inadequate, experiencing the first blow to their self-esteem. She hypothesized that boy children (and men who had never resolved this narcissistic injury) would defensively deny the existence of the vagina. This would reinforce their self-esteem by devaluing their mothers and other females.

Later Horney (1933a, 1933b) emphasized the influence of postoedipal cultural experience in the genesis of masochism, passivity, narcissism and penis envy. For her the villain was patriarchal culture and society. She found no evidence that the origin of these traits lay either in biological realities or in infantile fantasies.

Horney's theory about the aggressive role of a male-oriented society has been popular with some feminists because it allows for a cure of what are considered undesirable feminine traits. That is, they think that the character of individuals can be altered by changing society and its stereotypical male and female roles. By contrast, Freud (1930) had theorized that culture reflects the external projection of intrapsychic phenomena and structures, by which he explained cultural taboos, such as the incest taboo (Freud, 1912b). The occurrence of the incest taboo is a projection of the superego which mandates against parent-child sexuality.

Even if we are not prepared to decide on this issue, Horney's theory leaves us with a dilemma. Homo Sapiens require a long period of nurturance by their mothers, who have been the principal transmitters of language and culture. (This has been changing slowly in modern Western culture as more fathers are involved in the early care of their infants.) The dilemma, therefore, is in trying to understand what part mothers played in creating the problems of chauvinism in men and subservience in women.

Are women themselves, even those in positions of power, vested in a female adaptation that is passive and masochistic? If indeed they are, why? Does the answer lie in the biological matrix? Freud said that "anatomy is destiny," by which he meant that the presence or absence of a penis is the decisive issue. We know now, from the observation of infants, that the answer is far more complex.

Ernest Jones

One male contemporary of Freud's, his biographer Ernest Jones, interested himself to some degree in the psychology of women. Using data from adult patients in analysis, he disputed Freud's contention that there was no femininity in girls until the phallic phase of development (Jones, 1933). He believed that little girls identify themselves as such even before they become aware of the existence of a penis (Jones, 1927). Later, he expressed the notion that basic femininity developed instinctually (Jones, 1935). It remained for later investigators to prove him correct with the use of data from the direct observation and treatment of children.

Clara Thompson

Clara Thompson, an analyst who reached conclusions similar to those of Karen Horney, explained penis envy and masochism in women on the basis of the socioeconomic inferiority of women and as a consequence of their restricted lives (Thompson, 1942). She stated that the frustration of a woman's ability for self-realization led to her increased dependency, and she agreed about the characteristics that Freud attributed to women. She felt, however, that masochism, passivity and narcissism derived from the historic restriction of women's intellectual development and the external limitations and sanctions imposed on the expression of their sexuality.

Now women are allowed and encouraged to develop intellectually in some cultures, and fewer women are socioeconomically underprivileged. The double standard of sexual behavior, if not dead, is dying. Are women who are no longer culturally restricted psychologically any different? Are some of the present day lay thinkers correct? Is woman doomed to dependency, passivity and masochism as long as she has a womb and elects to use it to bear children? Are the daughters of nontraditional mothers who themselves have opted for a career instead of motherhood different in their basic characteristics?

Melanie Klein

Melanie Klein (1928, 1932) was primarily concerned with human development in the first year of life. She believed that the infant/mother relationship during this year influenced all of sexual development. Along with Deutsch (1925), Lampl de Groot (1928), and Brunswick (1940) she acknowledged the influence of the preoedipal mother. Unlike them, she did not assign a dominant influence to the oedipal father in determining the sexuality of his young daughter.

She insisted that girls and boys distinguish themselves from birth. She postulated that the essential femininity of the small girl is due not only to the primary awareness of the vagina but to an early conscious awareness that her father has a penis, which Klein believed occurred in the absence of actually seeing the genitalia of either parent. Rather, she ascribed it to early fantasy formation. This implies either a cognitive capacity in infants which later investigators have been unable to prove, or it requires an innate biological or instinctual awareness (that we are as yet unable to substantiate).

Contributions to the nature versus nurture argument with regard to sexuality come from two sources, observation of the early mother/child dyad, and experimentation in monkeys. Harlow (1962) and Harlow and Harlow (1966) demonstrated that infant monkeys separated from interaction with their mothers, but satisfied in their needs for food, clinging and warmth, do not take up their proper sexual roles when exposed to peers. He also demonstrated that infants of dominant mothers attain dominance in peer groups, not because of their own behavior, but because of the subtle interventions of the mother. Proper sex and gender orientation among baby monkeys depends on the dyadic relationship with the mother and clearly is independent of verbal symbolization.

Thus we see that even in Freud's lifetime, in-depth studies of women by women challenged some of his basic assumptions of female passivity and masochism, and most importantly, of the necessity for women to change genital primacy from the clitoris to the vagina. However, Freud's hypothesis of the centrality of the oedipal complex and penis envy was left essentially intact.

LATER CONTRIBUTIONS FROM PSYCHOANALYSIS

Later contributions to female psychology, still utilizing only data obtained from the psychoanalytic treatment of women, posed a more direct threat to Freud's basic assumptions. More specifically, they challenged the concepts of clitoral primacy, feminine masochism, the temporal relationship between genital awareness and oedipal development, and impact of castration anxiety on the ego. At the same time, they stressed the significance of the preoedipal mother, identification of the young girl with a nurturant and childbearing mother and her presence in the ego ideal, importance for women of later developmental events (e.g., pregnancy), the centrality of separation-individuation from the mother and the special role of the early fantasy of having a baby.

Phyllis Greenacre

In 1950, Phyllis Greenacre took up Freud's admonition to ''turn to one's own experience, the poets or science to know more about femininity'' (Jones, 1955, p. 421). On the basis of the reports of her adult female patients, she substantiated the existence of early vaginal sensations and vaginal awareness before puberty. She noted that this occurred especially in girls who had been subjected to more than average stimulation of the rectum or anus, and that urethral irritation stimulated other adjacent structures. She also observed that vaginal awareness preceded awareness of the clitoris, although it was vague, diffuse and amorphous. From her patients she learned that castration anxiety did exist in women and that it contributed to, but did not singularly initiate, female oedipal development.

In another departure from Freud's thinking, Greenacre (1948) said that oedipal resolution is incomplete in both sexes, with differential effects on superego formation. She noted that girls, having been hurt and disappointed by the discovery that males possess a penis, might well be more fearful of new injury, and that they seemed more worrisome and fearful than their male peers. Hers was the original discovery of the unconscious fantasy of castration as a punishment for masturbation in females, as was her observation of the unconscious fantasy of an illusory penis coexistent with castration fantasies. Furthermore, she explained the fantasy of an illusory phallus existing in the oral, anal or the genital apparatus as a consequence of the poor somatic differentiation of vagina, urethra and anus, as well as the coexistence of vaginal sensations with oral sucking behavior and sensations. However, Greenacre (1952, 1953a, 1953b) also noted that the fear of loss of love was greater than castration anxiety in females.

Greenacre recognized two phases of genital awareness in little girls, each with a different meaning. In the earlier, pregenital phase, the realization of genital difference was more meaningful in terms of the child's sense of self-worth and attempt to differentiate herself from her mother. That is, narcissistic issues and problems of self-object differentiation are of central importance at this time. It is only in the later phase that the issues become oedipal and that the narcissistic injury is conceptualized in sexual terms.

Greenacre was the first investigator to see a *positive* consequence for little girls in the discovery of anatomical difference between the sexes. Specifically, she noted that the failure to compete anatomically was compensated for by growth in intellectual sublimation and by turning to creative fantasy life. When women were discouraged from intellectual pursuits, creativity was transferred to the function of childbearing.

On the negative side, Greenacre noted that the vagueness of female genital awareness was associated with a vagueness in feminine ambitions. Characteristic problems in abstract and analytic thinking were related to women's incomplete body image. Later psychoanalytic data (Keiser, 1956) confirmed Greenacre's hypothesis about the influence of body image on ego styles and interests in both sexes, and most analysts have observed that bodily trauma or illness invariably results in an alteration of the ego, which takes the form of either a deficit or a compensatory hypertrophy of one or more ego functions. In short, Greenacre understood and accepted the anatomical differences between the sexes as pivotal, with wide-ranging consequences for general maturation and ego development.

Much later, Lerner (1974a, 1974b) took this a step further by postulating that cultural and interpersonal factors, such as parental mislabeling and ignoring female genitalia are the major determinants of penis envy and learning inhibitions in female children. Little girls are frequently told only about their vaginas but are not acquainted with the complexity of either their external genitalia or their hidden reproductive organs. By contrast, boys are almost universally aware of their penises, which are often called by a variety of euphemistic names. Although boys are seldom told about their testicles, and it is doubtful that they know any more about their vas deferens, seminal vesicles and prostates than little girls know about their ovaries, uteri or fallopian tubes, the genital apparatus of boys is certainly more visually apparent and can be more easily explored tactilely. Therefore, males are more likely to incorporate a picture of their genitalia into their body schemata and internal self-representations than are little girls.

It is also true that a mother handles little girls and little boys differently. Mothers hold little girls closer to their bodies, carry them around both for longer intervals and for greater periods of time, and are less prone to let them separate and be as active motorically as little boys. Moreover, fathers will more often intervene in the mother's closeness to the son than to the daughter. This too contributes to body schemata and sense of self-esteem, in that boys invest their motor systems positively when they see themselves as active, strong and agile, whereas girls invest their motor systems positively when they see themselves as graceful, delicate, cuddly and clinging (Green, 1976; Korner, 1973; Murphy, 1962).

Judith Kestenberg

Judith Kestenberg (1956a, 1956b, 1975), an analyst of children and adults, has been particularly interested in the nature of endogenous sources of femininity and their expression in childhood. She takes for granted that the oedipal yearning for father is the prime mover of female heterosexuality. She states that interest in the external genitalia peaks in the early phallic phase and is accompanied by penis envy. Her hypothesis is that the high value placed on the penis is a reflection of the female wish to be penetrated and impregnated.

Kestenberg's (1956a, 1956b, 1968) contribution was to elucidate the role that the girl's "productive inside" plays in her development, aside from the fact that it provides a receptacle for the penis. Like Erikson (1968), who wrote of the centrality of inner space in females, Kestenberg initially observed that there was an "inner genital space," which she considered the "cradle of maternity" in both sexes. She agreed that both girls and boys vacillate between the positive and the negative aspects of the oedipal complex (i.e., attachment to both parents with corresponding hatred and rivalry). She felt that the oedipal wishes to give or to receive a child are simply later manifestations of the desire to nurture a child, as the child itself has been nurtured in the dyadic relationship with its mother. Developmentally, she placed the wish to have a baby very early (age one to two and one-half years) before full separation from the mother has occurred and long before the oedipal period.

Kestenberg believed that a female child moves full cycle from sharing a placenta with her mother to wanting a new one of her own in adulthood. She speculated that the baby girl's genitalia, swollen at birth, leaves a somatic imprint. In addition, she hypothesized that the mother and the daughter feel a oneness due to the maternal encouragement of similar rhythms of movement, and she thought that the infant girl might have difficulty in distinguishing between her own internal space and that provided by her mother.

Kestenberg felt that the integrative task for the female child was to establish the separateness and privacy of the generative space over that of the alimentary and excretory organs. Early identification with the mother helped to establish the little girl's own nurturant understanding, intuition and empathy. The acknowledgment of her childlessness constituted an important early loss (Kestenberg, 1975). Intense penis envy and turning to the oedipal father to obtain his penis and baby was an attempt to eradicate the feeling of empty inner space.

In addition to her other contributions was Kestenberg's formulation of female masochism, which related to the adult woman's later capacity for pain tolerance, self-sacrifice and endurance to her functioning as a wife and mother. The woman will symbolically restore the relationship with her preoedipal mother in her own attainment of motherhood. Kestenberg also noted the wish of men to have a baby that grew out of their own preoedipal relationship. For Kestenberg this wish is not a consolation prize for the lack of a penis, since it applies to both sexes. Rather, it is a maneuver to restore the early blissful relationship with the mother of early infancy.

Helene Deutsch and Judith Kestenberg had made similar contributions to the understanding of pregnancy. In addition to restoring an old close relationship to the woman's mother of early childhood, pregnancy offered an opportunity to resolve conflict between the two. Deutsch (1944, 1945) divided pregnancy into two periods: The first, in which all interest and investment are focused on the mother/child unit; and the second, when the mother begins to experience her baby alive within her. At this point, she relates to the unborn child as her phallus and it is treated as if its role were to fill the mother's empty inner space.

Deutsch (1944) and others (Chertok, Bonnaud, Borelli, Donnet, and Revault D'Allones, 1969; Jessner, Weigert, and Fay, 1970) concentrated on the massive regressions of this stressful period. They noted that pregnant women are more dependent, need more nurturance, are often more emotionally labile and self-absorbed, and have other physical complaints such as easy fatigability, nausea with or without vomiting, feelings of bloating and heaviness, gastric distress, swelling of the legs and weight gain, which interfere with their normal functioning.

But Kestenberg (1956a) also recognized that pregnancy could be a major integrating force. By studying patients in analysis at two-week intervals to assess pregnancy progressions, regressions and new integrations, Kestenberg (1975) found a sequence of oral, anal and urethral regressions in the first, second and third trimesters, respectively. She also found that all regressions were subordinated to inner genitality and formed a progressive move toward femininity. Her observations revealed, in addition, that phallic and oedipal fantasies were interwoven but not predominant, and that yearnings for the oedipal father often defended against more primitive yearnings for the preoedipal mother.

Kestenberg further found that motherhood represented yet another significant stage in the intrapsychic development of women. The identification with a loving preoedipal mother paved the way for the acceptance of the baby and served to reinforce the mother's new identity. To be tenderly cared for, the fetus had to be purged from associations with malevolent objects. Thus, the task of the expectant mother is to transfer investment from the cherished internal baby to a new and separate object. Often, there is in reality a reevaluation of the expectant mother's relationship with her own mother and a "rapprochement" (Mahler and Furer,

1963). Moreover, to be a "good enough mother" (Winnicott, 1965) depends on the female's resolution of her own preoedipal development. In brief, a "good enough mother" provides adequate nurturance while neither overwhelming nor neglecting the child: She neither allows him to become overly frustrated nor prevents frustration entirely.

Margaret Mahler

The best understanding of what is entailed in the preoedipal dyadic relationship for both sexes is furnished by Margaret Mahler and her associates (Mahler, 1963, 1967; Mahler and Furer, 1963; Mahler and Perriere, 1965). Beginning with the study of infants at one month of age, Mahler labelled, described and attempted to understand the process of psychological unfolding within the mother-child relationship which must take place.

Phase one, labelled as "autistic," includes infants up to one month of age. It is a period in which the infant seems primarily concerned with its own bodily sensations. Phase two, called "symbiotic," lasts from two to six months. In this period the mother must act as the stimulus barrier, relieving the baby's tension states and attempting to ameliorate his displeasures of hunger, wetness and cold. Some failures inevitably occur, to which the infant responds by splitting the image of the mother into two parts, good mother and bad mother. During this phase the infant perceives its mother's face, breast, eyes and hands and begins to smile in response to her appearance. The adequate mother smiles back with pleasure, thus both reinforcing the smiling response and encouraging socialization. But the infant does not as yet discriminate itself as separate from its mother. Infants are also affected by the way they are held, and mother and child must mutually negotiate the intricacies of their distance and closeness. For example, the mother who is comfortable holding her infant close to her will frequently raise a child with good self-esteem, self-image and the ability to nurture others. Yet, in this early symbiotic period, speech, like mobility, may be inhibited or hypertrophied to preserve the illusion of unconditional unity. The child who must shape himself to suit his mother's needs will have trouble later in maintaining a self picture as separate from the mother.

After the age of four months, the stage of "separation-individuation," the baby begins to separate from its mother. Between four to six months is the so-called "hatching" phase, in which the child becomes alert, persistent and goal-directed. Between six and ten months, the child passes through the "early practicing subphase," at which time he begins to creep and crawl and recognize his bodily parts. When the mother is not in the room, the child's activity level drops and he or she assumes a fixed inward stare. It is hypothesized here that the child is attempting to visualize his intrapsychic image of mother.

The "practicing subphase proper" occurs between ten and twelve to fifteen months. During this stage the child is upright, seems impervious to knocks and bumps, and behaves as if the world were his. The child is entirely focused on its needs and pleasures and seems oblivious to dangers or limitations. This stage is followed by the "rapprochement subphase" at age fifteen to twenty-four months. During this period the child has a growing awareness of others and a need to recognize and relate to them. He initiates more separation from mother but also tries to share with her. When the mother is absent, he is restless and active. Eventually there is a rapprochement crisis, and it is during this crisis that separation anxiety, castration anxiety, and oral, anal and genital pressures converge to set the child squarely "on the road to object constancy" at three years.

In the third year of life, the child is interested in bodily functions. He now has an image of a mostly good mother, and concomitantly, the mother has an internal image of a mostly good child. If she supports mastery and independence the child will continue to have confidence and good self-esteem.

Edith Jacobson

An important ego function for the child's development —identification—has been recognized and described in great detail by Edith Jacobson (1964). It is a complex process whereby the child's self-images assume the characteristics of the child's object images and the child's object images assume aspects of its self images. For example, the three-year-old who insists that she has fur in her pubic area is imposing her view of her mother's body upon herself. The bright and grandiose two-year-old who insists that mother can fit into her pajamas is superimposing her self-image onto her mother. This is a partial process, meaning that it is amenable to reality testing. Gradually the early merging of self and object representations gives way to the child's wish to be a realistic likeness of the parent. The needed separation of the self and the object representations is aided by the mother's empathic understanding of the child, and by her ability to distinguish the child's needs as separate from her own.

Identification with the real parental figure helps to neutralize aggression, which further helps to establish object relations and other identifications. A woman who has become identified with the nurturant qualities of a good mother and allows her child to separate and individuate will herself become a mostly good mother. Thus, the preoedipal mother has a very complex task. Her abilities will have been determined in large part by her own early childhood experiences.

The investigators whose observations have been reported in Section 2 of this chapter contributed greatly to our own thinking, especially in the following areas: the importance of the period of separation-individuation from the mother in the preoedipal phase of development, particularly the convergence of castration anxiety, oral, anal, and genital aims and wishes (Mahler's "rapprochement" period); the timing of separation-individuation and the entrance into the oedipal phase of development; the very early awareness of the vagina; the early primary femininity of little girls; the pertinence of the wish for a baby to replace the preoedipal mother-child relationship; the profound effects on ego functioning of the early relationship with the mother, and its consequences for the vicissitudes of penis envy, castration anxiety and the oedipal complex; the salience of the mother in the ego ideal; and pregnancy as a significant developmental stage in female psychology.

CHAPTER 2

Contemporary Contributions From Direct Observation and Research

ADULT STUDIES

Alfred Kinsey

In 1953, Alfred Kinsey and his associates published the book *Sexual Behavior in the Human Female*, which followed a similar volume about men. Using questionnaires and interviews for their investigation, they noted that, contrary to Freud's theory, women reported masturbation throughout the life cycle. This activity, as in men, was independent of the availability of a partner. Moreover, sexual satisfaction in women was considered a very active rather than a passive process, which also contradicted Freud's formulation of their giving up "active phallic masculine" sexuality in favor of a passive, receptive adaptation. These nonanalytic data led to direct medical observations that have supported similar findings obtained from patients in analysis.

William Masters and Virginia Johnson

More dramatic data has come from the laboratories of Masters and Johnson (1966), whose reports were drawn from direct observation and laboratory measurement of human sexual response. First, they clarified the function of the clitoris as the erotic focus for sexual stimulation. Far from being a vestigial, inadequate organ, the clitoris, despite the role of the vagina, is the trigger zone for sexual release in the adult female.

Careful measurement revealed that there is no difference in "clitoral" or "vaginal" orgasm. Although in intercourse the vagina is stimulated by the action of the thrusting movements of the penis, a significant number of sexually active women were not able to achieve orgasm without simultaneous clitoral stimulation. The reason for this is not physiological, but anatomical. The closer the proximity of the clitoris to the vagina, the more likely that orgasm can be achieved without direct clitoral stimulation.

A majority of women reported stronger, more prolonged orgasms with masturbation, but preferred vaginal/penile orgasm. Perhaps the most important finding is that, far from being endowed with a weaker sexual urge than men, as Freud had hypothesized, women are capable of achieving multiple orgasms. Men, on the contrary, require a physiological period of recovery between orgasms. This observation led to the speculation that much of the denigration and subjugation of women may have evolved from the masculine fear of the female's sexual insatiability (Sherfey, 1966).

Masters and Johnson also demonstrated that women require more continuous stimulation to achieve orgasm and that arousal may be lost with interruption. Furthermore, simultaneous stimulation of more than one erotic area may be necessary in many women to achieve a summation of excitement for orgasm.

These data have caused some consternation. Psychoanalysts have always considered the hallmark of maturity in women to be the achievement of "vaginal orgasm." Therefore, Masters and Johnson's finding that "an orgasm is an orgasm'' (quotation ours) has precipitated rethinking about both female sexuality and female psychology.

Mary Jane Sherfey

Mary Jane Sherfey (1966, 1973) was the first investigator to draw some theoretical conclusions from the observations and measurements of Masters and Johnson. She reaffirmed that physiological evidence does not distinguish vaginal from clitoral orgasm. She cited their observations and measurements as proof that clitoral stimulation, direct or indirect, is a prerequisite for orgasm in the female. She therefore refuted, on the basis of new evidence, Freud's contention that women, in the course of maturation, must change their leading erotic zone from the clitoris to the vagina. She further pointed out that there can be no such thing as clitoral fixation and that it does not represent a psychologically pathological state.

She also argued again, citing the Masters and Johnson data, that the female's capacity for orgasm is limitless. She speculated that men are threatened by this and must keep it in check. However, although males have been noted to have breast envy and envy of pregnancy in women (Jacobson, 1964), no one has as yet written about their ''orgasmic envy.''

CHILD STUDIES

In addition to the direct observation of adult sexual behavior, a body of data has been obtained through direct observation of children. These data also support our formulations from anamnesis and analytic reconstruction.

Eleanor Galenson and Herman Roiphe

Galenson and Roiphe have furnished the most extensive reports of direct child observation. Roiphe (1968) proposed the existence of an early genital phase between sixteen and twenty-four months of age, characterized by behavior indicating genital arousal. He predicted moderate to severe castration reactions in those children exposed to the genital anatomical differences between the sexes at that age. Much evidence for this is presented (Roiphe, 1968; Roiphe and Galenson, 1972, 1973), including the occurrence of fears and phobias as well as direct questions and concerns by children.

But the data in no way can be construed to mean that Freud was incorrect about the pivotal importance for female development of observing the absence of a penis. Roiphe emphasized that these children, studied in a therapeutic nursery, had suffered an important earlier trauma to their body image, such as a serious illness, a surgical procedure, or disruption in the mother/child relationship due to prolonged separations from or depression in the mother (Roiphe and Galenson, 1972).

Galenson and Roiphe (1974) also noted that, whereas children six months of age played with their toes, fingers and bodies in a general way, the child of twelve months of age compares its own facial features with those of the mother. Soon the child includes the rest of its body in specific sequence: facial features, then anal, then urinary, and finally, genital ones.

The emergence of anal awareness was indicated by attentiveness to toileting, interest in toilets and garbage cans and the use of anal language, which was accompanied by behaviors understood to be anal derivatives, e.g., putting things in and out, emptying and filling, scattering and smearing. Urinary awareness was indicated by an interest in faucets, hoses, and pouring liquids, and in the urinary function of peers, animals and dolls.

Genital awareness began between fifteen and nineteen months of age, characterized by focused genital play, was accompanied by an inner-directed look suggesting primordial fantasy formation. At such times the child is absorbed, seems to derive pleasure and shows evidence of excitation, with skin flushing, perspiration and rapid respiration. In addition, affectionate and erotic gestures toward other people now occurred with genital manipulation. Little girls were observed to use nursing bottles, blankets and stuffed animals (transitional objects) for masturbation, which ordinarily, are later discarded.

Galenson and Roiphe believe that sexual drive organization plays a central role in early sexual identity and that it influences ego development, particularly with regard to object relationships. They postulate the early castration complex with its component penis envy to be a central factor for the girl's developing femininity. All of this precedes the oedipal period by many months.

In comparing genital development of girls and boys, Galenson and her associates (Galenson, 1971a, 1971b; Galenson, Blau and Vogel, 1975; Galenson and Miller, 1976; Galenson and Roiphe, 1976) discovered that their courses were initially alike: Both sexes began masturbation at about fifteen months of age and initially behaved similarly during the early weeks following the discovery of genital anatomical difference. However, later divergence developed: Only boys turned to play activities which were usually considered masculine, such as interest in cars and ball-playing, and showed signs of hyperactivity and masturbation that was continuous and vigorous. Moreover, only a few boys suffered severe overt disturbances, whereas all of the girls revealed marked reactions to the discovery of genital differences.

Although the authors emphasized, once again, the particular selection of their sample, they felt that their data support Freud's view of the girl's discovery that she is castrated as pivotal to her development. They postulate, however, that this event takes place earlier than Freud suggested and that the sense of loss depends on many factors, including earlier bodily experiences, the availability of the father, and the mother's attitudes, both conscious and unconscious. They described temporary affective disturbances and even frank depression in preoedipal girls aware of castration, as well as a negative effect on verbal symbolism, a spurt in fantasy life and attempts at graphic representation. Since they did not describe the emergence of passivity or masochism, it is difficult to judge whether this affective disturbance reflects a permanent or a transient loss of self-esteem and narcissistic injury.

Henri Parens

Henri Parens (Parens, Pollock, Stern, and Kramer 1977), also basing his conclusions on observations of children, cited three possible entries by young girls into the oedipal conflict. The first is via the wish to have a baby, which can occur preoedipally and does not necessarily relate to the wish to have a penis; the second is a result of a psychologically-determined and gender-related constitutional predisposition to heterosexuality; and the third is via the wish to have father's penis-baby. All pathways are mediated by ego predispositions and hormonal and neurological changes. He also suspected that there may be constitutionally preprogrammed differences in the primary ego apparatus pertaining to perception, synthesis, cognition and motility.

Recent neurological data reveal that, in right-handed individuals, the left or dominant side of the brain is responsible for concrete forms of cognition, spatial relations, mathematical concepts, sequencing and planning, whereas the nondominant side deals more with abstract cognition, creativity, appreciation of art forms and intuition. Since these are processes that go on preconsciously, it may be that the sex of the individual in some way determines which side of the brain is likely to be more active. Nonetheless, Parens accepted the main pathway to the oedipal complex, the one postulated by Freud, namely, the recognition of anatomical genital differences, followed by castration anxiety, penis envy and the wish to have a baby (Parens, 1971).

Robert Stoller

Robert Stoller (1964, 1965, 1968a) introduced a new concept, "core gender identity," defined as the individual's sense of his or her own sex. He emphasized early postnatal rearing as the most important determinant of core gender identity, although its development is influenced by several sources: sex assignment at birth determined upon examination of the infant's external genitals; attitudes of the parent, especially the mother's and the infant's eventually developing these perceptions into fantasies; "biopsychic phenomena," such as the habitual patterns of handling the infant that permanently modify the infant's behavior; and the developing body ego especially with sensations from the genitals, which help the baby itself to define its own sex.

Stoller (1968a) believed that there is primary femininity. The little girl is happy to be female and perceives herself as intact. She holds herself differently from the boy, and daydreams, plays, wears clothes and uses a vocabulary different from boys, all by the age of two years. These behaviors and attributes precede the discovery of the anatomical

difference between the sexes. Stoller argues that there is no
need to postulate that the discovery of the absence of a penis
is the force of motivation for the development of feminine
characteristics or gender identity.

Stoller (1964) also studied the phenomenon of transsexualism in men, which he defined as the presence of
feminine characteristics in males, occurring in the first year
of life. Not only are these men mistaken for women, but
their "feminine behavior" is markedly exaggerated including total body exhibitionism and hyperemotionality as in
the female. He postulated that such femininity is not the
result of oedipal or even preoedipal conflict, but is the
product of failure of the infant to sense himself as separate
from its mother's body. He felt that this process is non-
conflictual and gratifying. It is hard to understand why, if
this is the case, their "hysterical" femininity seems so false
and caricatured. Rather, we tend to believe the data of
Person and Ovesey (1974), which indicate that there is an
early deprivation that leads the male transsexual to attempt
symbiotic repair by becoming an exaggerated caricature of
his mother.

From Stoller's (1972) studies of transsexual females, he
postulated that the mother/infant symbiosis in such individuals is severely disrupted. The mother is within reach but
unavailable, leading to a lifelong yearning for a feminine,
mothering woman. Warner and Lahn's (1970) study with
psychological test results supports this hypothesis.

In conclusion, Stoller (1968b, 1975) has provided valuable data based on studies of gender identity aberrations.
These support the hypothesis that the establishment of core
gender identity in females (primary femininity) *does* precede
their discovery of absence of the penis.

John Money and Anke Erhardt

Money and Erhardt (1972) studied hormonally- and genetically-aberrant children. They usually had been given a

sexual designation (male or female) by the attending physician, based on a guess after observation of the external genitalia, and were then named, dressed and reared on this basis. Later genetic studies revealed that, in many cases, the original guess was incorrect, and that the gender identity corresponded to the gender in which the child was reared. Moreover, the child's gender identity could not be changed after two years. They found that genetic males with prenatal complete absence of gonadal hormones externally appeared to have female anatomy; that they developed a self-image of being female and were recognized as such by others, if they had been reared as females. In contrast, genetic girls hormonally androgenized prenatally and reared as girls, although in latency showed "tomboyish" traits (including more physical contact play and a preference for "boys' " toys with disinclination for dolls), still chose heterosexual objects and viewed themselves as female. The investigators concluded that feminine gender identity is primarily dependent upon the sex of rearing, and not upon prenatal hormonal or genetic factors.

They also studied genetically male individuals who did not have hormonal androgens prenatally. Those born with normal female external genitalia and reared as females showed preferences for doll play and later wishes to have children. Ninety percent of these individuals said that they were content with their female roles and eight percent had already established heterosexual relationships when followed-up in early adolescence.

However, those with some prenatal androgens and born with anomalous external genitalia, neither definitely male nor female, were also in the group. In several infants raised as boys, sex reassignment was attempted at the end of their second year of life because of the impossibility of surgically producing normal male genitalia. These children reacted to the attempted change in sex reassignment with a profound

psychological disturbance. Again Money and Erhardt concluded that primarily postnatal factors in humans lead to the
establishment of gender identity. They nevertheless believed
that cognitive development, and particularly language, is
responsible for the critical and specific age of eighteen
months after which sex reassignment is impossible.

James Kleeman

On the basis of James Kleeman's (1971a, 1971b) direct
observations of infants, he stated that as soon as the girl is
given a female name, she is bombarded by verbal and nonverbal messages that convey a sense of femaleness in whatever way defined by her family. Observable differences
between male and female children from birth occur in a
number of spheres: motility, play and toy preferences, fantasy, autonomy, dependence, exploratory behavior, and responses to frustration and aggression. They also differ in
perceptions of what constitutes a fearful situation. Kleeman
felt that although there are innate differences between male
and female infants, the learning experience is more crucial
for the formation of gender identity. Learning, after all, is
the ability to modify behavior in response to experiences.
Memory stores that modification over a period of time.
Children "learn" that parents relate to each sex differently,
that their expectations are different, and that different types
of behaviors are rewarded or discouraged accordingly. (Parenthetically, we might cite a jingle for little boys from the
generally read "Uncle Wiggly" series:

> Oh fie, do not cry,
> If you get hurt, say "oh"
> and let it go.
> Be a man if you can.

A better known rhyme is:

> What are little boys made of?
> Frogs and snails and puppy dogs tails,
> That's what little boys are made of.

> What are little girls made of?
> Sugar and spice and everything nice.
> That's what little girls are made of.

Additionally, only Little Miss Muffet fears the spider and runs from it.) Apparently, these learning experiences for boys and girls are sufficiently dissimilar to produce observable differences in dependency and aggression.

Kleeman attributed primary femininity to core gender identity and to its origins as cited by Stoller, but added that cognitive functions play a prominent role. He felt that even identification is a process secondary in importance to core gender identity. He saw the labelling of female as the organizer of behavior to the opposite-sexed parent before the oedipal phase, and noted that the parent's recognition of the child as a girl organizes an entire set of cues and directives that increase the development of core gender identity by eighteen months of age. He observed that even boys reared only by mothers have a primary identification as boys and cited Kohlberg's (1966) thesis that this occurred because the boy is labelled as a boy, which is selectively reinforced by adults. This reinforcement overrides his predominant contact with a female model, and all learning visually, kinesthetically and tactilely is organized by the mental representation of being a male. He also cited Stoller's (1968a) data that even girls born without a vagina feel feminine and that primary femininity is independent of the internal female genitalia.

Kleeman's (1971a, 1971b) studies also suggested that the young girl from one to three years of age feels pride in her femininity, and does not believe that she is inferior or anatomically deprived; it is only after the observation of sexual differences that this may occur. He disagreed with Freud that feelings of inferiority, penis envy and castration anxiety are prerequisites for the emergence of femininity, citing language and modes of communication as crucial in the transmission of gender identity. He felt that gender identity results from a positive direction in the family and is not merely a normal unfolding of predetermined lines of development. Kleeman noted that the categorization of gender, largely a cognitive function, started around fifteen months of age and reached a crescendo in the final third of the third year. Like Stoller, he believed that experiences of sensation in the genitalia contribute to the primitive body ego, the sense of self and to gender awareness.

Kleeman (1975) observed two different patterns of onset of genital self-stimulation in girls: (1) began around eight months of age, and gradually increased with discontinuity until a peak in the middle of the second year of life; and (2) rapidly rose in the middle of the second year of life followed by no interest in exploration or stimulation afterward. It is generally true that genital play is decreased or absent when mothering is inadequate, but there can be little girls with excellent mothering without evidence of genital play.

Usually girls, in contrast to boys, start self-stimulation later and are less vigorous, less focused, stimulate themselves with less frequency and show less self-absorption in the first year and early part of the second year of life. After this girls are capable of intense and vigorous genital self-stimulation in the second half of their second year, but they are more vague about their anatomy than boys. This is true visually, tactilely and in naming of genital parts. The material presented here, based on direct observations of adults and children, represents a conglomeration of studies on one or another aspect of female sexuality.

The work of the above authors confirms, for one thing, our clinical impression of the importance for gender identity of the relationship of the preoedipal child to its primary caretakers. Their research also raises an assortment of questions about the role and timing of castration anxiety in female development as posited by Freud. On the basis of these and other findings, we will present a coherent theory of female psychology and sexuality, only portions of which have been directly documented. In that our theories evolve from psychoanalytic data only, it is our hope that the aforementioned investigators and their successors will provide the systematic observational data to confirm our hypotheses.

OTHER STAGES OF DEVELOPMENT PIVOTAL TO FEMALE PSYCHOLOGY

Latency: Virginia Clower and Harold Blum

"Latency" generally refers to the period from about five to seven years of age until adolescence when apparent sexual development begins. During "latency" the child devotes most of its energies to work, play, peer relationships and the acquisition of the skills of his culture (Erikson, 1959). Female psychology and sexuality continue to evolve during this stage. Freud had believed that female clitoral masturbation ceases in normal latency girls. This is true for some girls, but as Virginia Clower (1975, 1976) has shown, it is not the norm. Girls continue to masturbate but do so differently than boys: The erotic focus is the clitoris, and the mode involves indirect stimulation of the mons pubis, the labia and the introitus via rhythmic movements and thigh pressure. Clower's own clinical work, as well as information from direct observation of girls in nonclinical settings, convinced her that any girl who has abandoned genital self-arousal entirely is suffering from an interference with further normal development. This formulation entirely contradicts Freud's notion that it is necessary for girls to repress awareness of and pleasure in the clitoris in order to develop into feminine women.

Blum (1976), in further study of latency girls, made an important contribution related to superego formation, establishment of an ego ideal and the problem of masochism in women. Contrary to Freud's notion that women have a weak superego, Blum pointed to the strength of superego functioning in latency girls: Their sexual and aggressive activities are controlled; and they tend to be conformists who are industrious in work and whose instinctual impulses generally are channeled into socially acceptable goals. Blum also emphasized the importance of distinguishing between male and female superego systems in relation to biological, cultural and developmental factors. He warned that different precepts and values should not be confused with inferior psychological structures. For example, if the ego incorporates the ideal of passive dependency, a strong superego will enforce this value. Compliance would therefore represent a feminine value rather than a deficient structure. Blum stated that even if rejection of a castrated mother would lead to internalization, this might not necessarily result in a defective self-representation, but might lead to the formation of a harsh superego. Both girls and boys have superego precursors, such as sphincter morality (the injunction to control one's bodily functions), and they identify with the superego of both parents and the ideals of idealized parents. An inconsistent or punitive superego will undermine ego functioning in both sexes, and introjection of a bad "mother" will interfere with the formation and function of the maternal ego ideal. Maternal ideals and aspirations are deeply embedded in the female superego and contribute to the capacity for nurturance and to humanitarian concerns. One has only to observe the behavior of the average latency-age girl with small children to see the "ideal mother." Internalization of the ideal mother is linked to wishes for an ideal family.

Blum added his voice to the argument that being sexually receptive or nurturant is not equivalent to masochistic submission. Masochistic traits and fantasies are the legacy of conflicts in early childhood. Intense masochism is not characteristic of normal femininity, but is associated with an impaired object relationship. He stated that masochism is the weapon of the weak, used for seduction of the perceived aggressor. At one time masochistic fantasies and identifications were reality-based. That is, sexual relations were to be passively endured without hope of pleasure for the woman. In addition, childbirth was difficult, and sick, unwanted children were the rule. But maternal self-sacrifice in such situations is not masochistic; the masochism of the martyred mother is not evidence of mature maternal love. Blum also pointed out that penis envy does not adaptively foster femininity, but is an impediment to it. That is, when penis envy causes profound narcissistic injury and reactive masochism, it interferes with the development of the mature adult woman. These observations of latency girls also support our formulations about latency culled from the analyses of adolescent and adult women.

Adolescence: Samuel Ritvo

Adolescence is ushered in by the biology of puberty. With bodily and hormonal changes comes an intensification in sexual and aggressive urges directed toward infantile and incestuous objects. These ties must be abandoned and the urges shifted to nonincestuous peer objects.

Physically, secondary sexual characteristics develop, masturbatory activity increases, females begin to menstruate and males begin to experience ejaculation with orgasm. Males show off their new masculinity whereas females become more shy and modest. Both sexes become concerned with bodily changes and physical attributes.

Samuel Ritvo (1977), in discussing adolescence, stated that there is a widespread, if not universal, practice of concealment during this stage, which has its early roots in the repression of pregenital strivings, particularly anal ones. Concealment may be a defense against early exhibitionistic wishes, and from the ego's side, may reflect a lack of pride, confidence and self-assurance. Ritvo noted that the manner in which a girl resolves the problem of a new body image, negotiates regressive pulls and is able to separate from incestuous objects, will govern her approach to heterosexuality. She now has to bring her masturbatory fantasies into the actuality of an intimate sexual relationship. Ritvo believed that reaction to the absence of a penis is universal, and that penis envy may combine with a heightened body narcissism to create a provocative, assertive, seductive adolescent. Intercourse may take on a competitive quality.

In some cases, the adolescent girl tries to compensate for the loss of her mother by turning to a man as a substitute. Much of what is taken to be sexual behavior on an adult genital level among adolescents is actually behavior revolving around holding and being held. What looks like sexual promiscuity often is less genitally sexual than it is the search for the comfort of being held by the pregenital mother.

Ritvo felt that adolescence must be accompanied by a change in the ego ideal. The adolescent must give up the mother as the only source of her ego ideal and modify that ideal in terms of her own emerging interests, talents, capabilities and capacities. Autonomy requires giving up the wish to be mother, and the substitution of an ego ideal which embodies the common and desirable qualities of both mother and adolescent daughter.

Adolescence will be discussed further on, particularly in reference to severe psychiatric disturbances (e.g., anorexia nervosa) occurring in this period (see Chapter 5). In addition, we will furnish clinical material from our own analytic practices of adolescent girls in treatment. Moreover, there are other (generally post-adolescent) adaptational tasks which lie ahead for women.[1]

Among these are pregnancy, motherhood and becoming a grandmother (see Chapter 7) as well as the experience of mutilating genital or breast surgery (see Chapter 8).

[1] Nancy Chodorow (1978) has made an extensive contribution to the theories about mothering. These have meshed so closely with our own formulations that we have chosen to include her work directly as we discuss our own.

CHAPTER 3

Metapsychological Considerations Toward A New Theory of Female Sexuality

Roy Schafer

Roy Schafer, an analytic investigator primarily interested in metapsychology, has discussed problems in Freud's theoretical generalizations on the development and characteristics of women. Schafer's approach is from a theoretical rather than clinical point of view. He has selected three problem areas representative of the difficulties he sees with Freud's psychology of women: the misconception of women's morality and objectivity; neglect of women's preoedipal development; and what he calls the problem of naming (pejorative labelling).

Freud (1924) characterized women as being less moral than men. Schafer (1974) noted that Freud was referring merely to a certain quality of moral rigidity more generally characteristic of men than of women. Men seem to have a more abstract and so-called "objective" morality, and are less easily swayed by emotional appeals or subjective intuitive impressions. Freud estimated that so-called "hysterical" features (behaviors determined by emotional concerns) were more commonly encountered in women, and

45

that so-called "obsessional" features (behaviors determined by objective consideration and intellectual assessment) were more characteristic of men. Obsessional features included the use of rationalization, intellectuality and reaction formation, among other defenses, and were accompanied by isolation of affect.

Schafer has taken issue with Freud's judgment about the quality of morality because he feels that it is meaningless to measure differences in morality on a single scale. Moreover, he raises a psychodynamic objection: Obsessive morality is founded on intellectualization and reaction formation against anal-sadistic tendencies. Therefore, circumvention is necessary, which includes continuous atonement and magical undoing. A superego based upon these factors is not a model of genuine morality and involves the risk that the underlying irrational and savage rage may erupt.

Freud assumed that holding onto one's moral standards regardless of the consequences in personal relationships is a sign of a firmer, and therefore, a better morality. Furthermore, he stated that for men the major threat to an intact morality is castration anxiety, and for women it is the fear of loss of love. Schafer argues, rather, that castration anxiety is a more narcissistically detached concern than fear of loss of love (of another person), and thus provides a more impersonal foundation for moral activity.

Freud (1933a) concluded that, for the sake of being loved, women will sacrifice whatever autonomous sense they have of what is right for them and for others. He ignored the observable clinical fact that castration anxiety continuously incites men to violate conventional morality. Thus, Schafer has drawn attention to what is surely a paradox in Freud's formulations. Freud (1933b) also stated that one aim of a therapeutic analysis is to reduce superego influences. Surely he did not mean to reduce any morality. Another paradox is that a harsh superego can result in criminality. Schafer thinks that Freud drew the wrong conclusions from his theory. If a woman has a less stringent superego, she may be better suited than a man to develop a moral code.

In addition, Freud (1931) said that women manifest less ego development than men, that is, their judgment is less objective and their comprehension not as lucid and acute. He also felt that castration anxiety is the greatest spur to ego development. Schafer suggests that there are no quantitative differences in ego development, but rather qualitative ones. Again he sees a paradox. If women are, as Freud believed, more intuitive and empathic than men, is that not a reflection of acute comprehension? He concludes that Freud's estimates of women's morality and objectivity are logically and empirically indefensible.

In discussing the problem of neglected prephallic development, Schafer has pointed out that in ascribing primary importance to the achievement of genital heterosexuality, Freud was under the sway of an evolutionary value system. Freud (1923b) held that not only was superego structure the outcome of the oedipal complex, but ego structure as well. Although Freud described the influence of oral and anal phases on ego development (e.g., acquisition of language, consolidation of narcissism, early character formation), he neglected their effect on the formation of the oedipal conflict. Schafer notes that Freud took for granted catastrophic penis envy in little girls, but that he was remarkably incurious about the background of these reactions, and that his theoretical revisions did not adequately take them into account. Schafer also argues that one must understand the roots of female self-depreciation and envy, and why it is so important to little girls that there be no difference between the sexes. In effect, Schafer says that he cannot accept that de novo, without priming, the female child experiences a sense of profound shock, and that this occurs simply and only because she realizes that she has no phallus, or that this single shock explains, and thereafter controls, the totality of female development. He questions the origin of the precarious sense of self-esteem in the female child that causes collapse so rapidly and completely. He speculates that the anlage for this exists in the nature of the relationship of the young girl to her mother.

Turning to the problem of naming, Schafer is interested in designations such as "feminine" and "passive" versus "masculine" and "active" that are found in Freud's descriptive and explanatory propositions. When Freud spoke of "feminine" he referred to how the lady should behave and look; any departure was not feminine, and therefore phallic. Maleness implied active mastery and accompanied the possession of a penis. Femaleness meant passivity and compliance along with (because of) the lack of a penis. For Schafer these definitions imply and enforce a denigration of women.

Schafer also has drawn attention to the complexity of the issues involved: Does the penis penetrate the vagina, or does the vagina receive the penis? In addition, we may add that there is hardly anything passive about the sucking movements of the vagina. Is the anatomical orgasmic platform formed in the vagina by engorgement and retraction for the tighter containment of the penis more passive than penile erection? Are active thrusting movements of the pelvis as obligatory and involuntary in females approaching orgasm as they are in the male partner? Schafer asks if it makes any sense to call a mother "passive." Mothers involved in rearing their children are active, engaging, initiating, directive and educative. Thus, Schafer also observed that Freud did not give much thought to the subject of mothers.

Schafer as a theorist has raised another interesting question. If indeed women are passive, doesn't it require a distinct inhibition to assume an inactive role, and isn't this a very active process? One example comes easily to mind. A small child begins exuberantly to explore his or her environment, as yet unaware of danger. The mother, desirous of preventing injury to her child nevertheless forces herself to inhibit the wish to scoop the child up to safety. Most mothers similarly assume passive behavior with active vigilance, ready to rescue if they are needed, but appreciative of the child's need for motoric mastery. Thus, the mother's behavior is both active and passive, as is her intrapsychic organization in general.

Laila Karme

For Laila Karme (1981), the question is not whether penis envy exists, but whether penis envy is a universal phenomenon. In contrast to Freud, she suggests that penis envy has multiple intrapsychic determinants which differ from patient to patient, in patients she has studied. In cases of severe penis envy, she has hypothesized the following meanings: "(1) the penis as umbilical cord, a means of attachment to mother; (2) the penis as a baby, a means of completing mother and/or herself; (3) the penis as an object that can unite with and separate from mother with pleasure to both and without damage to either; (4) the penis as the undamaged, undamageable external version of the womb; (5) the penis as breast; (6) the penis as a defense against murderous rage; (7) the penis as a weapon of competition for mother with father and brothers, all of whom had penises; (8) penis envy as a means of blocking the wish for sexual expression for fear of losing the mother by inhibiting sexual responsiveness for pleasure; (9) penis envy as part of a general feeling of envy of both men and women" (p. 443).

She has also noted other well-known determinants of penis envy: the penis representing the self or another object; penis envy as an unconscious pledge to a jealous and possessive mother image to deny sexual pleasure with the penis; as the unfulfilled wish to have permission from other to be sexually operative and responsive; as a reflection of identity, narcissistic sensitivity and problems of aggression; and as a defense against the expression of envy derived from preoedipal narcissism and possession of the omnipotent object.

Summary and Conclusions

It is no wonder, then, that Freud set the oedipal conflict at center stage in his formulations. Despite having formulated a coherent metapsychology about female development, Freud still had to ask, "What does a woman want?" (Jones, 1955). We do not think it presumptuous to suggest that the general answer is a simple one. Women want to be considered as separate, autonomous individuals with their own set of characteristics determined biologically and stemming from their early infantile relationships. They do not want these characteristics to be pejoratively labeled or considered to be merely a compensation for their damaged anatomy, not less good nor less desirable, nor less important, merely different.

To recapitulate briefly, Freud felt that in females recognition of the anatomical difference between the sexes caused a kind of castration shock followed by penis envy, which invariably ushered in the oedipal conflict. In the prior phallic period, the little girl had masturbated with her clitoris, which she regarded as a small penis. With the discovery of her "damaged state," she angrily rejected her mother who had failed to provide her with a penis. Thus, she had to turn to her father, at first desiring his penis and later desiring his baby as a consolation prize.

The resolution of the oedipal conflict in boys, Freud stated, leads to the introjection of a harsh superego based in large part on their castration anxiety and the reaction to their feelings of destructive rage and guilt toward the father, the competitor. He thus reasoned that, in the absence of castration anxiety, the superego of women would be weaker, less objective and more subject to the vicissitudes of emotion. Another determinant of the weakened sense of morality in women was their willingness to sacrifice what might have been objective judgments for the sake of gaining love. He postulated that women, failing to introject a positively regarded mother as an ego ideal, would be masochistic and passive, feel inferior and damaged. To compensate for this, he supposed that they needed to become narcissistic and exhibitionistic. He also assumed that, because of this weak introject, women would not be as capable as men of rational thought or abstract processes. For Freud, the proper resolution of the female oedipal conflict resulted in the giving up of clitoral masturbation and other ''masculine'' identifications. Women would therefore be nonassertive, less intellectual, and funnel their creativity into childrearing. They would turn to the vagina as the primary source of sexual pleasure, the clitoris becoming, in effect, a vestigial organ. He considered femininity to be the attainment of vaginal orgasm.

Freud thus provided us with a heuristic theory without which there might have been little motivation to accumulate data. Given the findings from experimental research, child observation, psychoanalytic exploration as well as new theoretical considerations, we are in a position to amend, extend and change Freud's hypotheses about female psychology. For example, Freud wrote extensively about the pregenital phases of development, but did so primarily in terms of

instinctual vicissitudes rather than object relations or development of ego function. He virtually ignored the preoedipal mother, about whom he had no direct observational
data. His clinical analyses ended with attempts at resolution
of the oedipal conflict. Moreover, he was unable to analyze
his own preoedipal relationships without a separate analyst
(maternal transference object) and a profound regression
that can only take place in the presence of a therapeutic
alliance and with the interpretative help of a trained individual, male or female, who is not regressed in his or her
own ego functions.

CHAPTER 4

What Does A Woman Want?
Preoedipal Considerations

In our formulation of the determinants of female development, we shall start from birth. The child of either sex has
a prolonged period of dependence on, and an almost exclusive relationship with, the mother. During this time, the
female child develops a core gender identity and an early
primary femininity, which is readily observable to the untrained eye. This primary femininity has its roots in the
labeling of the child as a girl, with all the associated verbal
and nonverbal cues, as well as in the biological, chemical,
anatomical, visual, tactile and kinesthetic cues.

The mother immediately handles male and female children differently. She holds her daughters closer and for
longer periods of time than she does her sons. Chodorow
(1978) states that the young girl has a far more difficult
time separating from her mother because the mother treats
the daughter as a narcissistic extension of herself. This frequently is a repetition of the way the mother was treated
by her own mother. Chodorow thinks that this accounts for
the turning of the little girl to her father and, subsequently,
to other men. The female child must escape her mother.

Person (1982) says that young girls fear abandonment
by the mother, and this accounts for the fact that women's

53

primary anxiety is almost always predominantly related to fear of loss of love. Fear of the loss of the dependency object and her love is later displaced from the mother onto all subsequent love objects. Person notes the fear of competition, almost ubiquitous in women, is also a derivative of the fear of loss of love. We feel similarly that it is not merely a castration fear nor a defense against the wish to castrate men. Nor is it necessarily a defense against murderous rivalry with the mother.

Freud (1925a) stated that girls are less fearful than boys during the oedipal period because they already are castrated. We think that girls are *more* frightened during the oedipal period because the erotic rival of the girl child is also her source of dependent gratification. This intensifies her fear of retaliation and leads to several reparative fantasies.

The shadow of the preoedipal mother falls constantly upon the girl's representational world during the oedipal period. It leads to fantasies that both form and deform the oedipal complex. In the treatment of women, it is repeatedly evident that a long period of analysis frequently must be devoted to unravelling the girl's relationship with her mother and undoing the reparative preoedipal fantasies developing out of this relationship. Such fantasies alter the oedipal complex and interfere with the female's ability to relate to men. They include fantasies of the phallic mother, of an illusory phallus, of the vagina dentata and the maternalization of the father. In addition, castration anxiety and penis envy must be understood in terms of their relationship to the mother as well as to the oedipal father.

As the father enters the girl's life he is often confused with the phallic mother. It is clear that different types of mothering influence all of the girl's responses later in life, whether the mother is intrusive, phallic, masochistic or narcissistic. This also puts a stamp on the girl's identification. It is responsible for bisexual identification as much as is the identification with the father. The following material describes and gives case illustrations of reparative fantasies used by the preoedipal girl to maintain her closeness to her mother and her own sense of personal integrity.

FANTASY OF THE PHALLIC MOTHER

The fantasy of the phallic mother is that she has a hidden phallus which endows her with strength, power, and an additional ability to control her little girl. She frequently is seen as intrusive and penetrating. In other cases, the girl holds the hope that the mother will endow her with a phallus.

Case Illustrations

Case 1

A professional woman in her twenties saw her mother as the all-powerful ruler of the family. This mother subjected her daughter to daily enemas until the child was seven. The patient saw the enema tip as her mother's phallus, which led to her fecal retention, making the repeated enemas necessary. She developed a fantasy at the age of seven that she really was a boy with a phallus inside (in the anus). During her analysis, after an extremely resistant period of a power struggle (similar to her enema experience) and replete with many transference ideas and sadomasochistic fantasies (including that the analyst would force words into her and make her vomit), an intense longing and a desire to be held by the female analyst developed. In these fantasies the patient endowed the analyst with breasts and an actual phallus, or a very large head, or an amazon-like quality. She had a longing to identify with all these features. Indeed, she revealed a masturbatory fantasy where a man would enter her rectally or from the rear vaginally, forcing out her clitoris into the form of a penis.

Case 2

An unmarried graduate student, with three older and successful brothers, had a sickly, depressed, incompetent mother. She fantasied that the analyst would give her a penis in the form of imparted knowledge and magical powers, which the patient felt that the analyst had and which she could use for her work in an associated field.

She talked about herself as Athena, born parthenogenetically from the forehead of Zeus. In addition, this patient was amnesiac for masturbation in childhood and anorgasmic both by masturbation and in heterosexual intercourse. With what she felt was the tacit permission of the analyst, she began to experiment with masturbation. She became orgasmic while mounting a pillow. This led to her recovery of the memory of masturbation while riding a horse and to the revival of the fantasy that the horse was her phallus. The galloping of the horse represented her thrusting pelvic movements.

Her earlier fantasy was that she had a horse phallus. When pressed by her family to pursue female academic goals, the fantasy changed to one of overpowering men by her "larger" brain and verbal ability. Coincidentally, she stopped horseback riding and indeed forgot about her horse, which was kept at the family farm. This patient's analysis had to be interrupted when she saw the analyst in the Intensive Care Unit after an accident that threatened the analyst's life. The transference was actualized because now the analyst was seen as the weak and damaged mother. The patient was subsequently successfully analyzed by a male analyst to whom she was referred.

FANTASY OF THE ILLUSORY PHALLUS

The female's reparative fantasy of an illusory phallus is the end-product of many determining factors, including identification with the phallic mother; identification with the father; the wish to have mother as the love object; denial of anatomical differences, which is generally associated with a feeling of inferiority; and penis envy. The fantasy of the illusory phallus may be located anally, vaginally, orally, or internally in the uterus, as the baby inside, in the head (I.Q.), or with the total body as the phallus.

Case Illustrations

Case 1

A professional woman with several sons entered analysis because of a fear of orgasm in intercourse. She was afraid that her husband's penis would enter her vagina and injure her internally. This fantasy included the "irrational" idea that it would protrude from her mouth. She was initially unable to fantasize while masturbating, although she was orgasmic in masturbation. After a period in analysis when her initial resistances centered about fears that her analyst would force-feed her, she developed a trusting relationship. She then revealed strong wishes to bite off her husband's penis and to suck on the analyst's breasts. Her earliest idea of pregnancy was of oral impregnation: She would swallow something her mother would feed her and thus have a baby or "something growing inside."

Oral incorporative wishes for a phallus related to a severe feeling of deprivation of maternal care during the first four years of her life when her mother was severely depressed over her own mother's dying. The patient, raised by maids, saw little of her mother, who worked and spent her free time with the patient's grandmother. The patient developed a very early and intense maternal wish for her father, with a fantasy of sucking on his penis. She was identified with him and had yearnings to be like him in order to attach to her mother. However, she projected her own rage onto the phallus and to men, whom she saw as depriving, much as she had seen the mother of her past.

(An example of the fantasy of an illusory phallus located in the anus was written about in the prior section, on identification with the phallic mother.)

Case 2

A young professional woman, unable to be as successful as her adored and dynamic father, began a love affair with an older man in whom she saw the qualities of her father. This man's inability to extricate himself quickly from a marriage that had been dead for many years, but not legally severed, was a source of disillusionment to the patient. For almost a year their sexual relationship had been very gratifying. She now developed vaginal pain, which she initially related to intercourse. Gynecological workup revealed no medical cause.

One day it occurred to her that she might have something "psychological," like vaginismus. She began to realize that the pain also occurred whenever she was having "anything feminine" done to her body (electrolysis, hairstyling, cosmetic facials). At those times she had a sensation of fullness, as well as pain, in her vagina. The fantasy was that she had "something" in her vagina that she could not identify. When asked to think about what that might be, she was reluctant to do so, stating that the symptom was better than some of the illnesses and injuries she had developed previously during the course of her analysis. Her theory was that these prior distresses had taken something from her, whereas her current complaint had given something *to* her.

In order to test the psychogenic nature of her complaint, she contemplated using her vibrator to masturbate, which she rarely did in the course of an ongoing sexual relationship. Years earlier in her analysis, when she had first acquired the vibrator (one designed to be inserted into the vagina), she had jokingly referred to it as "my do-it-yourself own little penis." In the session in which she suggested returning to it, she made a slip, saying that she did *not* have a vibrator, the opposite of what she meant. She then recognized her fantasy of having a hidden penis that she could summon to consciousness, when she was not involved with a powerful man whose penis she could conceptualize as her own.

Case 3

A patient in the course of her analysis developed uterine bleeding which necessitated the scheduling of a hysterectomy. She reacted to this with terror and helplessness and spoke of the loss of her "baby machine," which she frequently slipped and called her "boy machine." She had several children and did not intend to have more. Associations to this resulted in her relating inferior mental capacity to the loss of her ovaries, about which she felt "testy." Exploration of this feeling led her to equate her ovaries with testicles and her uterus with a penis. When she had become pregnant she had felt "full and complete" and able to tolerate orgasm in intercourse. Without pregnancy, she was anorgasmic during intercourse. Further associations led to her fear of loss of her female analyst during surgery, and then, to an anamnesis of her mother's illness when she was quite young. During that time her mother was hospitalized for three months, having had a mastectomy with complications, including postsurgical depression. It was during this period that the patient experienced conscious wishes to be a boy, followed by wishes to have a baby boy.

Case 4

A professional woman in her early thirties sought analytic treatment because she had reached the time in her life when she and her husband had agreed to start a family. While not masculine in her appearance, she wore pants, never used makeup, and chose a mode of dress not appropriate for her professional role. She felt that she needed analysis because she had too much anxiety and too many "psychosomatic symptoms" to be a capable mother.

Within the first year of her analysis her symptoms cleared, and she became pregnant. A talented seamstress, she made herself a wardrobe of beautiful feminine maternity clothes. She also began to use makeup and wore her hair in a loose and casual style. During the course of her pregnancy she was orgastic in intercourse and, for the first time, was able to allow her husband to touch her clitoris and labia. Although she denied any fantasy about the sex of her unborn fetus, she kept referring to it as "him" and dreamt about having a boy. This baby represented her illusory phallus.

As her date of delivery drew closer she began to experience panic attacks, which were far worse in quality and duration than the anxiety that had first brought her to treatment. These included screaming night terrors of being ripped apart during the delivery. She wondered aloud about whether the doctors would be able to "put everything back in again." This educated woman believed that her uterus would come out with the baby and would have to be sewn back. Such distortion of the usual suturing of the perineum was related to her strongly invested fantasy that loss (birth) of her baby would result in the loss of her phallus.

Delivery was uneventful. She began to nurse her son and was regularly orgastic during the course of nursing. She then refused to have sex with her husband, convincing him that as long as she was nursing, sexual relations were forbidden. When challenged about this lie, she angrily said, "I don't need his penis while I have my son."

Case 5

A young woman dancer, in the course of her analysis, suddenly became preoccupied with a weight gain of two pounds. She related this to the spoiling of her firm, almost breastless, erect body of which she was very proud. The weight gain had followed a dinner party at which she had been attracted to and slept with the man who would become her future husband. She enjoyed the cuddling of their physical relationship, but at the point at which she was almost orgasmic would feel herself stiffening her body in a ballet pose. An anamnesis revealed her wish that everybody admire her superb athletic body, which so much resembled that of a preadolescent boy.

The patient's mother, who had been intrusive and obese, had put the daughter on a strict diet from early life and called her by a nickname that was masculinizing and similar to the mother's brother's name. The mother had taken great pride in grooming her young daughter in athletics and dance, and the care given to the child's body exceeded that usually given by mothers, both in quality and duration. The patient became aware during her analysis that her mother had regarded her as an extension of her own body and as "her little prick." The patient herself also viewed her body as a phallus and described it in those terms. As her analysis progressed she was able to become more comfortable with her feminine attributes. Her fantasy of a body phallus was thus related to identification with her narcissistic mother's use of her as a phallus.

The fantasy of an illusory phallus is usually combined with the fantasy of a phallic mother. The phallus endows the girl or woman with a sense of completeness, and thus a sense of continuing union with her own mother. When this fantasy is analyzed or disrupted by a real event (approaching birth of a child, death of the mother), the patient initially experiences intense castration anxiety, which presents clinically as panic followed by a period of depression.

FANTASY OF THE VAGINA DENTATA

The fantasy of the vagina dentata, or vagina with teeth, really represents any formulation in which the female patient sees herself or her mother, with whom she is identified, as destructive to men.

Case Illustrations

Case 1

The patient, a 41-year-old professional woman, had an intrusive, domineering mother who successfully "castrated" her father at home. The mother, with whom the patient identified, had deprived her child of a warm father, a man who had fled from his wife's insults. As the patient's coldness towards men was analyzed as the repetition of what she had seen at home, she slowly became able to be warmer to them and met and married a loving man. During this period she developed a fantasy that her vaginal secretions would damage her husband's penis. She also dreamt that he was decapitated when he leaned under the hood of their car in an effort to repair it. She experienced transient vaginal spasms, which she associated with the feeling of swallowing and joked about the fear that her spasms would "cut his penis off." The fantasy of the vagina dentata was associated to her identification with her mother's "insulting mouth," which had "cut Daddy to shreds" and which she displaced to her vagina.

Case 2

A college student sought treatment for many problems, among which were depression and aimlessness. She had a repeated history of having been physically abused by her mother to the point of needing medical attention on many occasions. Her father remained passive in the face of his wife's attacks upon him and his daughter. In fact, he maintained a separate residence to which he could flee. The mother was a seductive woman involved in many love affairs, who, in the patient's words, "chewed men up." The patient originally reported having been raped as a young adolescent, when, in fact, she had set up the seduction. Later she told her parents of the event, causing the young man to be socially ostracized, but had little awareness of her destructive wishes towards him. She repeated this behavior once more in later adolescence, at which time she caused a trusted protégé of family friends to lose his job and their support. Since this second episode she had had only one heterosexual experience, during which she felt severe vaginismus. Her initial history included fear of penetration and bodily damage, and analysis revealed her wish and belief that she could sexually "chew up men" the way her mother had.

Case 3

A very sophisticated woman physician who knew about the sexual transmission of her disease during its active state, developed herpes vaginalis. Intercourse was very painful for her during the periodic recurrences of the disease, but it was precisely at these times that she chose to sleep with men she wanted to punish. In one case it was a man in whom she was interested, although he had made it clear that he was not intending to leave his marriage. She had intercourse with him while infected, even though she knew that his wife, with whom he was still sexually active, was pregnant. She was also aware that herpes vaginalis during pregnancy would necessitate Cesarean section and "might damage the baby." On another occasion she seduced her employer because he had not been a strong enough advocate of her professional advancement. Overcome with rage, she saw her genitals as instruments of active aggression and retaliation.

The origin of her vagina dentata fantasy was the failure to replace her mother with her father. While mother had been considered phobic and useless, she worked in her father's office and was his constant companion. Yet, he was never willing to take her side against a mother who arbitrarily picked on, confused, deprived and publicly shamed her. In her case, she both punished the man as the maternal substitute as well as the fetus of the maternal substitute, which she saw as phallic. Hell hath no greater fury than a woman scorned.

FANTASY OF THE MATERNALIZATION OF THE FATHER

This is a fantasy that occurs under several conditions, singly or combined. First, the father may be the actual maternal surrogate or primary caretaker. Second, the female child with an unsatisfactory relationship to her mother may turn to her warmer, more affectionate father earlier than is expected in normal development. Third, when the father is sexually seductive the child may defensively perceive him as castrated in order to avoid the danger of the felt seduction. When the mother is experienced as more phallic than the father, the father may then be perceived as more nurturant than the mother.

Case Illustrations

Case 1

A married mother of three children came to treatment for severe depression related to her inability to receive maternal care from her husband. He was described in the same terms as she had described her mother in early life, namely, unempathic, begrudging, unavailable, self-centered and disinterested.

Her mother was remembered as spending most of her time in bed, taking care of her body and eating chocolates which were locked in a closet away from the children. The mother would emerge at dinner in a seductive hostess gown and attempt to monopolize the father's time. However, he did find time to spend with his daughter, helping her with toileting activities and later with homework. It was he who stayed up at night to take care of her when she was ill. He awakened her for school and had breakfast with her, the two tiptoeing and whispering so as not to disturb the mother.

The patient's father died during her latency, after a long illness about which she had been deceived. She was sent away during the terminal part of his illness. Several weeks after the funeral her mother left her with an aunt and went abroad to recuperate from "her tragedy." During the patient's depression she described periods of feeling dead, of not being "lucid," losing objects, being forgetful and not able to say what she wished to say; therefore, she was easily misunderstood. In one session, when she was severely regressed, she became panicky because she could not see. She remembered that during a period of her father's illness he had confused her with her brother, which her mother said was due to his problems in thinking. When she related this she cried hysterically and was herself unable to see. She thus realized that her father had been blind. During this agonizing anamnesis she was able to recognize that she identified with her neurologically impaired father. Hospital records confirmed his terminal course as had been reconstructed in her analysis. As the patient was able to separate herself from her introjected father and accept his death, she was able to function more appropriately.

Her marriage represented a renewed attempt to obtain maternal care from a man. She had maternalized her father. Her choice of a narcissistic object who resembled her mother blocked this solution and she clung to her maternalized father whom she kept alive inside herself.

Case 2

A young woman in her late twenties suffered from anorexia nervosa, the result of prolonged wearing of a Milwaukee brace (Bernstein and Warner, 1983). Her father had developed a spinal tumor when she was very young, and her mother, who had to work in order to support the family, turned away in disgust from both of them. The father was at home for prolonged periods in the girl's childhood and adolescence. The two were very close, but, she finally felt that she had to leave home if she were going to make a life of her own. Her anorexia became a medical emergency when she was forced to give up her own life to come home because her father again was symptomatic. A large part of her initial difficulty with the Milwaukee brace was that it confirmed an identification with a sick and possibly dying father. It had always been her fantasy that he would be paraplegic and slowly starve to death.

Case 3

A married psychologist in her thirties, with two children and a "weak" husband, entered treatment because of feelings of unhappiness, incompleteness and emptiness, accompanied by worries about being a bad mother. Initially a strong transference developed in which she alternately devalued and idealized her female analyst. During this period she spoke extensively about her phallic mother who had fled from her children when they were very young, leaving them in the care of relatives. During this period she had many memories of her father lying on a bed with his penis exposed and frequently having her in his lap while he had an erection. He also fed her sweets and took her on long walks. Both agreed that the mother should not be told. She recalled that he bought her a fur coat when she was ten years old. During these memories she characterized her father as a weak, insignificant and silent man, albeit affectionate. There were hints that one of the reasons he worked so hard was to be "out with the boys or other women."

During her latency the patient allowed herself to be touched and approached from the rear by men and boys. She developed a fantasy that she was really a boy, and with menarche she experienced distinct relief that she now had evidence of being female. She was married in her twenties to a weak and ineffectual man, who was capable of caring for her financially. When he seemed interested only in sex, she felt extraordinary urges to castrate him. During the analysis she had multiple dreams of her female analyst holding or rubbing against her. In session she became quite frightened when she had a fantasy (after hearing the analyst move in her chair) that the analyst would get up and touch her genitals. This patient also was afraid to look at the analyst. In fact, looking and being looked at represented derivatives of extensive but repressed primal scene experiences that she was able to remember in the course of treatment. In these experiences her father was seen as the aggressor, but she was confused as to which parent had a penis. Since her father was perceived as the aggressor, she had defensively viewed him as weak and castrated in order to avoid her own fearful wishes for him. In the transference she later began to perceive the analyst as more female. She fantasied that the analyst was married to a weak, ineffectual man, about whom the patient was very curious and would "peek at" if he came by. At the same time her dreams involved her ability to wrest a strong man from another woman.

Case 4

An unemployed married mother of four young children became depressed postnatally and angry that her husband had forced the fourth pregnancy upon her. In actuality, it turned out that she had unconsciously arranged this pregnancy and refused the option of an abortion. The patient was the only child of an unsuccessful and alcoholic father who ostensibly ran a neighborhood business really run by her mother, who also had an auxiliary business. The father had been accused by the mother of having multiple affairs, and when he was not present at work, she would take the patient to search for him in hopes of catching him with other women. On such occasions, the father was often found lying about the house only partially dressed. One night, during her early adolescence, he actually came into her bed and put his arms around her. When the patient asked him about his poor relationship to the mother, he said, ''She's so frigid she keeps her diaphragm in the refrigerator.''

The father pressured his daughter into dressing like an adult prematurely and seemed more comfortable with this child-woman than with his wife. He also forced her into premature sexual experiences which he enjoyed vicariously, much as if he were an adolescent. When she returned from dates he would inquire, ''How far did you go?''

Her mother was sharply critical of her looks, behavior and aspirations. Once, while preparing a lunch for her mother, she substituted white glue for mayonnaise. Unlike the mother, her father praised her, adored her, thought she was wonderful and bought her little treats. He also gave her money which her mother refused her. As much as she hated her cold and aloof mother she admired her effectiveness; fond as she was of her father she despised his weaknesses. In adolescence she became a member of a motorcycle gang and convinced the members to physically beat him up.

Her husband was quite narcissistic and did not function up to his professional potential. His parents, however, were both very warm, giving and nonjudgmental. Her husband's hobby was collecting weapons. He taught their son to kill animals in the neighborhood and once, in a jealous fury, threatened the patient's life. She stayed in the marriage, always hoping that when he was less preoccupied with his own problems he would be more giving. At the same time, she was aware of vicarious excitement and fascination at his violence. In addition he made a great deal of money in a quasilegal manner and, although indicted, avoided prosecution.

After her mother's death, which followed the patient's divorce, she was very ambivalent about her father. On the one hand, she hated and resented him. On the other hand, she wished to help him both emotionally and financially because, "If he ever had a dollar in his pocket, he gave it to me."

CASTRATION ANXIETY RELATED TO FEAR OF MATERNAL LOSS

We believe that castration anxiety in females occurs only in the presence of the fantasy of an illusory phallus and is always related to fear of the loss of mother. This is diametrically opposed to Freud's view that castration anxiety is not found in women. Other workers have related castration anxiety to identification with the father, or to its presence after awareness of the anatomical distinction between the sexes and the feeling of inferiority in girls.

Case Illustrations

Case 1

A two-and-one-half year-old girl, who had essentially given up being nursed, was willing to try new things and separated easily from her mother, had a rapprochement crisis which began with a fear of the bathtub. Insisting that a dog would bite her bottom in the bath, she started to have wetting and soiling accidents, began to cling to her mother, demanded to be frequently put at the breast, and was observed masturbating with evidence of some anxiety. It was discovered that she had observed her brother in the bathtub one day when the family dog had jumped against and opened the unlocked bathroom door, and that for a period of about two weeks thereafter she reverted to infantile behavior with both obvious castration and separation anxiety. This gradually resolved itself; the child lost her phobia and then resumed active attempts at mastery and increased independence.

When the child heard of this episode a year later she said, "The dog unlocked the door with his paw. Everyone was watching television and I was lonely." It was evident to her mother, an analyst, that her biting dog phobia represented a projection of her own wish to orally incorporate her brother's penis. She felt that her brother was closer to her mother than she and attributed this to his being the proud possessor of a phallus, whereas she had "lost" hers when the dog bit her bottom.

Case 2

A young married woman with two latency age daughters came to treatment for failure to complete her thesis and inability to assert herself at work as an art historian and painter. She chose a woman analyst feeling that she could more easily and safely talk about her "female" problems. The early part of her analysis was filled with obsessional ruminations as she tried to work on her thesis and involved herself in a myriad of nonprofessional activities in which she could comfortably behave like "a bitch." She also was intrusive in the life of her eldest child, whose passive-aggression really did interfere with the patient's work. In addition, she had a poor sexual relationship with her husband, who she felt frightened easily and could not tolerate "normal aggression." When her husband entered treatment and became more desirous of a sexual relationship, she fled from this and refused to have them seen jointly by either therapist or a sexual therapist.

The first element worked through in her analysis was her terrible disappointment in and pressure on the eldest daughter. In this context she revealed that her father, a successful New England farmer, had always treated her like a boy and demanded that she awaken at four in the morning to do multiple farm chores, like barn cleaning and animal feeding. Although horses were available she had to walk many miles to school and was assigned the task of cleaning her father's boots, which he demanded look like those he had kept polished while he was in the army. He often beat her for failing to meet his expectations. By contrast, her mother was a gentle, quiet, intellectual woman who taught her about art, philosophy and music.

The second issue to be resolved in the analysis was the provocative part the patient played in her extracurricular activities, which interfered with her work. Although once she did not take charge of her seriously ill mother's convalescence but used the time to complete her work, this was followed by a series of self-sabotaging maneuvers. These included handing in her thesis so late that it could not be seen by several members of her committee, out of fear of having it ripped apart; keeping her thesis from being published because of the danger of exposure and loss (while publishing another book much less important to her); and rejecting the helpful efforts of her husband, out of bitterness and fury at his presumed attempt to invade her world and take away what belonged to her. At one time he had been considered very helpful in her work, but much as her vagina was closed to him, she began to close off the rest of her world to him. This thesis represented her illusory phallus, to which she clung with great anxiety. She feared exposure would lead to its loss and be felt as castration. The defensive use of her thesis as an illusory phallus and the symbolic reunion with her dead mother protected her against oedipal rivalry. The unfortunate price that she had to pay was her high level of castration anxiety, which interfered with her ability to work.

PENIS ENVY IN PREOEDIPAL FEAR OF MATERNAL LOSS

In our experience severe penis envy is not always related to jealousy of the father or to the wish to have his penis. Rather, it is often related to problems with the preoedipal mother, who the girl fantasies prefers men. Thus, if the girl child had a penis, she might be able to capture and keep her mother.

Case Illustration

The following session, presented almost verbatim, is from the termination phase of analysis. The patient, an unmarried professional woman, is the child of a dynamic father and a depressed mother who married in order to satisfy her own dependency needs.

This session took place after a missed session following a weekend. The patient missed the session in order to pick up a fur coat that her mother had bought for her, and entered wearing the new fur coat. She began by complaining that her mother picked on her, making various criticisms about the coat, the major criticism being that it was made of male rather than female skins.

During the weekend she reported that she had had three nightmares. The first was, "I lost my tongue." To this she associated the dreams she used to have at the beginning of analysis about losing her teeth. The second was, "I had a short fur jacket instead of my long coat. A. (patient's boyfriend) was wearing a false fur coat but he didn't realize it for a while. I was driving with my mother who was competing with me for A." The third nightmare was, "My left leg was amputated. A wooden leg had grown in. Now my right leg had to be amputated. I heard the electrical saw and I woke up screaming. Half-awake, I told this dream to A. and he said, 'castration dream.' He touched my vaginal area and said, 'No need to worry; all you have is a hole.' " The patient then "slugged" him very hard. (She had never hit anyone before.)

(Patient): "I remember another dream. I was taking care of a baby. I kept dropping it and it was getting all bashed up. I asked my brother for help. Then I was holding an egg. I kept dropping it also. The baby's parents were about to come home. I didn't know what in the world I would tell them. Then my brother produced the baby. He had hidden it and substituted the egg so I wouldn't hurt the baby.

"Another dream, too. The Jews were being persecuted. We were getting away on a boat. My mother had a chest of silver and pearls. I was supposed to exchange what I had for my mom's but I didn't want hers. Why did that missed session remind me all over again about castration?"

(Analyst): "You lost your 'good mother' who has given you a penis and allowed you to keep it."

(Patient): "I've been thinking about having a baby a lot. That will be at least two to three years away, if I can get organized with the job that I want within the next six months. Can I borrow your pen? I thought of a call I have to make. I usually have my own pen in my bag, but I can't find it."

(Analyst) (handing her the pen): "Why should this have happened now?"

(Patient): "I'm not concentrating well. When A. and I were making love I was obsessed by a blouse I had bought. I bought a bunch of things I really didn't need from a lady who sells out of the house. I couldn't decide if the blouse would fit right. While making love, I was obsessed about the blouse in the box in the closet. I never seem to be happy with what I've got."

Interpretation of the Session

The first nightmare, about the loss of a bodily part, the patient readily related to lifelong dreams of losing her teeth, which she realized were castration dreams. The second nightmare was related to an amputation of her fur coat to one-half length, and her boyfriend had a false fur coat (a fake penis) without realizing it. The patient's mother was competing with her for her boyfriend (oedipal rivalry). The third nightmare involved the core problem coming close to consciousness, with an amputation of her leg after a previous amputation had grown out. Her boyfriend A. correctly interpreted this and evoked in her an uncharacteristic violence.

She then remembered another dream. In this case she had care of a baby (substitute penis) that she kept dropping. In an attempt to help her, her brother substituted an egg which she continued to drop. She was worried about what to tell the parents about their baby. This represents her parents' baby, the brother who appeared in the dream and saved himself. Indeed, she had repeatedly stolen from this brother, specifically, an easter egg which she had eaten.

The fifth dream was about being persecuted. (Her mother had escaped Europe before the second World War.) In this dream her mother had a chest of silver and pearls (jewel case = female genitals) (Breuer and Freud, 1892). She was supposed to exchange what she had, a penis, but she didn't want to. She wondered why the missed session reminded her all over again about castration.

The interpretation was that the analyst was seen as having given her a penis. Loss of the analyst threatened her with loss of this gift. She spoke about fantasies of having a baby (substitute penis). She suddenly needed to write something down, which related to her job, and asked to borrow the analyst's pen (penis), stating that she usually had her own in her bag (vagina) but that she couldn't find it. When the analyst wondered why that had occurred, she avoided answering the question directly and revealed two further pieces of data. First, she had bought clothing that she did not need and could not understand why. This behavior was an attempt to repair the sense of having been castrated. Second, during sex she was obsessionally concerned with the blouse that did not fit her, in the box in the closet (a condensation of an illusory phallus in her vagina and a female genital representation with which she was uncomfortable). The session closed with her recognition that she never seemed to be happy with what she had.

This is a patient who alternated between extreme penis envy, which she often attempted to repair by the acquisition of transitional objects (fur coat) and the fantasy of an illusory phallus about which she developed extreme castration anxiety. Both of these are related to her longing for her mother and her wish to satisfy her mother's need to keep the patient close and unseparated. (Her mother bought a fur coat for this successful professional woman, an item either she or her successful boyfriend could have afforded to purchase.) The fur coat is probably a transitional object for the mother as well, since the mother was separated from her own mother as a child. The complexity of themes in this single session illustrates a large part of the tapestry of the female experience that is reenacted in an analysis.

This session reveals the many determinants of penis envy. Freud repeatedly showed us that parapraxes, dream symbols, and even transient symptoms were multidetermined. Yet Freud rested his entire theory of female development upon a single event, namely, the discovery of the anatomical differences between the sexes.

Schafer (1974) believes that Freud was centered on the importance of anatomy and reproduction as a consequence of his commitment to an evolutionary model and a societal value system that placed priority on procreation. Ernest Jones (1935), Freud's biographer, coined the word "phallocentric" as characterizing both Freud, the man, and his theories.

CHAPTER 5

What Does A Woman Want?
Oedipal Considerations

THE CROSSROADS OF SEPARATION-INDIVIDUATION

At approximately eighteen months, the expectations, ideals, values and aspirations, as well as the rewards for and the prohibitions against behaviors, differ markedly for each sex. There is evidence that girls have early, if poorly defined and differentiated vaginal sensations, and that these clearly precede clitoral sensations. Self-stimulation is seen from birth, but it is unfocused until this time. Children tactilely explore their own faces and bodies and those of their mothers, although visual comparisons of others to the mother follow later. Core gender identity is now firmly established and unalterable, without severe psychological disturbance. This occurs even in the absence of normally formed genitals or in the absence of the parent of the opposite sex. In cases where core gender identity is abnormal (transsexuals), there is a disturbed mother-child relationship. At this critical period children begin to traverse the crossroads of separation and castration anxiety.

At this point we must diverge from the classical Freudian viewpoint that the anatomical difference between the sexes is most frequently noticed at age three, ushering in the female oedipal complex. Our analytic data confirms the direct child observations of Galenson and Roiphe that this occurs at eighteen to thirty months, which coincides with the final separation-individuation from the mother (Mahler's rapprochement phase). During this early period, the observation of anatomical differences between the sexes does not seem seriously to affect the little boy, but it always seriously affects the young girl, who often experiences castration shock.

This castration shock could be accounted for by prior narcissistic injury. We propose that the narcissistic injury with which the young girl already is coping is the loss of the mother as separation-individuation proceeds. This is more serious for girls since they have been held closer to the mother traditionally, whereas boys' independence generally has been fostered earlier as part of the parental conception of core gender identity and because boys in general are biologically more active.

DEFORMATION OF THE OEDIPAL COMPLEX

Vagueness of Female Genitalia

Female children have a further problem as a result of their normal genital anatomy. Their vagueness about the configuration of their body is abetted by parental mislabelling. Even with attempts at proper labelling, girls are vague about the labelling of their genitals, which are not easily inspected. We suspect that this contributes to a deficit in body imagery and impels a continuing tie to the mother for a sense of physical completeness. This necessity for maintaining closeness to the mother also deforms the oedipal conflict.

Case 1

A three-year-old-girl, daughter and granddaughter of physicians (including grandmother and mother), was adequately and formally introduced to all parts of her anatomy, which were correctly labelled for her. At age ten, while describing the discomfort of a small girl in a wet, sandy bathing suit, she easily labelled the child's rectum, but referred to her genital area only vaguely by saying, "Maybe she has sand in her rectum or in front of her where it is open."

This little girl had a persistent clinging attachment to her mother. She expressed fantasies of wanting to have a baby that she and her mother could play with, but she was also a tomboy who cultivated an interest in the sports in which her father and brother were proficient. When ill, she would ask her mother to leave the parental bed and come into her bed. It was not until the age of ten, when her father was encouraged by her mother to take a more active interest in this child as a female, that she turned to him with expressed preference for the first time.

At this time she asked her mother if she would inherit all the mother's jewelry when the mother died. She herself became interested in jewelry and feminine clothing. She flirted with her father and attempted to take over from the mother the task of massaging his back. She coaxed her father into dancing with her and began to tell him that her first child would be a girl. She reported a dream in which she entered a room and found a beautiful box with her mother's initials, which she took as her own.

The above illustrates delayed oedipal phase behavior as well as typical behavior of latency, including the girl's flirting with her father and reporting dreams and oedipal fantasies about having a child, rather than revealing the romance fantasies about latency.

Severe Trauma

This period also affects children of both sexes who already have experienced a challenge to their intrapsychic body image secondary to family physical or psychiatric illness, surgery, or other such trauma. These "castration shock" reactions can precede the oedipal period by several months.

Case 2

The patient was a 21-year-old college dropout, who worked at a menial job while living with her boyfriend. She sought treatment because of a profound depression. Her boyfriend was continuing on to graduate school and did not wish to marry her unless she returned to school and found a career.

The patient was the daughter of professional parents, the middle child of three siblings. In high school she had been an excellent student. A favorite teacher suspected that she was abusing drugs, a fact that her parents had not noticed. They had been complacent about her life until the presenting depression and had tacitly allowed her to abuse drugs and drop out of college.

At first meeting it was clear that she was a loving, kind and empathic individual, yet very untrusting of people and without friends. She seemed to be hiding a horrendous secret, the nature of which she was not conscious. She described it merely as "some awful shadow from my childhood." Ostensibly, both siblings were functioning well, although each was doing very "offbeat" things considering their middle-class, professional background. The first task accomplished in the analysis was to confront, clarify and make conscious her anger at her boyfriend, who was the only one she had ever trusted. The patient then was able to continue their relationship on weekends and moved back to her parental home in order to return to a local college.

In analyzing the family interactions it became apparent that the older brother, who was acknowledged to be hyperactive as a child and "weird" as an adult, was really overtly psychotic. He had always been prone to rages and succeeded in manipulating the family to support him financially, but they avoided confrontation with him. The patient then remembered that the brother's severe drug and truancy problem during her high school years had humiliated her. She dealt with her shame and dysphoria by using drugs, which also represented an identification with him. Her distress with him and her family's inability to control him sent her off to a college almost chosen at random, and their inability to be involved with her led her to seek the safe haven of living with her boyfriend.

She remembered that her brother had been a psychotic child who had brutalized her while her parents looked away. On one occasion he had put a caustic alkaline household cleaner into her bath and on another, attempted to kill his mother in the patient's presence. Despite this the parents often left her alone in the house with him, and she became a terrorized child who constantly searched for protection. Some of her needs were met by a maternal grandmother to whose home she could flee.

The job that she chose initially after dropping out of college was one in which she looked after a baby with whom she identified, providing her with the vicarious mothering that she had needed in her earlier life. It seemed that the patient's oedipal period was consumed with the one aim of protecting her physical safety. She saw men as dangerous and relationships with them to be avoided. She perceived that her mother was depressed and ineffectual and longed for a parent to protect and to love her. She had found this parent in the person of her boyfriend, in whom she saw both paternal and maternal features.

When this patient entered adolescence she might have had a chance to work out her oedipal conflict, but her brother again became an overwhelming threat to the patient and to her family. Thus, her oedipal triangle, so long postponed, seemed to occur for the first time in the transference between her boyfriend and the analyst. Even at that time the problems of penis envy and castration anxiety were subordinated to the patient's needs for physical safety. With the help of the analyst she was able to confront her parents with the extent of her brother's psychopathology, which they continued to deny. Her younger sister, however, confirmed it although she had escaped without the severe traumatization that the patient had endured, having been born during the brother's latency when his symptoms were less overwhelming. The patient also was naturally gentle, whereas her younger sister was quite aggressive, tough and strong, and often protected the patient from their brother.

When the patient was ready to apply to graduate school, she was intensely competitive with the analyst rather than with her mother. She had done extraordinarily well upon her return to college, which her parents had not acknowledged. The patient was faced also with the decision of whether or not to move back to her boyfriend's home in another city while she attended graduate school. During this period, while struggling with her fear of the analyst's retaliation and rage, she developed a phobic symptom. She became afraid that her furniture would be broken in transit to another city. This represented a displacement of her castration anxiety.

She then had a fantasy that she would be unable to have a baby. Nonetheless, in a counterphobic manner, she became pregnant. This represented a wish for reunion with the analyst as mother. It was also understood as a coercive effort to get the analyst to intervene and to keep her from moving away. Her fantasy was that she would have her baby and take care of it with the analyst's help. Her parents maintained their usual neutrality in this situation while her boyfriend prevailed upon her to terminate the pregnancy until a more appropriate time. In her own mind she blamed the analyst for the termination of the pregnancy.

She elected to try summer school in the city where her boyfriend lived. The summer went well and the patient decided to remain with him. She discontinued analysis, but commuted to psychotherapy sessions once a week. She then kept in touch by mail, proudly reporting her progress and independence. She barely communicated with her parents but became closer to her sister. Her family eventually did put controls on her brother, who had increasing difficulty coping in life. The patient's boyfriend, who was not panicked by this psychotic man, was able to be helpful to him. This assuaged the patient's guilt over her brother, whom she feared and hated but knew was ill.

Case 3

Traumatic surgery simultaneous with the entry into the oedipal stage can deform the oedipus complex, causing increased dependent clinging to the mother in order to undo the abandonment that surgery represents. In the following case, the patient's negative feelings towards the abandoning mother were displaced onto her father, thus changing the constellation of her oedipal conflict.

The patient was a 27-year-old married physician and mother of two children, who had entered medicine because of her desire to be a surgeon. She sought treatment for anxiety attacks which followed the birth of her second child, who had a severe congenital illness requiring surgery. The patient had a history of more minor but similar attacks related to the witnessing, but not performance, of surgical procedures on others and in relationship to an injury to herself.

She was the only daughter of two professional parents. She hated her father, whose ''son'' she had been during latency. She had provoked him into beating her up severely and repeatedly at that time. This interaction ended with her menarche. Her father was a phobic man who often had fainting spells. She described her mother as a perfect beauty whom she idealized, but with whom she felt she could never compete. An early memory was of a surgical procedure performed on her at home on the kitchen table, into which she had been tricked and during which her parents had left the house. Her first dream was of being chased by the Nazis, a man and woman whom she recognized as her parents. In the dream, she shot and killed one of them, but could not recall which one. During childhood, recurrent dreams were of being chased by the Nazis and of skiing off a cliff during which she physically fell to the floor. Her associations were to the movie, *Spellbound*, the first movie to which she had ever been taken. She identified with the male patient, and with the good mother-analyst who helped recover memories and made things all right. She dreamt of her father as the surgeon at her operative procedure.

Her earliest memory was of having slept in her parents' room during summer vacation, having fallen out of bed, knocking a blue ball handle off the night table and splitting her lip. This was a screen memory. In reality, she had fallen out of bed that summer, but had been cut at a different time, and the knob of the night table had been broken by household help. It was her exposure to the primal scene that was screened by this memory, in which she was castrated (bleeding from the mouth), and the more passive parent lost her "blue ball."

As her sexual experience became less constricted she allowed cunnilingus in a passive position, had a powerful orgasm, and was surprised to hear herself say, "Please don't leave me." She thus became aware of her profound separation anxiety. She had had the unconscious fantasy that she had been prepared to be eaten on the kitchen table during the surgical procedure of her childhood. As the analysis progressed, the patient came to realize that her father was the warmer, more accessible parent whom she hated for having castrated her. Her mother, though the more indifferent, narcissistic parent, had in reality not been responsible for leaving her during the surgical procedure. It was, rather, her father's inability to tolerate her screams that caused them both to leave the house.

Her traumatic surgery and rage toward her father were preoedipal legacies, as was her need to cling to her mother in an attempt to negate the abandonment of surgery. The illness (castration) of her youngest child led to the reexacerbation of her oedipal and preoedipal problems, and the patient's entire analysis was preoccupied with issues of rage, abandonment and mutilation. In order to preserve an oedipal relationship with her father, the patient continued to blame her mother for the abandonment and mutilation during her surgery. Her physical battles with her father were not related to the usual adolescent denial of oedipal feelings, but were really a reenactment of the perceived violence of the primal scene. In reality, the analyst (mother) was spared battles with the patient, who battled with her husband instead.

Separations from the analyst were always perceived as abandonments and were tolerated poorly. During one period of separation from her analyst, the patient became enraged and almost started a love affair. She had a dream that she had fled from the Nazis into the arms of the object of her romantic feelings who had protected her. The analysis of that dream led to the recollection that it was her father whom she had killed in the initial dream. This patient protected the image of a good mother because abandonment before separation-individuation is more traumatic than oedipal phase castration.

Separation from the Mother

We have presented cases in which surgery, trauma and illness in a child or family member have deformed the oedipal conflict. These occurred because of separation from the mother when the child was on the verge of the rapprochement phase and coincident with the imminent entry into the oedipal conflict. Prolonged separation from the mother in any form, as a result of illness, death, or even pregnancy, can also deform the oedipal configuration.

An example of the deformation of the oedipal conflict caused by prolonged separation from the mother is as follows:

Case 4

The patient was a 19-year-old college student who sought treatment because of depression and an inability to write creatively. She had been both an excellent creative writer and an actress of some talent as a child. She did not pursue a theatrical career because she "could not learn to sing." The patient was the youngest of four children. Not long after her birth, her mother suffered a postmenopausal depression for which she had an initial brief hospitalization, followed by a prolonged hospitalization when the patient was two years old. During this period, the patient was cared for by her father and her three older siblings and an aunt. Her earliest memory was of being distressed upon her mother's return. Although her mother tried to establish a good relationship with her, the patient always perceived of her as critical, unreliable and demanding. After her mother's return home the patient's father became progressively more involved in his business activities. In addition, the family, who had always been religiously orthodox, now became fanatic in their religious practices. The patient would sneak off to do forbidden things, which she realized represented her wish to defy her mother. Her family disapproved of her choice of a college far from home.

The patient's analytic treatment was marked by an immediate worsening of her symptoms of work inhibition and depression, and she began to develop social anxiety. Her parents pressured her to return home and even refused to pay her school tuition. Nevertheless, she opted to remain in New York, although she talked about getting better psychiatric treatment at home. She took a part-time job and moved to a slumlike area, which the analyst viewed with great concern. But the patient seemed oblivious and even counterphobic about the dangers involved. She entered a series of unsatisfactory and even sadistic relationships, turning to the analyst to protect her, yet was resistant to her help.

The first relief of symptoms occurred with the development of a paternal transference, in which the analyst was seen as a father who had in the past been maternalized. The interpretation of the transference occurred when the patient realized that she was discussing the practicalities of her life (financial and career goals), much as she had listened to her father discuss his business goals with all of the children during her mother's absence. Being little, she sat on his lap at that time, enjoying the physical comfort which he provided; thus, she would not interrupt his conversation with her older siblings.

Shortly thereafter, the transference changed to a maternal transference with many memories of the good (not absent) mother of her childhood. In the course of her involvement with a musician, she "discovered" that she had a good singing voice, and began a full-time job in order to be able to pay for singing lessons. Upon being told by her teacher that she had considerable operatic talent and ought to train in that direction (rather than toward musical comedy), she recalled that her mother had been a light opera singer. The man with whom she was involved at the time periodically abandoned her, and she began to distance herself from him as she had from her absent mother. One day, she said innocently, "I thought of something very psychological." She then revealed her increasing insight that her relationship with this musician, as well as with other men, paralleled the relationship that she had had with her mother, not the one with her father. She was then able to develop a relationship with a very maternal man who eased her financial pressures and was very devoted to her career goals. When his job eventually demanded a change in schedule and the two had less time to spend together, she was able to maintain object constancy and feel good about herself. For the first time in her life she thought about marriage and indeed she planned to marry this man. Moreover, despite illness of both parents at this time, she was able to make arrangements for their care without having to sacrifice her own life by returning home.

This case illustrates how, as a result of prolonged separation from the mother in the preoedipal and oedipal periods, this woman could not permit herself to fall in love with an appropriate maternal man like her father. Initially this choice was forbidden to her because of severe oedipal guilt, since she had been obliged to assume her mother's role in the household during the oedipal period.

Case 5

One female patient, a 25-year-old professional student, was a middle child in a family of sons. She remembered many things about her early childhood, with the exception of her mother's pregnancy and the arrival at home of her younger brother. She came to treatment because of intense examination anxiety and was angry at being in a "second-class profession." The thought of allowing her to study law, medicine or engineering had never occurred to her family, since she had been her father's girl, helping him in his office.

Her father had always been busy and aloof whereas her mother, a depressed housewife, was quite involved with the children. Although the patient's comments about this were always derisive, her secret ambition, revealed in dreams, was to marry, have children and be taken care of as her father had cared for her mother.

The patient also had recurrent dreams of pregnancy. She envied her female analyst's career, ostensibly one to which she aspired and because she did not attain it, felt cheated. When her analyst became pregnant, the patient neither commented on the pregnancy nor revealed her knowledge of it by dreams, parapraxes, or associations. During the analyst's sixth month of pregnancy she confronted the patient with the fact. The patient felt shocked and rationalized that she had only perceived the analyst as tending to wear looser clothes because she had gained weight. But, two weeks later, the patient, who had an active sexual life and had always used birth control pills, also became pregnant. Although the realities of her life seemed to require her to have an abortion, she was loathe at first to seek this solution. When she finally made arrangements, she told her parents and was horribly disappointed when her mother refused to defer, even for one day, a trip that she had planned.

She remembered her mother's pregnancy with her younger brother, and although she had experienced the mother's delivery as an abandonment, adored her baby brother and had, in fact, played the role of mother to him. He had never forgotten this and was closer to the patient than to his biological mother.

The patient's abortion was followed by a serious depression. Meanwhile, the analyst's pregnancy was followed with great interest and adoration, and she, of all the analyst's patients, made the most inquiries about the awaited baby. The cold, aloof and obsessional demeanor that had thus far characterized the analysis melted away. She was anxious lest the analyst abandon her, but grew reassured as time passed. She began to wear attractive and feminine attire as well as jewelry. She felt confident that she would marry and spend time at home raising her own children. Her fear of surpassing, and thus destroying her mother, as she perceived her father had done, was analyzed. (It was his work preoccupation that had actually related to the mother's depression.) When this was analyzed, she was able to handle a difficult job without anxiety. She also made friends with both sexes. Finally, on the day of her last session she brought the analyst a scarf as a gift, which, interestingly was the same color as the maternity dress that the analyst had worn during a prior session with this patient. This final session had taken place on the day that the analyst had delivered her baby.

Case 6

Death of the mother or mother-substitute during the oedipal period also significantly alters the oedipal constellation.

A 30-year-old woman physician had become depressed after the death of a beloved mother-substitute when she was five years of age. She made a rapid positive transference to what she perceived was her good mother in the analyst and subsequently gained twenty pounds, which she had also done years earlier, shortly after menarche. Her dreams were replete with themes of pregnancy, delivery and nursing. The baby in these dreams resembled the analyst as well as the aunt who had died when the patient was five. The patient recalled that up to the age of two and one-half she had had a close relationship with both parents who were warm and empathic. But she was "suddenly" sent to nursery school because her mother had to return to work, maintaining two jobs while her aunt became the babysitter. Her father, who was unable to earn the livelihood that the family had anticipated, became depressed.

Before this period the patient recalled herself as a lively, vivacious child who would talk easily to any man she met. However, after age two and one-half she became frightened, feared being alone, was afraid of the dark and had multiple nightmares. One recurrent dream, experienced as pleasant, was of playing on the beach with a little boy, while a brontosaurus head peered protectively over the pair. The patient associated the brontosaurus with her protective father of her first two years. When he suffered his first severe depression, he was no longer able to relate to his little girl, and with her mother working, she turned to her aunt for maternal nurturance. When her aunt died, the patient had not been told of the impending death, but was aware that her aunt had grown an enormous abdomen. Her fantasy was that her aunt was pregnant with her father's child, although this "pregnancy" turned out to be a terminal ovarian cancer. In times of separation from her analyst the patient often "forgot" to use contraception which, however, did not eventuate in pregnancy. These symptomatic acts were viewed as attempts at reunion with a good, preoedipal mother-analyst.

Physical Illness or Disability

In addition to changes in the configuration of the oedipal conflict wrought by family illness or trauma, surgery and prolonged separation from the mother, there are cases which present with a deformed oedipal configuration secondary to severe prolonged illness. An individual who has been overwhelmed by the catastrophic events of early childhood experiences changes, not only in the oedipal complex, but also in ego functioning. For example, an individual with disturbances in motor function, such as paralysis from early life (polio), may hypertrophy the functions of verbal ability and creativity. A child with dyslexia may turn her attention to motor skills, thus becoming an expert in a sport, while creativity and verbal ability will suffer. One analytic patient, a successful attorney with a reading disability, hired a reader and spent all of her spare time bowling with her law firm's bowling team and supervising bowling teams for disadvantaged youngsters.

Physical illness or disability may stimulate the ego's defensive functions. For example, counterphobia is often the basis for the choice of a medical career. This may be combined with a loving rescue fantasy and a reaction-formation response. One of the authors (Bernstein) recently surveyed a class of medical students. Originally 90 percent affirmed that they were aware of a severe physical illness or an injury requiring hospitalization during the first three years of life. As the subject of how this may have influenced their choice of a medical career was discussed, another 5 percent had recovered the memory of an important early illness. The other author (Warner, 1970), while acting as a psychiatric consultant in a school of nursing, saw 400 students for consultation and 40 students in treatment. A history of a severe illness in each student or her mother in the first five years of life was almost universal.

Case 7

A female patient with a learning disability and multiple congenital disorders thought that she was "dumb" in comparison to her brilliant brother. This perception occurred *before* the observation of the anatomical differences between the sexes. After observing these differences, she developed her entire personality around a core fantasy of obtaining a penis by incorporation (oral, anal and phallic) in order to fill this "hole in her head." This is an unusual clinical picture. The more common presentation in female analysands is that they perceive genital castration and penis envy first, which leaves them with an ego deficit in their cognitive self-image; they feel less smart than men.

Case 8

One woman analysand had a severe orthopedic injury and failed to grow in early childhood. This resulted in a protracted hospitalization during which she was virtually immobilized. She taught herself to read and concentrated on the development of her cognitive functioning. Unable to participate in much physical activity, she became a planner and a designer in addition to her medical career. She developed phallic and "macho" character traits and became very competitive in her own activities, striving to outdo her peers. This represented a deficit in self-image compensated for by a denial in fantasy (A. Freud, 1966), in which her unconscious fantasy as a "big shot" was the opposite of her conscious perception.

The Wish for a Baby

Lacking the penis as a transitional object, and struggling with residual problems of separation-individuation from mother, the female child enters the oedipal phase of development. She forms a number of fantasies whose ultimate purpose is to maintain her union with her intrapsychic representation of her mother. Although vague about her own anatomy and the facts of reproduction, very often female children express the very strong wish to have a baby. This does not represent the longing for father's penis or a substitute for it. It is one fantasy which initiates the entrance into the oedipal conflict and can act to deform it.

Case 9

The patient had a narcissistic and often absent father and was raised by a depressed and suicidal mother. This patient was openly competitive with men, and inhibited and sabotaged her husband's career. Having been sexually frigid because she "hated to be reminded of a vagina," she was eager to be pregnant and became sexually interested and orgasmic during pregnancy. As delivery approached, however, she became panicky and had dreams that her body would be ripped apart and that she again would be left with the empty vagina that she hated.

Although she insisted that the sex of the child was of no concern to her, she had repeatedly dreamt of and referred to the baby as "he," and had only chosen a boy's name. Nursing her newborn son restored her equilibrium and diminished her anxiety, but she again refused sex with her husband. She stated that while nursing her infant she felt whole and kept her son close to her, trying to discourage his early attempts at mobility. Yet, at the time of weaning, a major portion of her analysis was complete and she was able to tolerate separation from him. She looked forward to returning to part-time work and enrolling her son in a nursery school.

Despite her strides, her son had a school phobia. (She jokingly commented that she had undoubtedly convinced him that he was her penis.) Gradually, when she was no longer ambivalent about the separation (a mother's ambivalence will inhibit a child's separation), there was no problem in getting the son to go to school. But he then showed cognitive failures despite a high intelligence. Since these had resulted from the mother's early handling of her son and were not remediable without treatment even though her attitudes had changed, the child was also analyzed. In his analysis, he relived and repaired some of the old problems surrounding separation and individuation that had left developmental deficits in cognition.

The above is a case in which more superficial evaluation would lead to theorizing about penis envy, castration anxiety and the wish to have a baby. Deeper analysis revealed that this patient's penis-baby was a replacement for her mother. While nursing her baby, the patient was symbolically, blissfully reunited with her own preoedipal mother. The symbiotic relationship had taken place before the occurrence of her mother's clinical depression, and entrance into the oedipal phase began with her express wish to have a baby. Turning to her father, who was not available as a love object, she was able to interest him in her academic achievements.

The patient had competed successfully but destructively with men throughout her school years. Destructive rage and its projection onto men defended against her longing for a father at the period when her mother was ill and absent. This, in turn, protected against a deeper longing for her mother, whom she perceived as abandoning her during the rapprochement subphase of separation-individuation.

After a prolonged analysis with an intense, dependent and hostile transference to her mother-analyst, the patient initiated the final repair of her defective self-representation. She felt incomplete without her mother or a penis-baby, until analysis of the transference was completed. For the first time in her life she was able to make friends with women and to continue lasting relationships with them. She entered a profession which required her to care for immigrant children who had suffered severe loss and abandonment. They even spoke the languages that she had spoken during her oedipal and early latency years.

Case 10

The wish for a baby may not arise out of identification with the mother and desire for reunion with her or out of the pure oedipal wish to have the father's baby. The following case is that of a patient who wished to have the baby her mother was incapable of having, in order to keep her mother homebound and within the family.

A 45-year-old woman presented with the complaint that her husband had been sexually impotent for the past ten years. The couple had two teenage children, which made her reluctant to separate from her husband despite severe frustration. Both children had an illness that was known to worsen in severity with succeeding pregnancies. Therefore, after the second pregnancy, the patient had a tubal ligation but continued to desire more children. She blamed her husband for the genetic problem, and it later proved to be her chronic anger with him that had caused his impotency (which promptly remitted during his second marriage). The patient subsequently remarried a man who was raising young children of his own.

The patient had grown up in an enormously wealthy European family, the older of two siblings taken care of by a nanny, "Fraulein F." They were isolated from their charming and successful father as soon as they became old enough to demand attention, and were exiled to a nursery which he formally visited once a day. Their mother was an extraordinarily beautiful woman who would come to play tea-party with the children and their dolls after the governess had carefully put away all the toys. But, she soon became involved in charitable activities and was rarely at home. The father, who did not have to work very hard, was known to visit the house during the day, and the patient developed the fantasy that he was having an affair with "Fraulein F." She began to implore the mother, at every opportunity, to have another child or to remain at home during the day, to which the mother laughingly replied that she was too old to have more children and that it would spoil her appearance. The patient even questioned "Fraulein F." about the laughter she had overheard between her and her father. The mother once appeared at home, and finding the two together, fired the governess. However, "Fraulein F." maintained a close relationship with both children, which lasted throughout their lives. She would never say why she had been fired nor give the patient any information about her mother or father. They would only talk about a great many other things.

During the course of her analysis the patient recovered the fantasy that she could have her father's child for her mother, thereby keeping the mother home and bringing the father back to the nursery. The man she had married was deliberately selected because he came from a wealthy family, and the patient imagined that there would be no obstacle to having many children.

In our experience, the young girl's wish for a baby grows out of either the need to repair the premature separation from the mother or a positive identification with a good preoedipal mother leading to firm feminine gender identification.

Case 11

The following is the case of a woman who could not establish firm gender identification or develop the wish for a baby until the damage she had suffered in a poor relationship with her preoedipal mother was analyzed.

The patient was a 38-year-old business woman who had had many prior years of analysis with a male analyst. Work in the analysis seemed to have been centered around her relationship with her father and her penis envy. It did not help her to adjust at work where she had to compete with men; nor did it help her failing marriage. The patient thought that she should have a child as the time for childbearing was rapidly nearing an end, but she did not have emotional desire for a child or any maternal feelings. Because the patient did not progress in her analysis, she accepted the suggestion of a friend to seek consultation and treatment. She wanted a female analyst.

The patient's initial psychiatric illness occurred after a fight with her mother, which she perceived as an attempt to ward off the mother's invasiveness into her life. Following the fight, the mother had a heart attack and never fully recovered. As a result, the patient's father blamed the patient for the mother's slow, downhill course that led to her progressive invalidism and death. The patient suffered a severe loss of self-esteem and had feelings of depersonalization; in addition, she was depressed about the loss of her job.

Her work with the female analyst was primarily centered around the relationship with her mother. She had been an only child, whose birth caused her domineering, European father to forbid her mother to continue working, although the family had multiple servants. Initially, the patient perceived her mother as the neutral parent and her father as alternately critical and unavailable. He had wanted a son.

The patient's primary relationships in childhood were with animals: first, with her dog and later, with her horse. At other times she would withdraw into a fantasy world of lush optic imagery which she created (and utilized much later in her work). She recalled times in school when she physically felt that she was incapable and "in a gel."

Her initial transference was cold and aloof, although she did not experience it as such. Analysis of this transference led her to recognize that her mother had criticized and "neutered" her. For several sessions, she physically tried to hide her hands from the analyst's view, fearing derision and criticism because they were not manicured. However, eventually the patient, who had never felt pretty, was able to buy feminine clothes, get a stylish haircut and wear nail polish. The patient began working more regularly and made an effort to expand her network of female friends. At this point in treatment she recalled closeness to her father as a young child. However, showering with him after swimming ended abruptly when she was about five years old, after she pulled his penis in the shower.

She recalled a period of militant feminism early in her career, during which she felt more respected and competent, and she became able to give up the wish to return to this adaptation and feel competent with her growing femininity. She began to write a book in which lurking, ferocious dog images recurred and recognized this as a symbol for her mother. Weird and dissociative episodes described in her book correlated with feelings of being disconnected from the analyst, especially during vacations. As she learned that the true source of her anger was her preoedipal mother, she became less angry and more accepting of her husband, a rigid and obsessional man.

After two years of treatment she began to become emotionally involved with her friends' children and considered becoming pregnant. She wished to terminate treatment, allegedly because of time and expense. A date was set, several months in advance, and she continued to feel good about herself, was productive and optimistic. The major unresolved issue in her life was the failure at reconciliation with her now critically ill father. Nonetheless, she was able to handle this without losing her self-esteem. She became emotionally close to and helpful to both her mother-in-law and a sickly maiden aunt.

During the summer she failed to become pregnant as she had planned. Again becoming irritable with her husband, unsure of herself, less successful in business, and depressed, she returned for further treatment. The baby she had failed to conceive represented both her link with the future and her wish for reunion with a good mother. During the first several visits, the patient again seemed hardened, cool and masculine. Her first dream was, "I was a boy. Someone called a lady—you—to take care of me. The lady already had four or five other kids to look after. She said that I could come, but that she might not be able to pay too much attention to me. I awakened in tears."

The patient was able to associatively link the perceived abandonment by the analyst with her regression to a masculine identification. This was further confirmed in her mind by her failure to achieve pregnancy. The patient had not yet introjected a good-enough preoedipal mother to foster her feminine gender identity. Rather, this identity still depended upon the real presence of the good mother-analyst. Further analysis would be directed toward undermining the still present bad preoedipal maternal introject whose shadow still fell upon the patient's ego.

Summary and Conclusions

We have presented material from the analysis of female patients, which leads us to a formulation of female psychology that differs from the Freudian view. In our theory, the major determinant of female psychology is the temporal coincidence of the rapprochement subphase of separation-individuation with the oedipal complex. Galenson and Roiphe (Galenson, 1971a, 1971b; Galenson and Roiphe, 1976) have observed that boys are affected by this temporal coincidence and handle their maternal loss by using the penis as a transitional object. Thus, genital masturbation increases during this period. At the same time, girls have been observed to "turn inward." We have found that this inward-turning represents a period of reparative fantasy formation designed to effect continuing union with the preoedipal mother.

The fantasy of an illusory penis, with resultant castration anxiety, is one such reparative fantasy. It is also one of the fantasies that propels the female child into the oedipal conflict. A second fantasy is the wish for a child. This fantasy is not based on the wish for a substitute for father's penis, as Freud suggested. Rather, it is usually rooted in the need to maintain a continuing union with the preoedipal mother through identification. In fact, where this identification fails, there is difficulty in core feminine gender identification as well as an absence of the desire for a baby. The wish for a baby is the second mode of entry into the oedipal complex and the most common one, in our experience. The third mode of entrance into the oedipal complex is via the

preoedipal attachment to the father, who serves as a replacement for the preoedipal mother. Girls pay attention to
their fathers at ten to eighteen months of age, somewhat
earlier than boys. This attachment is maternal at first, and
only later becomes oedipal. The authors have found that
many female patients said ''dada'' or its equivalent before
''mama,'' even when the mother had been the primary caretaker and breastfed the child.

It is the function of the father to intervene in the symbiotic relationship between mother and daughter. There is
almost no little girl, or adult woman in analysis, who does
not remember her father prancing around, making silly
faces, bringing her all sorts of toys and fussing over her
prettiness, unless there has been severe psychopathology in
the father. The popularity of the soliloquy from the Broad-
way musical and movie, *Carousel*, reflects its universal
theme: The father to be starts a song with the words, ''My
son, Bill.'' He goes on to sing about what rugged times
they will have together, how he will teach him to fight, to
be a man and how his son can choose any job he wants.
He can even conquer the world with the help, urging and
pride of his father. Suddenly there is a long pause in the
music, and the words that follow are, ''My God, what if
he is a she?'' The lyrics change, as does the tonal quality
of the music. The thought content is about the prettiness of
the little girl, the need to protect her, the need of the father
not to be a bum, but to be able to support her and buy her
pretty clothes, and the anticipation that she will, indeed, not
marry just any man. Her husband will have to be special
and wonderful and not a bum like her father.

The first route of entrance into the oedipal complex is
via penis envy as recognized by Freud. Little girls, after
their discovery of the lack of a penis, do not necessarily,
however, angrily reject their mothers. They show some
disappointment and proceed with further separation-indi-

viduation from her. In discussing penis envy, Freud primarily focused on the desirability of the larger, more superior genital. He regarded it as inevitable that little girls would prefer a penis to their clitoris, and as yet undiscovered (so he thought) vagina. We know now that little girls experience vaginal sensations quite soon after birth and during the nursing experience. We also know that the clitoris, far from being an inferior sexual organ, is capable of triggering multiple orgasmic responses without a refractory period, unlike the penis.

In conversations with the authors, male colleagues have revealed an awareness of their envy of the capacity of women for multiple orgasms. We can also cite one case of symbolic acting out of this envy. A professional male found his lover to be multiply orgasmic which fascinated him at the time and gave him a sense of power due to his ability to induce this with progressively minimal stimulation. He was unaware of being envious, although he remembered noting that he had "only come three times." Soon thereafter, on the golf course, he coaxed his partner into an extra round saying, "just one more," until indeed, they had played thirty-six holes rather than the usual eighteen. He then realized the meaning of both his statement and his behavior in terms of his orgasmic envy.

Since Freud did not have this data available to him he thought that the lack of a penis always represented an undesirable and deprived state. Therefore, he saw all women as having envy of the penis and the desire to have their father's penis. He thought that the little girl, disappointed that this cannot occur, would opt for having her father's baby as a consolation prize. The authors feel that all women *do* have penis envy. The stronger and more pathological this envy, the more unsatisfactory has been the preoedipal relationship with the mother. For many girls the acquisition of a penis means the pathway to mother's love and attention.

The fantasy of impregnating the mother with the penis taken from the father is not an uncommon one. (See Chapter 10, Case 7.) Penis envy, when it is strong and abnormal, may also be the wish to repair the deficit experienced by the child whose separation-individuation from the mother does not proceed normally. This occurs with severe trauma or illness or premature separation from the mother because of her absence, illness or psychological unavailability. The availability of a father, for either sex, provides the necessary triangulation to make separation-individuation proceed more smoothly. The absence of the father, therefore, disrupts separation-individuation and may fuel penis envy. (See Chapter 10, Case 8.) Without the father to provide support for the little girl's femininity and self-esteem, there may be an increase in the sense of defect. This will result in the formation of an intrapsychic world with a body image that reparatively includes an illusory phallus.

At the time of the perception of the anatomical difference between the sexes, little girls have a surge in fantasy life, creativity and graphic representation. From this time onward they are more social and extroverted with friends. They do experience a temporary setback in verbal symbolization. Parenthetically, it is known that girls are generally ahead of boys in their early cognitive and verbal development.

Contrary to Freud's speculations, however, the little girl does not give up clitoral masturbation. Studies of the sexual patterns of adult women reveal that the clitoris is always the trigger organ, even in "vaginal" orgasm. There is only one type of orgasm. Physiological measurements do not show any difference despite the prior supposition that there were clitoral and vaginal orgasms. Studies show that women experience more intense orgasms with clitoral masturbation, but that they prefer those with vaginal containment of the penis. We speculate that there are two reasons for this: the preference for being held, and the need for the filling of the

inner genital space. It is not until intercourse and later pregnancy occurs that the ordinary woman repairs her perceived
defect in body image schematization and alters her self-
representation. Failing to have separated adequately from
a good preoedipal mother results in reparative fantasies that
are not ordinarily given up until motherhood.

CHAPTER 6

What Does A Woman Want? Postoedipal Considerations

LATENCY

Freud believed that after the resolution of the oedipal conflict sexual feelings were repressed. In males this occurred due to an introjection of a harsh superego. One of the difficulties in Freud's psychology of women was his belief that girls do *not* introject a harsh superego.

In our experience, although latency girls remain close to their mothers and fathers longer than do boys, they manifest a sharp increase in guilt and the introjection of a harsh superego. Little is known about the fantasies of latency age girls because adults are rarely their confidants. Latency girls tend to have at least one very close friendship with another girl. They are almost always involved in competition to maintain a best girl friend. The relationship of the latency girl with her best friend tends to replicate the ambivalent relationship with her mother of the former separation-individuation phase. From this point of view, it is a very painful period of development.

There is nothing latent about the sexuality of the young girl in her postoedipal period. Freud believed that masturbation was renounced by latency age girls. Clinically, from retrospective data, this is not the case. The only thing that is latent about latency is the communication to adults about sexual fantasies and sexual behavior. Latency girls tend not to free associate, have few reported dreams and have limited verbal communication relative to their drive states. They are far more invested in academic work and the development of hobbies. Latency daydreams of girls recalled during adult analysis tend to have a romantic flavor (Sleeping Beauty, Prince Charming), but may also be frankly sadomasochistic (rape and prostitution).

Mutual masturbation with other girl peers often occurs normatively in late latency and adolescence. It is a preparation utilizing available objects for later heterosexual behavior. In our experience homosexual behavior that remains as the preferred mode of gratification does not begin until mid-adolescence. Adult homosexual women do not report the normal pattern of close relationships with women that are typical of latency. Rather, they are estranged from female peer relationships and often develop crushes on older women. Heterosexual girls of latency age also may develop crushes on older women and older men, but these objects usually represent idealized parents. Ubiquitous to latency is the "romance fantasy," in which the young child daydreams that she really has a different set of parents who are famous, handsome, wealthy, creative and altogether marvelous. This fantasy serves to perpetuate the illusion of a perfect family. It is not until adolescence that it becomes necessary to give up attachments to incestuous objects or to their fantasied and idealized substitutes.

Interests and friendships that develop in latency are often maintained throughout the woman's lifespan, even though they may be suspended temporarily during the storm of adolescence. The work and working through of latency is seldom given attention in the literature on adult analysis. In fact, when female patients are analyzed by us, they behave like latency girls hard at work in the industrious endeavor of the analytic process. They frequently call their analyst their best friend, and reenact a mutual conspiracy of confidentiality that excludes the outside world. Again this recapitulates normal latency development. Those women without women friends, in the analyses we have conducted, universally develop friendships with women for the first time. A good analysis of a female patient involves the widening of object relationships, if they are constricted, as well as the development of new interests and the capacity to invest in work. The widening of object relationships with women ordinarily precedes the establishment of a good heterosexual relationship. Thus, the normal patterns of latency must be learned and traversed before the patient can pass on to the next developmental stage, adolescence.

ADOLESCENCE

Female adolescence, a major area of concern to the authors (Bernstein, 1975), is ushered in by the biology of puberty. With bodily and hormonal changes comes an intensification of both sexual and aggressive urges that still emerge in relationship to infantile and incestuous objects. These ties must be abandoned and shifted to peer objects that are nonincestuous, and the oedipal complex must be worked through for the second time. The problem for the female adolescent is that, in accomplishing this goal, she loses the support and structural organization received from having the parents as auxiliaries or backups. Thus, the adolescent is in a vulnerable state at the very time that major and definitive separation-individuation must be accomplished, synthesis of new objects must occur, heterosexuality must be firmly established and career choice must be made. Identification as an independent adult is, therefore, a very difficult process. As Erikson (1959, 1968) pointed out, this is a period in which struggle for solidification of identity is threatened by identity crises and identity diffusion.

The first crisis stems from the need to integrate a new body image. For girls this includes increase in body size, development of breasts, increase in the size of the genitalia, development of genital, axillary and other body hair, as well as the onset of menstruation. Menstruation is perhaps the most pivotal experience. It stirs up old anal and castration conflicts in the course of caring for the body and the menstrual flow. It also elicits a feeling of loss of control since the vagina is the one female orifice without sphincter containment. In addition, there are real problems introduced by the menstrual flow, including possible discomfort due to water retention and uterine cramping from increased presence of progesterone. Moreover, activities have to be planned around the control of menstrual flow. For example, although there should be no limitation of physical activities that do not cause more bleeding, some activities do precipitate a period of brisker bleeding which may present an aesthetic problem and require specific care. A young woman wearing an external pad, and not an internal tampon, will stain while swimming and be irritated while horseback riding. There is no question that additional attention must be paid to personal hygiene because even an internal soiled tampon will have an odor.

Intrapsychically, menstruation causes increased narcissistic investment in the girl's own body, a conscious or unconscious feeling of damage and dirtiness, increased castration anxiety and anal concerns over loss of control. A heightened feeling of shame and increased feelings of helplessness and passivity are also noted. Reports of feelings of disgust are quite frequent even though the girl may simultaneously feel pleasure at the entrance into womanhood. Ultimately, the physiological phenomena of menarche, menstruation and menopause have far-ranging consequences for the development of the female's representational world and her consequent psychology. The impact of menstruation often begins with the young girl's first awareness of her mother's menstrual cycle. The way in which the child experiences her mother's adaptation to menstruation, as well as the age of awareness, are pivotal. Even a young infant prior to cognitive awareness may experience the menstrual cycle in terms of the mood swings of the mother. In fact, recent medical data reveals a change in the character of breast milk during the mother's menses, which some infants reject. (A discussion of menstruation fantasies appears at the end of this chapter).

The establishment of an intimate prolonged relationship with a heterosexual love object is one of the major tasks of adolescence and early adulthood. This relationship has many components for both sexes. Confining ourselves to the needs of women, they are the following:

1. A subjugation and integration of pregenital impulses within genitality.
2. An ability to be cared for (receive nurturance) and to nurture.
3. An ability to share in a relationship as an independent and autonomous adult.
4. An ability to vicariously actualize certain masculine strivings through the pleasures of the man as added to her own. (It is equally important that males be able to vicariously actualize certain feminine strivings through the pleasures of their women.)
5. The achievement of orgasm in which there is a fusion with a beloved partner which parallels the very early blissful union with mother, without severe fear of engulfment and dissolution.
6. The ability to share the desire for generativity (Er-

ikson, 1959) and to establish a nurturant atmosphere for children.

7. The ability to have a firm parental identification in the absence of one's actual parent.

Pathology of Adolescence

Adolescence is not only a stormy developmental stage with many tasks, but one in which individuals are susceptible to several severe mental illnesses, including anorexia nervosa and schizophrenia; they are also at high risk of suicide. Since this first disease is most prevalent in adolescent girls, it cannot be ignored in any discussion of adolescence.

The most serious disturbances occurring in adolescent girls have to do with the struggle for separation from the mother, which is particularly marked in the syndrome known as "anorexia nervosa." The clinical picture includes anorexia, severe weight loss, amenorrhea, increased facial and body hair, hyperactivity, and an almost delusional conviction that the anorexic person holds concerning her body image. No matter how anorectic she becomes, she feels that she is too fat.

All anorectic female patients whom we have treated shared several characteristics as follows:

1. An intrusive or invasive mother who does not allow separation, and a distant father, who does not help the child to separate from the mother.
2. An illusion or a delusion about body size.
3. A denial of illness for a long period in treatment.
4. A prolonged sullen stubbornness and a paucity of associations followed by passive-aggressive behavior.

5. The presence or the development of a clinical depression followed by mobilization of rage.
6. A remarkable absence of oedipal problems, that is, once unlocked from the abnormal symbiosis with the mother, the patients negotiate oedipal problems for the first time without much difficulty.
7. The frequent overtly expressed hatred of female secondary sexual characteristics, accompanied by the wishes not to menstruate and to never bear children.

Hilde Bruch (1978) has written extensively on anorexia nervosa and the dynamics of this syndrome. The introjected mother is the person the adolescent is starving for, trying to control and to punish. Some of the vicissitudes of the illness, including no desire to ever have a baby or to menstruate, are not the results of an oedipal problem that occurs as a defense against the wish to have father's child. Rather, they are the consequences of a preoedipal fixation and conscious wish not to be like the hated mother. Unconsciously, the shadow of the mother has already fallen upon the patient's unconscious picture of herself. Self starvations really represent the starving of the internalized image of the mother. This is a residue of a severe separation-individuation problem. (See Chapter 10, Case 9.)

The adolescent girl must rework her early separation-individuation and oedipal conflicts in order to establish her identity and move toward the true enjoyment of genital heterosexuality. A brief clinical vignette illustrating a less severe problem in separation-individuation follows.

A precocious 16-year-old beautiful young woman, who appeared to be several years older than her age, was brought to treatment by her mother. She had arranged consciously for her mother to find her and her boyfriend involved in sexual intercourse. This occurred after her open requests to see a psychiatrist were refused. The patient was promiscuous, sexually active and anorgasmic, except with clitoral stimulation. She treated her boyfriend as a maternal holding and caring substitute, and had difficulty separating from him. She was confused as to her future wishes for motherhood or a career, and she appeared as vain as her youthful-looking mother. During a family meeting she was openly seductive with her father and flirted with him whenever her mother spoke. Severe castration and separation anxiety were uncovered as initial early impulsive and counterphobic defenses were interpreted. Although a pronounced oedipal conflict was in evidence, there was a far more serious problem in separation-individuation from a mother who was hovering and yet also disinterested in this adolescent's needs. Her firmest and most adult relationship was with her younger brother, whom she had mothered since early childhood and considered to be her child.

SPECIAL POSTOEDIPAL ISSUES

Masturbation

Preceding full genitality, adult women patients frequently report periods of mutual masturbation in adolescence with boys. The use of water, the transitional object or the hands has lately been supplemented with the modern-day vibrator. This is most often applied to the clitoris and labia but is occasionally (when shaped like a phallus) used intravaginally or anally. Women who use this method report that it provides very intense and rapid stimulation. When masturbation is rejected in latency, it reflects a rejection by the girl of her genitals and signals an incomplete resolution of separation from the mother. For a girl, a certain degree of turning away from the encompassing mother and failure to identify with her nurturing capacity is a necessary transient phase in futhering individuation and autonomy.

One of the necessary prerequisites for good heterosexual adjustment relates to masturbatory activity. Very often patients in analysis begin to masturbate for the first time. In total frigidity, which is defined as the inability to achieve orgasm via masturbation or with another person, a first step in treatment may be the experimentation with masturbation and orgasm by masturbation.

Methods

The dynamics of masturbation can be discussed by separating the methods of masturbation from the fantasies associated with the activity. These may or may not be consciously related, but are generally unconsciously related. The methods of masturbation reported in the analyses of adult women patients are multiple and originate in the various maturational phases. They usually represent condensations of preoedipal and oedipal wishes and conflicts, and may occur at primary fixation points or points of regression in the face of the oedipal conflict.

Little girls in earliest infancy can be observed squeezing their thighs together during diaper changes, while nursing, and while lying in their cribs. This behavior also occurs in the crib after eighteen months of life when the child seems to be focused on something internal. There may be increasing thigh adductions with increases in respiratory and heart rates and what appears to be a sense of release of tension (orgasm?). Adult women who use this method are either repeating intense early gratification or have regressed to the "no hands approach" to avoid the recognition of castration.

Galenson and Roiphe (1974) describe nursery girls who use their bottle or doll for clitoral stimulation. Girls in their cribs often rub against their blanket or wrap their legs around their blanket while pulling on it. All of these behaviors represent the use of the transitional object (child-mother) for genital sexual pleasure. Adult women use symbolic transitional objects (blankets and pillows) in the same manner. This usually represents the rubbing of the child against the body of the mother, which occurs in early infancy and is repeated later on with the transitional object as the substitute for mother. It reflects deprivation of longed for physical contact with the mother. Blankets and pillows are also used with mounting behavior accompanied by fantasies that involve the presence of an illusory phallus. They may also occur when there has been an actual threat to the use of the hands (generally made by the mother) when girls are verbal and masturbate. These mothers frequently are primitive and imply loss of the mind (total castration) or physical disfigurement as the penalty for masturbating. One patient, who lived in an extended family, had a grandmother who regularly lined up all of the grandchildren and smelled their hands.

Another analytic patient recounted a peculiar behavior of her mother with her granddaughter. The little girl was pulling at her crotch in her wet bathing suit and was told by her grandmother, "Don't do that. You'll get sick." When the patient asked how she would get sick, her mother replied that the child would go crazy. The patient then remembered that she had been raised in a home where she was never allowed to shut a door, suck her thumb or touch her genitals. With the onset of the oedipal phase, the patient recalled masturbating vigorously with a blanket between her legs while she lay face down. She had kept her hands exposed for her mother to see when her mother came in to check her at night. She also developed a sleep disorder and nightmares of losing her head or her hands.

Another method of masturbating reported by adult female patients is by inserting objects into the anus. This may or may not occur in women who have a history of receiving frequent enemas in childhood. The most common objects are the douche nozzle, the vibrator, a tampax holder or a thermometer. However, objects such as candles, bananas, shampoo bottles and eating utensils also have been used.

One patient reported the use of various objects. The meaning of this choice of behavior was not understood until she baked a Christmas cake for the analyst and then confessed that she had later used the wooden spatula to insert into her anus. She was symbolically taking the mother's fantasied penis and attempting to incorporate it anally.

The use of water from the bathtub nozzle on the clitoris is another not uncommon method of female masturbation. One woman in analysis reported that from the age of eight, after accidentally discovering a sensation of pleasure in her clitoris while running her bath water, she preferentially used this method to masturbate. Over an extended period of time, an anamnesis revealed several facts contributing to this behavior. She would watch her father urinate with great awe and attempted to urinate while standing and facing the toilet, at age three, after her brother was born. Having been told that this brother was born after her daddy planted a seed in her mother, she decided, thinking concretely, that seeds had to be watered. This masturbatory behavior represented a condensation of her wish for a baby and her wish for a penis.

Another patient masturbated in adolescence only during menstruation. She forced water into her vagina and actively expelled the remaining menstrual contents. This behavior, which was masturbatory, had to do with the purging of the secret of her father's love affair. She had colluded with him to keep this secret from her mother. In addition, she was never able to achieve orgasm and remained unaware of the physical signs of her own sexual arousal, such as erection of her nipples, lubrication of her vagina, a pleasurable feeling in the genitals, and vaginal contractions. This massive detachment was due to the need to dissociate herself from the sexual feelings aroused in being a secret voyeur of her father's sexual activity.

The most common method of masturbation reported by female analysands is that of clitoral stimulation. This may be accomplished by manipulation of the surrounding tissues to provide traction, or by direct pressure and rubbing of the clitoris. This is normative behavior since the clitoris is the trigger organ for orgasm.

Some women report insertion of objects into the vagina. In most cases, this is a way of simulating intercourse and of providing indirect clitoral stimulation where the clitoris itself is too tender for direct manipulation. This is also normative behavior. There are female patients who insert symbolic objects into the vagina. One patient customarily utilized a cucumber for vaginal insertion because she found the edges of a banana too firm and too painful. She later ate the cucumber. The use of oral objects was a condensation of the need for oral gratification from the mother, as well as oedipal gratification from the father.

Some patients require two zone stimulation simultaneously to achieve orgasm by masturbation. These individuals use stimulation of their nipples and clitoris, or anus and clitoris. Again, this represents the condensation of both preoedipal and oedipal gratifications. These are patients who have been frustrated in either the oral or the anal phase of maturation.

In our experience, female patients who use vibrators are heterosexual and use these instruments as a convenient shortcut when men are not available. Occasionally vibrators are used with the "machine fantasy," which will be discussed later.

Some women do not report masturbatory fantasies, but they masturbate without fantasy in any of the above ways. They may also use books, movies or pictures to stimulate masturbation, either because fantasy is completely repressed or they are impoverished and deprived and use masturbation only for tension relief, such as prior to bedtime. This represents the fulfillment of preoedipal needs for comfort and has nothing to do with the achievement of adult genital sexuality.

Some women report that they have never masturbated. These women may suffer from complete repression. They are frequently anorgasmic with men. One such patient in the course of her treatment learned how to masturbate for the first time, and prior to her ability to make a relationship with a man became orgasmic during clitoral masturbation. Patients who have never masturbated because of rigorous superego pressure, and who can begin to masturbate during an analysis, are in general healthier than those who cannot touch their genitals. There are some severely sick patients who masturbate and are easily orgasmic, but they have little capacity for relationships with people. Their sexual activity is entirely split-off from their object relationships.

Fantasies

There has been much written recently in the popular literature about the multiplicity of masturbation fantasies reported by women (Friday, 1973). The authors wish to discuss only those fantasies that have been culled from the material of psychoanalysis, the psychodynamic meaning of which they have been in a personal position to study at length and in depth.

Most masturbatory fantasies in women reveal the large preoedipal component of female sexuality and psychology. The fantasies are often condensations from several psychosexual stages of development. These fantasies generally are pointed to by the method of masturbation (noted above).

However, the method may not match the fantasy and only serve to preserve the more infantile layer, while the visual and auditory portions of the fantasy may portray higher levels of development.

Among fantasies involving oral gratification, the one of being sucked, licked or kissed in the genital area or breasts is the predominant fantasy. One such patient used this fantasy for self-gratification. When explored, the aim of the fantasy was that of being the nursing mother who was admired and fed upon. The patient never reported the presence of more than a man's clothed body and face in the fantasy. There was a noticeable absence of any visualization of the penis. With analysis of an early history of maternal deprivation, the fantasy mutated somewhat into being exhibited, loved and admired, and later penetrated by the loved man's penis. Unconsciously, with this type of fantasy, the woman is often identified with the suckling child. One of the several gratifications involved in this fantasy, perhaps the most unconscious part, is the pleasure in the role reversal with the man, frequently revealing a masculine identification as the route to return to union with the mother in the oral phase.

Fellatio fantasies are far less frequent. This fantasy is generally an oral sadistic one and not merely a nurturing one. One patient had a masturbatory fantasy of sucking on a candy cane which would turn into a penis. She would then tease the man in the fantasy about biting his penis off, at which point he would actively seduce her and bring about orgasm.

Sadomasochistic fantasies, among the most frequent in women, derive from the oral and anal stages of development. They occur in an infinite variety of form and content. They are concerned with being dominated, beaten, tied up, enslaved, used by many men, teased and ensnared.

Freud (1919), in his paper "A child is being beaten,"

reported a masturbatory fantasy in women. The child being beaten is often a brother or a sister and the perpetrator always an adult. The first phase of the fantasy is "my father is beating the child." More important and more uncon- scious, however, is the second phase of the fantasy, "I am being beaten by my father." Freud stated that the fantasy is a sadistic one, but one in which a sense of guilt invariably transforms sadism into masochism. The guilt stems not only from the forbidden oedipal genital wishes but is regressive, derivative of the earlier sense of jealousy and rivalry with the sibling, and even earlier, with the father. Although the fantasy has oedipal elements in terms of being punished for oedipal wishes, the true sadism derives from an earlier de- velopmental period when the father was the child's rival for the mother.

The same psychodynamic constellation is at the root of the great variety of other masochistic fantasies. The manifest content of these fantasies is of being forced into submission, seemingly by the substitute of the oedipal father. The ma- sochism experienced as pleasure, relieves the sense of guilt inspired by the underlying sadism directed at the father as original rival for the mother.

One patient, who had the fantasy of being dominated by a large and powerful male lover, was forced to actually enact this fantasy as her sole means of achieving orgasm. This patient had indeed been her father's "little girl" in- consistently and intermittently during her life. Her father, however, completely dominated the family. His every wish was her mother's command. This caused the mother to neglect the needs of her several children, whom the patient, as the oldest child, then mothered. This patient was not jealous of her siblings, who received no special benefits and fared worse than she. But, she was intensely jealous of her father and yearned all of her life for her mother. She had overtly competitive and destructive fantasies towards men,

and she interfered with their getting attention from her female friends or female employers. She was happy only when
she ingratiated herself as a protective woman. Only under
those circumstances could she relate to men in other than
a sadomasochistic manner.

Fantasies of anal penetration by the penis or a substitute
(dilator) have two roots. First, these fantasies are submissive
in the same sense of the sadomasochistic fantasies discussed
previously. Second, they have their origin in the anal phase
of development and are usually connected to enema experiences. During enemas, little girls experience rectal and
vaginal sensations. These enemas are generally given by
the mother. Although the enemas are experienced as as-
saults, the sensations may be quite pleasurable. They are
always associated with a sense of humiliation, shame and
being robbed, and often, with being raped.

One adult analysand reported daily enemas given to her
by her mother in a forceable manner. At the age of five the
patient developed temper tantrums and demanded a stop to
the enemas. She did say, however, that her father might
administer the enemas, which, at the mother's behest, he
did. The patient's principle masturbatory fantasy on entering
analysis was of being gently dilated with increasing size
anal dilators by her lover. She also used this fantasy in
intercourse. The dilators actually resembled black penises
and were very similar to those she had seen as a child in
her father's medical office. They were, in actuality, vaginal
dilators. The patient had overcome her sense of humiliation,
submission and passivity by the seductive use of her father.
She had transformed any and all vaginal and clitoral sensations into anal fantasies. She never at any time had anal
intercourse, but she did prefer penetration from the rear.

The fantasy of being in the male role is not an uncommon
one in female analysands. This fantasy represents an attempt
at preoedipal gratification by identification with the phallic

mother or the father in order to establish a reunion with the preoedipal mother.

One analytic patient, a very dynamic business executive, was married to a maternal and protective man. Although capable of orgasm during intercourse with the male in the superior position, after clitoral stimulation the patient continued frequent masturbation with the fantasy of being in that position. This fantasy was so fraught with anxiety and guilt that she was unable to enact it in her marriage until it was analyzed. The source of her excitement in the fantasy was in imagining that her husband's penis, on which she was mounted, actually belonged to her and that she was inserting it into him.

This patient, rejected by her mother, was treated as her father's son. She became involved in all of her father's interests that mother admired, hoping in this way to be accepted and loved by her mother. She saw her father's masculine traits, and his penis, as ways of "getting into" mother who was always so "sealed off." The fact that her husband gratified, in reality, many of her real current needs for a good mother, did not repair her infantile, frustrated wishes. In this particular case, the patient never lost this masturbatory fantasy. However, she became able to enact it with her husband. She had told him the fantasy and he had smiled and said, "so what!" She was able to be more dependent on him in an appropriate way, and to see herself and behave in a more feminine way.

The authors have not had the experience of any patient able to remember the masturbation fantasies that actually occurred during the oedipal phase. These fantasies can be deduced from their later derivatives, or may be reconstructed during the analysis. There seems to be a massive repression of these fantasies in which the father was probably the conscious object. With the appearance of the introjection of the superego, it seems that the repression is extremely

effective in removing the actual father from the conscious
fantasy. The earliest fantasies that can be remembered in
the course of an adult analysis can be dated to early latency.
Even though latency girls do not discuss fantasies, adult
women analysands remember the fantasies of this period.
These so-called "romance fantasies" are the most elaborate
fantasies told, with the most drawn out scenarios. Both of
the authors have seen adult women conscious of incestuous
wishes towards the father, which escaped repression. In
these cases, the women were psychotic.

One patient was admitted to a hospital because of uncontrolled, indiscriminate promiscuity that had led to physical injury. She was never orgasmic during this sexual
activity. Her orgasmic masturbatory fantasy was of making
love with her father and of being impregnated by him. Her
overt illness began when her menopausal mother developed
a fibroid tumor of the uterus which looked like a seven-
month pregnancy. It had existed very close to this size for
five years. In the course of treatment, the patient gave a
history of repeated and deliberate primal scene exposure.
Her father had intimately fondled her from earliest childhood. She had sat on his lap and played with his erect penis.
Her oedipal fantasies were of penetration by her father's
penis.

A patient well within the neurotic range recalled that
during the oedipal phase she masturbated with great fear
that she might become pregnant. From derivative associations in an analytic session it became clear that she wished
for intercourse with her father, and to have his baby. This,
however, did not lead to the actual recall of the fantasies
during the oedipal phase.

Later latency "romance fantasies" elaborate the theme
of a loved, distant, handsome, sexually attractive male who
will bestow his favors on the little princess and make her
into his own protégé, coworker or child, thus turning her

into a beautiful woman. He may wake her from sleep and save her from a witch (bad mother) as in *Sleeping Beauty* and *Snow White*. He may take her from her state of maternal deprivation to make her a queen, as in *Cinderella*. He may remove her from the dominance of her own family at his peril, as in *Romeo and Juliet*. More modern day themes include the adulation of the male movie star or rock singer who will raise the girl into a desired position of exhibition-istic gratification.

The authors believe that the current popularity of the romance paperback novels is due to the fact that they represent latency masturbatory fantasies. Their themes are generally romantic and desexualized. In all of these stories, there is a longing from afar, idealization of the seemingly unavailable man, and a man who becomes the rescuer or the rescued loved object. Physical contact is not even discussed until the final first embrace on the last page. The rescued man may have a psychotic or a physically ill wife, or he is imagined to be in love with someone else, who turns out to be merely a childhood friend or a sister in disguise. Sexual activity in these novels is not explicit, but is left to the imagination.

Latency fantasies support the notion of the idealized princess favored by the prince or king who enables her to gratify her exhibitionistic, conquering, rivalrous feelings.

The commonest fantasies reported by adult female an-alysands, which once derived some of their excitement from the feeling of being wicked, are now openly accessible through the media of television, movies and magazines, and openly enacted. These fantasies include:

1. The seduction scene. In books such as *How to Make Love to a Man* (Penney, 1981), women are overtly en-couraged to make the plans and set the scene for behavior that will be irresistible to the male lover. The psychodyn-amics of the seduction scene in masturbatory fantasy are

really involved with the winning of the unavailable, forbidden or married man (father). Now women are being given
permission to have these fantasies, enact them and to take
the responsibility for them.

2. The rape fantasy. Fantasies of being raped, excluding
those where violence and masochism are the themes, are
also oedipal stage fantasies in which the girl-woman can
have the forbidden sexual gratification (with father), with
accepting the responsibility of her own temptation and
wishes. (We find no connection between the fantasy of being
raped and rape-seeking behavior.)

3. Fantasies of being watched. These fantasies of being
watched while making love are the reversal of primal scene
experiences or fantasies. It is the gratification of the voy-
euristic and exhibitionistic impulses, as well as the repetition
of the scene, with the opportunity for the patient to be the
chosen woman, that leads to orgasm. Women are rarely
genital exhibitionists. Their exhibitionism includes the total
body and involves decoration and varying degrees of socially acceptable nudity. Women are only rarely voyeurs.
We have seen two women patients who achieved some
pleasure when introduced to the use of binoculars and tel-
escopes by their male lovers. In neither case was this activity
accompanied by masturbatory activity in the women.

4. The prostitution fantasy. The prostitution fantasy is
also an oedipal fantasy that involves conquest of the oedipal
father while shaming him by making it a business trans-
action. In the fantasy of prostitution the woman does not
envision herself as orgasmic. The trigger to orgasm is the
excitement of the forbidden act and/or the conquest and
humiliation of the male.

One patient fantasied that she was married and that her
husband was overseas in the armed forces. She was forced
to prostitute herself to earn funds to put herself through
school. Two months pregnant, she would envision being

unclothed, admired, kissed, fondled and orally stimulated by a painter who paid her for her services. This fantasy bore no resemblance to her reality or to any book that she had read. In the course of her treatment, she recalled that her father had been overseas for three years when she was six years old, and that her mother and she would make monthly trips to the bank to deposit his armed forces salary checks into her joint account with her mother. During that time her only way of handling the sense of abandonment and rage at her father was to sleep with her mother or with a favorite doll held close to her lower abdomen. In her masturbatory fantasy she was safe from intercourse and "infidelity" because she was pregnant. The object of her fantasy was her ambivalently loved father.

Another analytic patient masturbated with the fantasy of streetwalking. She would set a scene of picking up a man who would be able to pay her extravagantly for her services and would make love to him until he was so aroused that intercourse was mandatory for him. She would pretend to be excited herself until this point was reached. During intercourse she would promptly become totally unresponsive and, thereafter, would force the man to leave. He would be puzzled and humiliated.

As a child this patient was repeatedly brought back from the parental bedroom by her father who would promise to stay with her while she slept. He would, however, leave her at the first opportunity. The patient was enouraged to intrude on the primal scene by her parents, who never closed their door. This tacit encouragement and later rebuff led to her feeling of being used for her father's pleasure. Her mother disliked sex and was not orgasmic. The father's excitement was linked to the arousal of his daughter. Later behavior of the father substantiated this. During her adolescence he bought her inappropriately seductive clothing and took her out on "dates." He never introduced her as his daughter which made her feel like a prostitute. The excitement and rage that the father's behavior had engendered led to a reverse situation in fantasy, whereby she rejected and humiliated him.

5. Group fantasies. These are also basically oedipal fantasies with homosexual and heterosexual elements, as well as preoedipal and oedipal features. The primary oedipal feature is the repair of the narcissistic injury caused by the patient's having been rejected by the oedipal father.

Frequent in adolescence is the fantasy of the "gang bang," in which the adolescent girl takes on and satisfies several boys or men. Two patients of the authors, who had actualized this fantasy, were both borderline psychotic.

In the fantasy that involves being made love to by two men, the psychodynamic element frequently is related to the primal scene, where one of the men in the fantasy may be a disguised version of the mother.

One young female patient, who was involved in homosexual behavior, had heterosexual fantasies during these encounters. The first man she had allowed herself to be attracted to was seduced by her former female lover. Her masturbatory fantasies at that time were of making love with the two of them. In these fantasies she was passive and was being stimulated by both male and female lovers. The psychodynamics revealed enormous wishes for her mother as a nurturant object and for her father as an oedipal aggressor. When the two of them were with her in fantasy she did not have to experience any oedipal guilt.

6. The stranger fantasy. This is another variant of the oedipal fantasy. It is of making love with a faceless or strange man. Not visualizing the object directly is a way of screening the fact that the object is the oedipal father.

7. Machine fantasies. Women analysands occasionally report the masturbatory fantasy of being stimulated by a complicated, multifunctional machine that can provide them

with oral, anal, breast and clitoral stimulation as well as vaginal stimulation. The psychodynamics of this fantasy generally serve the same function as the stranger fantasy. They are frequently found in patients whose fathers were aloof and cold and who treated their little girls mechanically. Parenthetically, these patients have general difficulty in object relations, which may have no bearing on their sexual functioning, or may be added to problems in sexual functioning. Frequently their expectation is that men will treat them as if they are feeling machines.

8. The femme fatale fantasy. This fantasy and its variants, being an admired actress, dancer, skater, singer, sportswoman or other type of performer at whose feet all men grovel, represent exhibitionistic and narcissistic wishes predominantly related to the oedipal phase of development. Desperate turning of these patients to their fathers for adulation indicates a severe prior narcissistic injury in the relationship with their mothers. That they visualize themselves frequently with phallic features represents an identification either with a mother who was seen as phallic or with the father in order to get to the mother. The reason that these women have to be the *most* beautiful, accomplished and talented is precisely because their sense of beauty, accomplishment and talent (self-esteem) has been so damaged. These narcissistic fantasies are meant to repair their defective sense of self.

9. Animal fantasies. Animal fantasies are generally disguised oedipal fantasies. One patient in the course of her analysis, reported the fantasy during masturbation that her french poodle was licking her genitals. This poodle, affectionately called "Pooey," was given to her by her lover. An anamnesis revealed that "Pooey" was what she had called her father when she was three years old.

The authors have seen two patients who urinated at orgasm and had the fantasy that this represented ejaculation.

In an editorial on Developments in Sexual Research in *Sexual Medicine Today* (1982), a publication of The American Medical Association, the occurrence of female ejaculation is documented in over 400 women. Stimulation of the Grafenberg spot, the once disputed erogenous zone in the vagina, produces a urethral discharge which is not urine. Study of this fluid reveals that it is prostatic acid phosphatase, the enzyme that is characteristically found in male prostatic secretion. The hypothesis of the article is that female ejaculation is a partial infertile homolog of male ejaculation. We have not treated a female patient who experienced the expulsion of a fluid other than urine, or who recognized or fantasied that it was ejaculatory fluid.

Most of our analytic patients have multiple masturbatory fantasies at different times in the analysis. These serve different aims. They mutate and change during the course of the treatment. Women, like men, often continue to masturbate despite the existence of an ongoing heterosexual relationship. Their fantasies vary with their immediate needs. There are no fantasies which are abnormal per se. Those that have been obligatory and rigid are usually less obligatory and more flexible at the end of an analysis. If an analysis has gone well, masturbatory fantasies no longer cause profound anxiety and guilt. Many of the fantasies can be actualized in practice and thus shared with a good male love object.

During the course of an analysis, heterosexual women in treatment with women may have masturbation fantasies in which the disguised analyst is the object of the fantasy. We have not encountered heterosexual women who report having had homosexual fantasies, except for the brief practicing subphase in late latency and early adolescence. These fantasies are more frequently oral in nature.

Dynamics

In our experience, women never renounce masturbation totally, unless there is a severe disturbance in the mother-child relationship. Patients who have given up masturbation lose orgastic potential in later heterosexual relationships. It is our experience that women who have not been masturbating during the course of psychoanalytic treatment must regain or establish this ability as a prerequisite for satisfactory analysis and heterosexual relations.

There is a single sexual phenomenon that is exclusively confined to women, one instance where anatomy is destiny, the simulation of orgasm. Obviously this is something that men are physically incapable of, even if they were so inclined. But women can and do simulate orgasm for a variety of reasons. Person (1982) has made a pivotal contribution to the understanding of "faking" orgasm. Although little attention has been paid to this phenomenon in the psychoanalytic literature, many analysts believe that it serves the function of pleasing and holding onto the male object. We have conceptualized it in terms of a general pattern of masochism, an extension of the biological tendency to nurture at the expense of the women's own pleasure. Person has brought to our attention a very significant additional psychodynamic, that of the "readiness to feel fraudulent." Women's lives are ruled by the necessity to avoid the loss of love, first of the mother, then the father, and finally, the husband or the lover. That women are willing to simulate, "fake" and lie to achieve this end indicates a superego deficit. The need to please supercedes, in women, the need to be honest to themselves and to others. These women do not feel guilty, but do feel a lowering in their sense of self-esteem. The loss of self-esteem is related to the inability to live up to the ideal of being the fully competent sexual woman.

One can conceptualize this phenomenon as either interpersonal or intrapsychic. Person feels that the governing
dynamic is the need for women to appear adequately sexual
to men in terms of men's fantasies about women. We believe
that it is important to women to be adequately sexual in
terms of their own intrapsychic (ego ideal) conceptualiza-
tions. The physical experience of sexuality in little girls and
the ability to experience orgasm during the oral stage of
development precedes interaction with the father, the oedipal triangle, and even the cognitive capacity to conceptualize about the expectations of others. In order to keep
their own feeling of worth and sexuality, they "fake" orgasm in intercourse. This avoids narcissistic injury from
failure to achieve the sexual gratification that may be beyond
their capacity because of neurotic conflict.

Some women are unable to surrender to the loss of
control in orgasm when in the presence of another person.
There are invariably women who have had disturbed relationships with their mothers, and who failed to establish
basic trust or an ambience of safety in which "letting go"
represented no threat. These are women who have often
been severely punished by their mothers for any assertion
or instinctual gratification, including thumbsucking, pleasure in toileting and masturbation. They often have been
forcibly and prematurely weaned, toilet trained, educated,
separated, individuated, and threatened with some symbolic
abandonment or castration if caught masturbating. They are
also women who have served as narcissistic extensions of
their mothers and so they allow themselves to become tools
of their husband's or lover's pleasure.

One analysand, a 25-year-old professional woman, related a history of always having to be a very good girl.
Dressed in white, always for her parents' pleasure in showing her off, she was never allowed to soil herself, even at
the beach. Her hands were painted with a noxious mixture

which prevented thumbsucking and nailbiting. She had no recollection of masturbating before marriage. Her poor marital relationship brought her to analysis. Her first dream involved severe anxiety over having to untie her hands and rescue a man.

In her marriage, this woman behaved as a little girl to a mother, seeking always to please and to mollify her husband. His rages and temper outbursts reminded her of her mother's similar behavior. Initially anorgasmic, she did achieve orgasm in early marriage via clitoral stimulation. Her husband would interrogate her about sexual response to him. As a result she began to masturbate and to fake orgasms, silently superior in the conviction that he never could tell the difference. Her masturbatory fantasies included the use of a blanket and the wish to be admired, exhibited, sucked and, finally, penetrated. The faking of orgasm was merely a model for the rest of her marital behavior. She would tacitly agree with his every wish, feel like a fake, and then come in touch with her feelings of rage, helplessness and a desire to hurt him. Feelings of desolation led to associations of gray days with her mother, who had neglected her to care for her demanding, stingy and overwhelming father. Her mother also seemed to "fake" her behavior with this father, since she spoke to him in a very different manner than the way she spoke about him to her daughter.

Her husband attributed her orgasms to his own sexual prowess. Her mother saw her neatness and lack of anger as a measure of the mother's dominance. The patient had formed the fantasy that in order to please and to hold onto her mother, she had to mask her own feelings and pretend to go along with mother's feelings. This same behavior was repeated in her marriage where she had chosen a man with the same needs to control and to suppress her.

This patient's history differs in one significant respect

from that of other analysands who fake orgasm. The others rationalize that their husbands will feel less male if they are not adequately female. However, this often is *not* the case. These husbands, when told of the previous "faking" behavior, commonly reply, "Why didn't you tell me sooner? Maybe I could have helped." In such cases, hidden behind the rationalization is an unwillingness to allow their husbands to gratify them as well as some pleasure in their masochistic stance and their ability to deceive. Indeed, these women only achieved pleasure at the expense of lying to and deceiving mothers who were generally repressive and utilized them as extensions. Thus the phenomenon of "faking orgasm," like any other symptom, has many determinants.

We have discussed methods of female masturbation and the variety of masturbatory fantasies that occurs in women. We have also discussed associated sexual behavior.

Menstruation

The occurrence of menarche and menstruation is not only part of adolescence but important enough in the psychology of women to be treated as a separate developmental phase with its own adaptive tasks. The reaction to menarche is determined by the young child's first exposure to menstruation.

The authors have never been able to recover, prior to the age of two-and-one-half years, the patient's explicit memory of the mother's menstrual flow. At this time, if the concerns of the little girl are still around toileting and sphincter control, the predominant experience is that of dirtiness, loss of control of bodily functions, and general aversion despite the mother's best intentions.

One patient's discovery of her mother's menstrual pads

in the wastebasket next to the toilet led her to the firm resolution that she would never menstruate. She was confused as to whether this was blood or feces and became quite anxious that blood meant death. She succeeded in suppressing her own menarche, and she was treated hormonally to no avail when she was 17 years of age. However, she was fully developed and sexually active. She wished eventually to have a baby, but was very frightened and disgusted by the dirtiness of the delivery procedure. She stated that if she had to have an enema prior to a vaginal delivery, she would rather have a Cesearian section.

In the course of her analysis she recalled that although there had been no particular trauma around toilet training, she had become inexplicably constipated. This turned out to be a consequence of her discovery of the soiled sanitary napkin. Fortunately, her constipation was handled in a noncoercive way by her mother. She had recurrent bouts of constipation monthly when she became an adolescent. She began to menstruate during the course of her analysis after much analytic work that dealt with other areas of control in her life, such as her compulsive neatness, cleanliness and orderliness, and inhibition of gross motor and athletic activities. She was afraid to get dirty or hurt. These inhibitions were defenses against her early traumatic experience. Before the early memory was recovered in analysis, the oedipal conflict had to be analyzed. This patient quickly and dramatically renounced her father as her oedipal object when, during her mother's pregnancy, she discovered the relationship between menstruation and childbearing. She did not experience men as hurtful or damaging. Rather, she experienced her mother as having some lack of control because she could not stop this "messiness."

During the oedipal phase, if the little girl becomes aware of mother's menstruation or if it is explained to her, it is experienced in terms of genital defect and castration anxiety as well as general bodily injury. One four-year-old girl came upon her mother's tampons in the bathroom cabinet. She already had a sibling and had been told factually about pregnancy and delivery, although not about sexual inter-course. As was her mother's practice, she was told about things as she questioned them, in concepts that her mother thought she could understand. After discovering the tam-pons, she was taught about menstruation in the following way: "There is a soft house inside the mother's belly for babies to grow in. That's the way your sister grew. Every month the house gets a nice lining in preparation for a baby to grow. If no baby grows, that soft lining gets cleaned out. Little blood vessels open to wash the lining away." The little girl listened very attentively but asked no questions. Unsure that she had understood, her mother asked, "Did you understand?" The girl replied, "Sure, every month you bleed to death."

Most girls learn of menarche during latency. They react to it in one of several ways, depending upon how they have traversed the prior preoedipal and oedipal stages. Some react with shock, disbelief and horror, and the wish that if it has to happen it be as late as possible. Those girls whose men-arches are most premature in relation to their peers often have great problems with shame, hiding, and the conviction that somehow, despite all their efforts, someone will know. Parenthetically, girls with early breast development have the greatest problems in adjusting in terms of peers, both male and female. The converse is true for boys, since the earlier the development the more valued they are in their peer groups. Within their peer group girls label menses in pejorative terms, such as "the curse," "anathema," "being unwell," "sick," or "wearing the rag." Some girls are very excited with the idea of menstruation as confirmation of their adulthood and femininity and as proof that they will be able to have children. Indeed, many girls who were tomboys, or sexually confused and fantasied being boys, welcome menarche as a means to the end of their confusion.

No matter what their prior attitudes, most girls initially are ambivalent when menstruation occurs. First menstrual cycles are frequently anovulatory and, therefore, painful. The girls must learn to manage the menstrual flow. There are many problems in choosing the means to contain the menstrual flow. Some girls, discouraged by their mothers from using tampons, are embarrassed by pads, soiled underwear, odor and the inability to participate in activities like swimming. Others refuse to use tampons because the use of an internal pad stirs up masturbatory and sexual anxiety and guilt, as well as causing pain. The universal fantasies are, "It will get lost in there and I won't be able to get it out," or "It will fall out in the middle of everything." This is, after all, usually the first direct handling of a poorly defined, inner genital space. No matter how carefully and explicitly girls have been taught about their inner anatomy, the recounting of how their fantasies defy their knowledge of reality seems comical to them.

There is a universal tendency towards concealment and secrecy about menses. One patient, whose reality testing was otherwise completely intact, revealed the paranoid delusion in adolescence that people could see through her clothes. Any time she did not have to be in school, she isolated herself socially, hid in her room and declined to eat meals with her family. She would sneak down late at night to eat.

When menstruation is established, the menstrual cycle is accompanied by mood swings, different fantasies and different levels of sexual arousal. In England the occurrence of severe premenstrual irritability and loss of impulse control has resulted in the fact that women cannot be convicted of willful homicide during the premenstrual period. One recent case report (Berlin, Bergey and Money, 1982) of periodic premenstrual psychosis in an adolescent girl was finally treated successfully with progesterone.

Another patient, a divorced mother of several children, reported agitation, irritability, impatience and destructive behavior as well as destructive acts, including automobile accidents, during the premenstrual period. The patient's father had died after a long illness when she was in early latency. She was delegated to care for the household and her younger siblings while her mother worked. Her mother was chronically tired, irritable, depressed and critical. She had an older brother who had no responsibilities, and she envied him and his masculinity. The patient had always had chronic difficulties related to concerns about her attractiveness. Her own marriage was dissolved for reasons about which she was confused. She attributed the rift with her husband, who had otherwise been an indulgent man, to a failure to agree on how strictly to manage the children. She alternated between idealizing and devaluing him. She returned to work at a very difficult and demanding job, although she did not have to. She thus repeated her mother's pattern of being chronically tired and overwhelmed. She stated many times, unequivocally, "It's a man's world."

Very careful attention to her difficulties revealed that they were clearly cyclical. She had some symptomatic relief when given antidepressant medication, but subsequently realized that for the first time she felt reliably normal. Initially she stated that this was true during "all" of her life. With some relief of what the patient and the analyst came to call the "rollercoaster syndrome," she suddenly realized that she had been "well" for the ten years in which she had taken birth control pills both preceding and between pregnancies. It was only after the birth of the last child, when at the advice of her gynecologist she began to use a diaphragm for contraception, that she "became crazy." It is clear that the difficulties with her husband were not constant, but occurred only in the premenstrual period.

The patient remained angry and confused about how this could have happened and ruined her life, without her or anyone around her understanding the true nature of her difficulties. Regardless of the hormonal mediators of this "disease," it was clear in treatment that her symptoms were entangled in the psychic web of her resentment and low self-esteem in regard to being a woman. This was exaggerated during the premenstrual cycle. (It is difficult to tell which is the cart and which the horse.)

Another patient, a diabetic woman in her twenties, had severe "premenstrual blues." She had become diabetic after her father left her mother. This was preceded by a love affair. Her mother was chronically depressed and reversed roles with the patient who parented her. In treatment it became clear that the patient's constant thought was, "It is better to be a man," or, as she once even more succinctly said, "Being a woman sucks."

Menstruation may be a disruptive factor because it is a reminder of castration and femininity. In our experience, premenstrual tension is not always correlated with rejection of femininity, but may also be correlated with disappointment about not being pregnant. A 35-year-old woman developed premenstrual tension and dysmenorrhea for the first time, after experiencing the problem of infertility. After operative intervention to relieve scarring and adhesions of the fimbria of her Fallopian tubes, which had occurred during a childhood illness, she conceived. Since delivery of her baby she had no further menstrual symptoms.

Dysmenorrhea, irregular menses and menometrorrhagia are often correlated with chronic depressive states. These symptoms are often relieved during psychotherapeutic or psychoanalytic treatment as the depression lifts.

Another patient with a history of a stormy rapprochement and severe castration anxiety welcomed her premature menarche. However, she did not menstruate during the summers when she was away at camp. This became explainable during the course of her analysis when, in the midst of an ambivalent maternal transference neurosis, she would cease menstruating during every prolonged separation from her analyst. (Her menses symbolized separateness.) Its absence reinforced the fantasy of symbiotic unity with her absent mother-analyst. Similarly, patients who succeed in achieving amenorrhea via the anorexia nervosa syndrome have problems in accepting not only their femininity, but their maturation to adulthood. They want to remain dependent children. They have never achieved full separation and individuation.

However, for many patients, menstruation is an organizing experience. A 21-year-old foreign student had been exposed to the marital breakup of her parents. Both parents subsequently had a variety of sexual partners, which confused and upset the patient. She stated that "My period reassures me that I am a woman in my own right, and that someday I will be free of the circus that my parents created." Other women welcome menstruation because it reassures them of their fertility and generativity.

CHAPTER 7

What Does A Woman Want? Other Unique Opportunities for Women to Rework Separation-Individuation and the Oedipal Conflict

Freud hypothesized that the desire to mother a child is secondary to the wish of the little girl to have a penis. This is the so-called "consolation prize" theory. Kestenberg (1956b) postulated that the desire of the little girl for an infant predated the oedipus complex and arose as a result of vaginal sensations experienced during the oral phase of development. Others (Deutsch, 1925; Johnson, 1963) have felt that the desire for a baby is a learned, culturally transmitted expectation of girls and women.

PREGNANCY

Pregnancy and motherhood are organizing experiences for the female. During an analysis, when a patient becomes pregnant, it is possible to study the fantasies, regressions, progressions and ego functions as they change during gestation.

Every prospective mother develops a set of fantasies about her unborn child, which begin between the awareness of conception and the first experience of feeling the baby move. These fantasies revolve around the sex of the child and the anticipated repetition of the relationship that the prospective mother had with her own family. In general, women who wish to replicate the preoedipal tie with their mothers wish for female children. Those women who wish for a reenactment of the relationship with their fathers hope to have male children. Around the centrality of this wish, the prospective mother weaves a set of conscious and unconscious fantasies which will later enable her to face the separation from her baby. The unborn child represents a part of her own body that she will lose. The loss will be experienced with separation and castration anxiety, and with some degree of depression known as "postpartum blues." This mild depression generally remits when the mother reinvests her baby, now outside of her body, with the emotional attachment that she experienced at the time it was within her.

During pregnancy women also have a complex series of fantasies related to body image, both before and after the delivery. Some women enjoy the dependency to which their obviously pregnant state entitles them. Others speak of a sense of inner fullness and euphoria, which is related to filling the inner genital space, and also to the fantasy of a reunion with the preoedipal mother. There are occasional women who react with rage and depression to their pregnancy, as it threatens their unconscious fantasy of being male. All women must cope with the changes in their breasts, bodily shape and weight.

In addition, there are many physical complaints related to pregnancy, some believed to occur on a psychogenic basis, and others related to known physiologic and metabolic changes. These include first trimester nausea and vomiting (morning sickness), frequency of urination, vaginal discharge, painful, swollen breasts, edema of the legs and general lethargy. There is also midtrimester gastric reflux with distension and heartburn. In the last trimester there may be difficulty in locomotion, sleeping and a recurrence of urinary frequency as well as constipation. Aside from the occasions when the symptoms are objectively severe, the degree of reaction to the minor discomforts is indicative of the pregnant woman's attitude toward and her fantasies about pregnancy.

One professional woman, during the course of an emerging and evolving oedipal transference, decided with her husband to have a child. She became convinced that she would be infertile. Analysis of her two-month "infertility" illustrated that this represented a fear of punishment for her wishes to have her father's baby. Underlying this was her fantasy that she had destructively damaged herself through early masturbation. She had also been a deprived and lonely child. Her dreams revealed that she envisioned a pregnancy as a voracious, destructive cancer that would eat her up from the inside. This represented a projection of her rage at her depriving, preoedipal mother. When she became pregnant she also became convinced that her baby would be a boy and that it would be born with a deformity. Analysis of this fantasy revealed it to be a condensed fear of punishment for oedipal wishes and an early memory of a lost brother who had died with a congenital illness shortly after his birth.

As her pregnancy progressed, she felt an increasing sense of inner contentment and a preoccupation with buying toys for her future son. She feared that her husband would be jealous of their son as she had been jealous of her brother after he was born and before he died. She felt that her brother's death was due to her own destructive wishes. As her delivery approached she experienced a rapidly evolving set of fantasies that she would be ripped apart and mutilated by the expected birth. As these were worked through, her castration anxiety gave way to severe separation anxiety which she faced during her separation from the analyst while she was in the hospital. The birth was uneventful. She gave birth to a son, and for two days thereafter worried about her competence to raise a child. This was related to her perception of her mother's incompetence in raising her. She felt a sense of depression. However, within the first week she became enamored of her newborn son and experienced a sense of satiety and near orgasmic pleasure while she was breastfeeding him.

During this pregnancy the patient worked through her oedipal guilt and separation-individuation, which had been incomplete. The pregnancy represented a new chance to traverse the crossroads of separation and castration anxiety, which is commonplace in women who become pregnant during their analysis. It is our belief that pregnancy, in general, affords a third chance for the working through of unresolved conflict. The first chance is during the separation-individuation and oedipal phases; the second is during adolescence.

A psychiatrist, herself in analysis, sought supervision because she had had two miscarriages secondary to a genetic abnormality transmitted by her mother. She found it difficult, during her own anxiety and grief, to cope with the verbal attacks made upon her and her unborn child by several of her very sick female patients. It was clear to her supervisor that she was tolerating these masochistic attacks through withdrawal. She did not confront them because they threatened the repression of her own rage at her mother. As her countertransference reactions were pointed out to her, and as she took them back to her own analysis, she again became pregnant. She did not abort this fetus, but had a period of anxious waiting for the results of her amniocentesis. If she were pregnant with a son, he would be likely to have multiple congenital defects. Therefore, she already had made the decision for abortion.

Under these objectively difficult and trying circumstances, the psychiatrist continued her practice and arranged her maternity leave. Her patients reacted predictably with rage and acting out behavior that threatened to be dangerous to themselves. She was able to confront them and to achieve excellent therapeutic results in enabling them to handle the anticipated separation. It became clear that she had conflicts about the defect in herself and in her mother. She was questioned about how she had handled certain conflicts in patients previously. It was apparent that she had been unable to be a "good enough mother" (Winnicott, 1965) in treatment situations. She was now able to provide a good "holding environment," while allowing her patients to experience an optimal amount of frustration. She was pregnant with a daughter. She managed the remainder of her pregnancy and her therapeutic work with ease. Clearly, her very traumatic pregnancy allowed this therapist to grow in a way that had not been possible in the past.

Three of the patients, whose analytic material is presented in detail, were pregnant during their analyses. (Further material on pregnancy may be found in Chapter 10, Cases 1, 6 and 10.)

MOTHERHOOD

When motherhood begins, a woman has another opportunity either to repeat or to rework her own early nurturing experiences. In studying the mother with her female child, we observe the pivotal importance of the early mother-child relationship for female psychology.

The female child's relationship with her preoedipal mother and the outcome of that relationship is pivotal for female development. Nancy Chodorow (1978) drew the same conclusion when she noted that the preoedipal mother treats her daughter as a narcissistic extension of herself, and her son as the object of her oedipal strivings. Chodorow's data were drawn from an excellent survey of the psychoanalytic and the sociological literature and from her own experience in a woman's group. Our data is drawn from the direct psychoanalytic observation of female patients during the regressive transference neurosis seen in psychoanalytic treatment.

There is one very interesting conclusion relative to mothering implicit in Chodorow's argument. She theorized that mothering is not a biological, hormonal or learned behavior; nor is it secondary to the wish to repair the anatomical absence of a penis. Her work suggests that women raised as narcissistic (symbiotic) extensions of their mothers wished to repeat this state not only in their heterosexual relationships but specifically with a child of their own. This is a conclusion that we have just begun to arrive at from our own data. We believe that she is probably correct, but such a wish is the most deeply repressed and genetically primitive factor in both our patients and ourselves.

The ability of a woman to be a ''good enough mother'' depends on many factors. These include her own early relationship to her mother, her state of separation-individuation, her ego ideal and superego, her own resolution of the oedipal conflict, and her idealized picture of her child. In addition, a good enough mother has established an intimate and sexually satisfying relationship with a man able to nurture and support her and their baby, as she nurtures and supports him and their baby. She has enough of a maternal indentification with a good mother to be empathic and intuitive. Thus able to respond to her child's needs, they are perceived as separate and not merely as a projection of her own needs. Her own core gender identity is secure enough to raise both a male and female child. She is sufficiently confident and autonomous to allow her mate to help her to decrease the symbiotic and regressive tie to her infant, when this becomes age-appropriate for the child. The mother feels actualized and gratified in her own life in areas other than childrearing. If this is not so, childrearing will be experienced as either masochistic submission or will be predominantly invested with narcissistic implications. By this, we mean that the infant, regardless of its own needs or wishes, will be used by the mother as an extension of herself. She attempts to repair her own sense of failure and her defective internal self-representation through this behavior.

Aside from women who face the economic necessity of working, there are growing numbers of women whose need for self-actualization propels them to careers outside of the family. Western society is moving, for the most part, toward the goal of zero population growth. This means that there are an increasing number of one and two-child families. Prenancies can be planned, and children can be comfortably spaced. Maternal mortality and morbidity has been sharply reduced in the Western world. The same is true of postnatal mortality and death in early childhood. Childrearing and homecaring no longer need be full-time work. Therefore, perhaps they are not so satisfying.

Freud originally stated that the goal of psychoanalytic treatment was to enable the patient to love and to work. Surely he did not mean to exclude women from this standard for psychic integration. Increasingly women who choose to stay at home are restoring work to that setting by gardening, preserving, baking bread and handcrafting clothing and other household items. Every woman cannot find fulfillment in that way, just as men cannot be arbitrarily assigned to a specific job or career without consideration for their specific talents, abilities or personal preferences.

We have stated elsewhere that we believe that children may not require full-time care by their mothers. We applaud the advent of maternity leaves, job sharing between women with families, and the future availability of good early schooling for children of all socioeconomic groups. When there is an only child or two siblings in a nuclear family, nursery school may provide a decided advantage.

One recent study documents the special difficulty with combined homemaker and work roles for women that we have seen in clinical practice (Moulton, 1977). In many families, a career outside of the home means that the woman is, in effect, responsible for two jobs. She keeps her home, shops, plans meals, cooks and serves, and is responsible for the needs of her children. These include visiting school, helping with homework and otherwise aiding her children, as well as providing income. Thus, a traditional marriage with the traditional sex role assignments still exists, even though the mother works full-time outside of the home. Often tension, exhaustion, irritability and depression result. Since emotional availability of mothers and their empathic and intuitive capacity is more important for childrearing than what is physically done for the child, depressed mothers, whether they are at home or working, deprive their children profoundly in ways that impair the normal unfolding of ego functions.

"What does a woman want?" The answer, according to the authors, is to be self-actualized, to love and be loved in an adult relationship that is interdependent, and to work in accordance with her own tastes and needs. This may be at home, or away from home, as long as it does not involve carrying a double burden.

Many so-called "feminists" have viewed women's

wombs as a burden. They have raised the question about whether the desire for children is a necessary concomitant of normal mature femininity. When the question is phrased that way, however, it cannot be answered. It seems that Erikson's (1959) assessment, which applies to individuals of both sexes, is valid. "Generativity is primarily the interest in establishing and guiding the next generation although there are people who, from misfortune or because of special and genuine gifts in other directions, do not apply this drive to offspring but to other forms of altruistic concern and of creativity which may absorb their kind of parental responsibility" (p. 97). He goes on to note that there is a stage of generativity in the life cycle and growth of the normal personality, male or female. If it fails altogether, the result is often a pervading sense of stagnation and interpersonal impoverishment.

The authors believe that the clinical material supports their formulations about female psychology. We have been deeply interested in the psychoanalytic treatment of women. It has seemed to us that women analysts are better able to understand other women than are most male analysts. Chodorow's work has led us to speculate that this must be a function of our own needs for narcissistic investment in a female patient (infant).

Parenthetically, we have received the oddest queries about our ability to work collaboratively. This capacity seems to be rare in women psychiatrists and analysts as well as in women in other professions. Dr. Ethel Person, Director of the Columbia Center for Psychoanalytic Research and Training, herself profoundly interested in the psychology of women, recently asked, "How do you work together?" We replied, "very well." She then said, "No, *how* do you work together?"

We have tried to be observers of the mechanism of our own collaboration. There is a simple and primitive explanation—we complete each other's thoughts. It seems to us that we alternate comfortably in the role of preoedipal mother and preoedipal child. We speculate that the reason why women have often been called each other's worst enemies is that they are generally competitive for the role of the preoedipal, omnipotent, all-powerful mother. We are not yet sure what specifically enables us to alternate in that role. Perhaps it is the fact that we each have large families and daughters of our own, and that we have been able to extend our mothering to each other's children.

ABORTION

All pregnancies do not lead to fruition. Abortion can take place spontaneously or as a result of direct medical intervention to terminate an unwanted pregnancy. It is our experience that, in either case, the patient feels a loss of a body part and becomes depressed. This depression, with guilt, is worse in the case of an arranged abortion, for which the patient must take the responsibility.

A 28-year-old woman physicist experienced multiple spontaneous abortions during the first trimester of pregnancy. This was due to known genetic disease. After each spontaneous abortion she was profoundly depressed, a result of the loss of the anticipated baby as well as the conscious experience of loss of self-esteem and derogation of her body image. Unconsciously, she felt each abortion as a castrating and mutilating experience. She had been reassured that her ability to carry a child of normal chromosomal makeup was in no way impaired. After each of the abortions, she had doubts about her ability to work effectively, and about her qualifications for her job. She wondered if she were "man enough" to carry on.

Another professional woman in her early thirties found

herself, to her surprise, pregnant by a male married lover. Severe agitation developed related to her wish to abort the baby before she became "irrevocably attached." An abortion was performed within one day. She had hoped that her lover would leave his wife and marry her. This did not occur. She was unaware of her wish to have a baby in order to recreate an old symbiotic attachment to her mother. She became so profoundly depressed that she entered analytic treatment.

This patient recounted a history of a somewhat sadistic and mostly absent father who had failed to break up an intense symbiotic attachment toward her mother. Her parents eventually divorced and her father died soon after. She and her mother had continued in a hostile, dependent, ambivalent symbiosis since that time. She yearned for a child to repair the ungratified longing for an unconditionally loving mother. Her relationships with men were unsatisfying because they also tended to become hostile and ambivalent. This was related to her wish for a mother in any man. Ever since the abortion, the patient felt severely castrated and complained that she could not succeed in her field. Nothing seemed to motivate her to increase her success.

A 20-year-old, single music student became pregnant shortly after leaving her parental home. She felt consciously that this pregnancy was an unwanted foreign object. She had it terminated as soon as possible. Shortly thereafter she experienced a profound depression that included panicky feelings of isolation and loss of her creative ability. This forced her to enter treatment. Over a five-year period, the extent of her symbiotic and narcissistic relationship with her mother was explored. This mother demanded that her daughter be a carbon copy of herself. When the patient rebelled, she worked through her separation-individuation problems. She married her boyfriend and suffered the loss of both of her parents who would not accept her way of life.

A college student, after two years of treatment, was able to establish her first relationship with a man. Although the two had definite plans to marry upon his graduation in six months, the patient felt unsure of holding onto him. This woman's parents had divorced during her latency. Her father had remarried, and she saw very little of him after the marriage. Her mother was clearly psychotic. Her older brother, to whom she was very attached, had left the family. Thus, he abandoned her in order to get away from their crazy mother. The patient became pregnant in order to hold onto her brother.

Realistically, it was disadvantageous for her to continue this pregnancy. Therefore she opted to have an abortion. After the abortion she became depressed and gave up playing a musical instrument which was her pride and joy. Her depression continued after her marriage. Although it lightened in intensity, it remained through her first planned pregnancy one-and-one-half years later, and through the birth of her daughter. She planned to become pregnant again so as to raise two children and get on with her career. She had a sense of continuing bodily injury and loss. This did not interfere with her life functioning, but she stated, "I have a sadness and emptiness during quiet moments which will never be repaired."

A medical student sought therapy because, despite her academic success, she was still dependent upon her mother. It was her mother's refusal to keep caring for her as if she were a latency-age child that forced her to seek help. She was quite comfortable in relating to men. She had a relationship with a lover who planned to leave the country upon his graduation. She considered this affair a convenience. She hoped that when the most difficult portion of her training was over, she would find and marry a more mature (maternal) man. Twice during the course of this affair she became pregnant. She had two abortions. It was medically confirmed that the cause of her pregnancies was a faulty birth control device. During each abortion she required the presence of a mother surrogate. In one case this was a fellow student who returned from another part of the country to be with her. Although both pregnancies were undesired, the patient became depressed after each of the abortions. In each case, the underlying issue was her failure once more to control her life. She feared that she had endured bodily damage and that she would not be able to have a pregnancy when one was finally desired.

One patient, who has been discussed previously, became pregnant in the course of her analyst's pregnancy. She had an abortion and suffered from chronic crying spells after the procedure. She too felt as if her body had been ruined. She feared that she would not be able to become pregnant again.

It has been our experience that out-of-wedlock pregnancies, terminated by abortion, always reflect a problem in the mother-daughter relationship. They are rarely related to the incestuous wish to have the father's child.

STILLBIRTH

Stillbirths present other problems. A baby born dead to the world is not a baby born dead to its mother. The fetus has been alive to the mother. It has provided her with fantasies. She has made a great investment in the fetus even before birth. Indeed, a name or names are usually chosen for one or both sexes well before the infant is due to be born. Stillbirths are generally felt by the mother to be the loss of a living infant. They are followed by crying and depression and a sense of loss of the union with a loved one. This repeats the early sense of union with the mother and its later loss. There is also a feeling of guilt and failure related to harming the infant.

One professional woman in her early thirties, close to terminating an analysis, became pregnant. She already had two healthy and living children, but she "knew" that this child was a girl even before amniocentesis was done, which affirmed this fantasy. She had named the baby after a beloved grandmother, but "strangely" realized that the infant's first two initials would be the same as her female analyst's initials. The pregnancy went well and termination was completed before delivery. Suddenly, she went into labor and had a severe hemorrhage which resulted in the baby's death. She nearly died herself but was saved after multiple blood transfusions. Her first wish, on being told of the death, was to join her infant daughter who was in heaven with her dead grandmother. A profound depression ensued which caused the patient to return to her analysis. She had to work through both the loss of her baby and the loss of her grandmother. However, on every anniversary following this stillbirth, the patient continued to have an encapsulated, short period of depression. This has continued despite the birth of two female infants. The guilt underlying this depression stemmed from the negative wishes related to rivalrous feelings with her mother, for whom she yearned. This mother was substituted for by her grandmother because of the mother's unavailability. The analysis terminated after her realization that she would have preferred the death of her unavailable mother to the death of her grandmother.

MENOPAUSE

Menopause is also a significant stage for women. Its outcome is dependent upon the psychic integration and sense of fulfillment that the woman has achieved during her prior development. The problems which commonly arise around menopause, whatever their medical or hormonal cause, seem to relate psychologically to the feeling of unfulfillment as a woman. In the words of one patient, "The curtain is coming down before the play has ended." Many women fear the loss of their sexual capacity, although for humans this capacity is more related to psychological phenomena than to the functioning of their ovaries. Some women experience a sense of genital deadness. Others are relieved and feel more genital excitement since they no longer are concerned about unwanted conception. Also, menopause often occurs when children are grown and the woman is relieved of the responsibilities of caring for them or of being available for them. In many marriages sex has been confined to nighttime because of the presence of the children. At night, one or both partners may be tired and disinterested. Thus, menopause may provide a freer atmosphere for sexual experimentation. Some women have described it as a "second honeymoon."

Other women experience the "Empty Nest Syndrome." These women's lives have been organized around their nurturant and household activities, to the exclusion of their own intellectual growth and development. With the leaving of their children, unless they are heavily invested in hobbies, friends, voluntary or community activities, a depression may ensue. Frequently, the only route out of this depression is a late-life love affair, a menopausal pregnancy or a vocational endeavor including schooling or finding a job.

Menopause may be a general reminder of aging. Erikson (1950) discussed the stage of integrity vs. despair. If a woman has been satisfied with her life and her reproductive cycle, she will not greet menopause with despair, depression or crippling physical symptoms.

One 52-year-old psychiatrist, in the terminal phase of an analysis, reported that she had "lost her period." This was accompanied by the feeling that she was "dead down there." She experienced a temporary loss of orgasmic ability during masturbation. She had never been orgasmic during intercourse. She experienced her marriage as a "dead issue." She developed the fantasy that her analyst was pregnant, then felt intense feelings of rivalry and jealousy.

As these were explored, the patient recalled that she had greeted her mother's second pregnancy with the same feelings of resentment. Her mother had given birth to a son when the patient was five (oedipal) and when her mother was menopausal. With the working through of her oedipal rivalry, she began, for the first time, to develop friendships with women. This was followed by her involvement in a love affair with a man with whom she became orgasmic in intercourse. He resembled her father. Her husband, whom she had married in order to escape her parental home, resembled her mother. She contemplated divorce and began training in a new psychiatric subspecialty.

GRANDMOTHERHOOD

In the experience of becoming a grandmother, through identification with her children or grandchildren, the issues of separation-individuation and the oedipal constellation present themselves for further possible revision. The identification with the grandchild is the most prevalent adaptation, probably because it allows for a new feeling of generativity.

It is often said that grandparents and their grandchildren get along exceedingly well because they have a common enemy, the parent. If the life cycle proceeds normally, the grandmother will perceive her grandchildren as a validation of her own narcissistic investment and success. In addition, the grandchild is thought of as a continuation of her presence in the world, even as her own abilities decline and as she becomes aware of her own mortality.

There is sufficient proof that mothers recapitulate their own relationship with their mothers in their relationship with their babies. One has only to examine the frequently true myth that grandmothers and granddaughters may be more alike than either is with the intermediate mother. Bibring, Dwyer, Huntington and Valenstein (1961) noted that Helene Deutsch (1945) and Karl Abraham (1925) spoke of a normal grandmother as having a postambivalent relationship to her grandchildren. One of the authors (Warner, 1967–1969), early in her practice, was receiving referrals of many involutional and older women with depressions. Their neurotic or psychotic despair occurred a few weeks to months after the birth of their grandchildren. These eleven grandmothers' postpartum reactions recapitulated their own difficulties with separation-individuation from their own mothers, their own postpartum symptomatology, and their difficulties in separating from their male or female children. Since this author was pregnant twice during the treatment of the majority of cases, it was possible to study, via the transference, a new version and recapitulation of the disturbed mother-daughter relationship and the symptoms that followed. These patients developed extensive concerns about the therapist's survival and the future baby's survival and health. They were also preoccupied with their own survival. All regarded the future baby as a rival for the therapist's affection. Being a grandmother is perceived as successful and happy only when the previous stages of feminine development have been more or less successfully traversed.

The old adage, "The apple does not fall far from the tree," is noted in the following vignette. An adolescent reported to her mother, "My G-d, Grandma [maternal] is even worse than you are." Not twenty-four hours later this young woman's brother was heard telling his sister, who had commented on his behavior, "My G-d, you're even worse than Mommy."

The adaptation to being a grandmother depends upon the vicissitudes of the woman's own preoedipal experience, its reworking in her adolescent years, and once again during her own pregnancy and motherhood. Old ambivalent feelings often reemerge and are repeated between the grandmother and her daughter or daughter-in-law.

There are many jokes about the mother/daughter-in-law relationship, which is often a difficult one and seems to worsen at the stage when grandchildren arrive. A grandmother was talking to her friend about her daughter and her daughter-in-law. She said, "My daughter just got a new fur coat. It is absolutely beautiful. My daughter-in-law made my son buy her a washing machine after the baby was born. Such luxuries! You would think that she was a princess, or something."

The enmity and devaluation revealed by this joke has several determinants. It represents an oedipal rivalry for the son. More deeply, it is the result of splitting of the negative feelings from the grandmother's relationship with her own preoedipal mother onto an object not as narcissistically invested as her own daughter.

CHAPTER 8

Mutilating Experiences Unique to Women

There is an increasing number of women who are afflicted by cancer of the breasts or genital organs. Their postoperative psychiatric morbidity exceeds that due to any other kind of surgery. While writing about the psychology of women it was imperative to understand the symbolic meaning of the mutilating experiences. We explored the meaning of these experiences in relationship to the psychology of the woman involved and drew some conclusions about the symbolic meaning of the breasts and uteri for women.

MASTECTOMY

Pfefferbaum (1977) recently noted that the prevalence of breast cancer in the United States was one in fourteen women. We have learned informally that the prevalence today is probably closer to one in seven or ten women. These women are also younger (in the thirties, forties and fifties) than were the patients of prior years.

Most women with breast cancer will be treated surgically with or without later radiation and chemotherapy. In most centers, both lumpectomy and radical mastectomies are not the procedures of choice. The most common procedure is

161

a modified radical mastectomy, which is the removal of all of the breast tissue, including the nipple and removal of all axillary nodes on the affected side. Some surgeons advocate prophylactic chemotherapy or radiation therapy even without the presence of lymph node involvement. All patients with involved lymph nodes are advised to have chemotherapy.

Ananth (1978) and Lewis (1978) have established the relationship between prior psychopathology and coping mechanisms to psychiatric problems following mastectomy. The commonest responses to mastectomy noted are anxiety, depression, anger, guilt, fear and regression. Jamison, Wellisch and Pasnau (1978) as well as Witkin (1982) have written about problems in marital and sexual functioning after mastectomy. They have related a better prognosis in these areas to several factors. These are: participation of the husband in the treatment decision, number of hospital visits made by the husband, early exposure of the husband to the mastectomy scar, and the quality of the marital and sexual relationship prior to the mastectomy.

Mastectomy is experienced by most women as a mutilation. It is understandably related to body image and fantasies about sexual desirability and adequacy. Beyond these understandable problems in reality, a woman's reaction to a mastectomy, as to any other surgical procedure, will depend upon her unconscious conflicts prior to the procedure. Once again, as in all female psychology, women's reactions to mastectomy have been understood primarily in terms of their relationships to men (oedipal). However, it has been our experience that the breast represents a tie to the mother through identification.

There is a popular belief, helped by modern pornographic literature, that the breasts are the catalyst for sexual desirability. Most men, in fact, do *not* experience a loss of sexual desire in response to their wives' mastectomies.

However, they do react markedly to the threat that their wives may die because of the cancer. In our experience women who have not yet married or had children have a more serious psychological reaction to the loss of the breast, even after reconstructive surgery, than do women who are mothers.

A woman in her late twenties, who was a school counsellor, discovered a lump in her breast early in her marriage and before she had children. It proved to be a carcinoma-in-situ without node extension and this was treated by a radical mastectomy, a mutilating procedure for which she was unprepared. She had always been a tomboy and had welcomed the appearance of her breasts and her menarche as proof that she was a woman. After her mastectomy, her marital relationship did not deteriorate. Against medical advice she even eventually had two children. She completely denied that she had had cancer and was furious at her doctors for her mutilation. She felt deceived because they had not prepared her for the possible extent of her surgery. She had had a large-breasted mother to whom she was very attached and who died shortly after the patient's own surgical procedure. Her first reaction to her mother's death was, "First I lost my breast. Now I lose my mother!" After her mother's death, during her mourning period, she would frequently think of being held and fed by her mother and would hold and feed her two small children. She began to mourn the loss of her breast and to become frightened that she really did have cancer, and that she too could die.

A 40-year-old woman analysand suddenly discovered a lump in her breast shortly after the death of a twin sister. She was treated by a modified radical mastectomy and elected to have chemotherapy, even though she had no node involvement. Her reaction to the surgery was one of bravery. This was related to her being identified as the brave twin. Her sister had been the weaker twin. After the surgery was completed she became very depressed and panicky that she would die, even though she had been given an excellent prognosis. Analysis of this panicky depression led to an anamnesis of a long symbiotic period with her mother who was a phobic and panicky woman. This mother was unable to visit her adult daughter in the hospital because the daughter's surgery made her feel ill. When the patient was a child, the mother had taken pains to make the world a dangerous place for her, thus assuring that she would have the child close to her daily. This panic was reenacted and relived after the patient's mastectomy. She remembered that her mother had become panicked whenever the patient was ill, and that her father would have to reassure her mother that the patient would not die. Despite this, the father had not significantly interfered with the symbiotic tie of mother and daughters. He was away from home for a four-year period in the armed forces. After discharge, he had a prolonged severe depression.

Although obviously our personal experience with mastectomy patients is limited, we have data to support our understanding of the meaning of the breast for a woman, from the analysis both of nursing mothers and of women involved in sexual play with their breasts.

Nursing mothers, as well as women who enjoy having their lovers suck on their breasts, in their fantasies are alternately the giver and the recipient of the breast-feeding. Several analytic patients have reported orgasms during breast-feeding of their infants. Infants are frequently referred to by pet names that are derivatives of the word "mother." Examples of this would be "mamala," "mamacita," "imi" (my mother). One patient whose husband suckled her breasts during the time that she was nursing, reported that her husband called her "my little mommy." Some patients become closer to their own mothers during the period that they are breast-feeding their infants. Other patients, especially those with greatly ambivalent feelings toward their mothers, try to exclude them during this vital period when they feel complete unto themselves within the duality of nursing mother and child.

The loss of the breast may frequently lead to fears of death, dying and loneliness, not necessarily related to the danger of cancer but to early fears of separation from the mother. This is again confirmed by analytic material from patients weaning their infants from the breast. Although many women experience some real relief from the burden of being the sole nurturer, it is not infrequent that women experience depression during the weaning period. One patient who had great difficulty in weaning her son, and did in fact become depressed during this period, reported many dreams related to a separation from her own mother when the latter became ill during the patient's childhood. These dreams occurred despite the fact that her mother was still alive, well, and staying with her during the weaning period.

HYSTERECTOMY

Ten percent of the adult female population in the United States will have a hysterectomy, according to Polivy (1974). This is the commonest surgical procedure that leads to a postoperative depression. We observe that psychiatric status of women after hysterectomy is related to their prehysterectomy status. Martin, Roberts and Clayton (1980) studied patients who had hysterectomies for diseases other than cancer. They commented on the relationship between hysteria (Briquet's disorder) and primary and secondary depression, and found that patients with depressive disorders often have somatization involving the female reproductive tract. Sloan (1978) compared hysterectomy and cholecystectomy patients (those who have undergone gall bladder surgery).

Although both of these procedures remove internal organs and have the same operative morbidity, the incidence of depression was much greater in the women who had undergone hysterectomy. This study did not involve cancer patients, who have additional reasons to feel depressed.

Drellich and Bieber (1958) noted that women with impending loss of their uteri had concerns centered around the loss of childbearing ability. Many women regretted losing their uterus because of other feminine functions that they attributed to it. Some regretted the expected loss of the menstrual cycle. Others expressed concern about the loss of sexual responsiveness (Zussman, Zussman, Sunley and Bjornson, 1981). Additional expressed fears included the fear of loss of strength and change of appearance, even though the uterus is an internal organ that in no way changes physical appearance. Ovariectomies (oophorectomies; removal of the ovaries), which would have resulted in hormonal changes, were not being done in these women.

The anxiety or depression experienced after hysterectomy has different determinants: Women who experience their uteri as an internal phallus respond with castration anxiety, which may show itself in a postoperative panic reaction, whereas women who conceptualize their uteri as an internalization of their mother, almost always react with depression, since the main unconscious conflict is that of loss of the mother.

A business woman, mother of several grown children, had a tubal ligation after the birth of her last child ten years ago. She had undergone a fibroidectomy prior to the birth of her third child. She had a fourth pregnancy, despite the presence of additional fibroids that often caused heavy menstrual bleeding and intermenstrual spotting.

One year after her mother had died from breast cancer, the patient was discovered to have an ovarian tumor. She was aware of the relationship between breast cancer in mothers and genital cancer in their daughters. Therefore, she had some concerns about her diagnosis, but was rapidly reassured when her computerized axial tomography (CAT scan) scan revealed a cystic lesion believed to be benign. When her surgeon said casually, "We might as well take out your uterus while we're in there," the patient became panicky and then severely depressed. Her own reaction made no sense to her in view of the prior tubal ligation and the nuisance of her fibroids. As she free associated to this strange reaction, she said about the projected hysterectomy, "It would be like losing my mother all over again." She cried for the remainder of the session.

In her next session she reported that she did not want to keep her uterus for purely neurotic psychological reasons. She discussed the problem with her gynecologist, who decided to examine her uterus during the surgery, and to make his decision by balancing his medical judgment with her emotional need. He would not remove the uterus if there was no medical indication. The patient underwent unilateral oophorectomy for benign polycystic disease of the ovary, but her uterus was left in place. She was out of bed on the first postoperative day, feeling well and planning to take up regular activities upon discharge.

One woman, recently menopausal, reported to her female analyst that her gynecologist had recommended a hysterectomy and salpingo-oophorectomy (removal of the Fallopian tubes and ovaries) for the treatment of a large fibroid tumor. She became quite panicky, first, anticipating postoperative pain, and second, because of the loss of her "child-bearing equipment," even though she could no longer have children. All associations at first centered about the loss of an internal phallus and the loss of her children in dreams. As this was slowly worked through, she began to speak of her mother, who was ill. She feared that she too would weaken and die like her mother, simply because she was losing the genital equipment that she felt endowed her with strength, energy and "bliss." This patient showed the dynamics of both castration anxiety and depression surrounding the loss of her mother. Her uterus represented, first, her illusory phallus, and then her internalized mother. An anamnesis revealed that the patient perceived her mother as a depressed, unavailable and phallic woman who had left the patient alone during the early years of her life.

The depression experienced after a hysterectomy may be more profound than after any other surgical procedure, including mastectomy. A woman in her late fifties, who began to experience menometrorrhagia (bleeding heavily and in between menstrual cycles) had been thought to be menopausal before this occurred. She agreed to a recommended hysterectomy, which in this case was a vaginal procedure that did not involve an operative scar. The patient had married children and grandchildren. She had established a relationship with her daughter-in-law, which repaired the loss of her mother who had died when the patient was pregnant with her daughter. Although the daughter-in-law was a constant visitor in the postoperative period, the patient complained long and loudly that she never came to visit. Despite more than adequate private nursing care, she was frequently in tears, expressing the feeling that the nurses were not concerned with her well-being.

The patient's mother had been a professional woman whom she admired and adored, but who often abandoned her. One particularly painful memory was of dressing herself for a party and finding, to her shame, that her dress was stained. The mother of the child whose party it was said to the patient, "Don't you have a mother?" This patient both found herself a new mother and carried inside of herself an image of her own mother. In addition, the patient wished to become her mother's child-bearer (uterus) in order to replace a highly valued younger brother who had died.

Although the patient did have a son, he was chronically ill, and so her fantasy was never fulfilled. In fact, her son's illness led her to fear that she would repeat her mother's fate.

The loss of the breast or uterus often has severe psychiatric repercussions. The problems secondary to mastectomy are those of changed body image, imagined loss of sexual appeal, and more importantly, the loss of identification and symbolic union with the nurturing mother. The latter is certainly comprehensible as the breast is connected with nurturance, especially for those women who have been nursed or have themselves nursed children.

It is perhaps surprising that hysterectomy patients have more severe reactions than mastectomy patients. This even occurs in response to surgery that may not be mutilating and which may have taken place after childbearing years. The uterus is sometimes the site of the illusory phallus; moreso, it is the symbolic link to the mother. These findings are consistent with the viewpoint of the authors. We have found that the desire to have a baby in order to maintain the union with the preoedipal mother is an early, strong and pervasive fantasy of the preoedipal girl.

CHAPTER 9

The Psychic Structure of Women

THE SUPEREGO

The resolution of the oedipal conflict, as in males, leads to introjection of the superego in females. The superego is the repository of all of the parental prohibitions as the child perceives them. It is the agency of the mind that says, "No!" to the instinctual drives residing in the psychic structure known as the "Id." This conflict between superego and id then leads the "Ego" to institute defense mechanisms to control the drives.

Women have a superego that is more concerned with considerations of object relatedness than is the man's. It is a less rigid structure and less obsessional. For reasons discussed previously, the female child is more attached to the mother. This attachment lasts for a longer period of time and occurs in the earliest period of life when the sense of reality is nonexistent or is just beginning to appear. During the oedipal phase, love and hate for the father occur when a sense of reality and separateness has already been established. When the father becomes an important object for his young daughter, it is in the context of a triangular relationship. The girl's relationship to her father involves not only competition with the mother for the father, but competition with the father for the mother. However, her attachment to her father does not substitute for her attachment to her mother as the primary caretaking object. For girls, there is no absolute change of object.

Fathers are generally relatively less available, both emotionally and physically. Because the young girl is not totally invested in her father, but remains attached to her mother, she does not have to completely repress her oedipal conflict. Many more women than men have an hysterical personality, retaining their oedipal emotionality and overt sexuality.

Since boys fear castration from the father because of their libidinal wishes toward the mother whose primary care they continue to need, their oedipal conflict must be completely and rigidly repressed. This results in a harsher, more rigid superego. Some girls, who are more thoroughly identified with their fathers, show this same harsh and rigid superego, and traditionally have an obsessional character structure.

A female business executive came to treatment for primary anorgasmia. Her husband quite correctly observed that she was less emotional, less warm, and less giving than he was. She was aware that her sense of right and wrong was "impossibly correct." The early part of her analysis dealt with her rigid obsessional character structure in which she was concerned with many details, avoiding all emotion. However, she projected her own harsh superego onto her husband, saying that he was critical and unsupportive. During a period when she had some difficulties at work, it was possible to see how her obsessive need to consider every bit of data had stood in the way of her ability to make a decision. She found it impossible to do what her husband did easily, "go with gut feelings." She really had no intuitive feelings.

The patient was the only daughter of an ineffectual

mother and a narcissistic father who were divorced early in her childhood. She was very frightened of her father's overt and blatant sexuality to which she was often exposed. Yet, he was the parent who could comprehend and share her intellectual pursuits and was effective in his career and life, whereas her mother seemed content to "just get by." Her father had had several marriages. When one situation did not suit him, he simply moved to another. There was a period of time when he ceased to provide child support because that would have compromised his life style. The patient was completely identified with his cognitive functioning and with his ability not to allow his emotions to interfere in his life. At one time or another, he had completely alienated all of his family of origin. Her mother, on the other hand, seemed saddled by her concerns for sick and poorly functioning relatives. The patient's oedipal conflict was a negative one. Analysis of her isolation of affect revealed yearnings for her mother, which she considered to be forbidden, and which led to her extreme ambivalence and indecisiveness. Almost paradoxically, she had selected a very maternal, emotional husband and had insisted on a female analyst.

THE EGO IDEAL

The ego ideal is composed of the representations of both parents and other important figures in the child's life, both real and idealized, as well as the idealized picture of the self gleaned from the parents. The formation of the ego ideal starts before the oedipal period and does not cease with its termination. More idealized images may be added to it throughout the life cycle. The ego ideal represents what one feels one should be.

This is quite different from the superego, which states

what one must *not* do or be. We feel that the major difference in the ego ideal of men and women lies in the longing and tenderness imbued by intrapsychic representations in women, as opposed to those in men, which are more isolated from emotional considerations. Living up to the ego ideal in women seems to provide greater love and self-esteem than is the case for men. In men, living up to the ego ideal is more a source of satisfaction and omnipotence.

In our experience, narcissistic injury in men often derives from the criticism of others, whereas in women it most often results from perceived failure to live up to the ego ideal. A large portion of this ego ideal consists of the picture of the girl's idealized mother. In the ego ideal of women, there seems to be less of a picture of achievement, even in very successful women, than there is of love and lovability. For example, female students are often much more preoccupied with whether their instructors like them than with their grades. This is independent of whether or not the instructors' feelings will in any way influence their progress.

The ideas of compliance and dependency are firmly embedded in the ego ideal of women. This is a result of the fact that they have functioned as narcissistic extensions of their mother, and in order to receive her love must be compliant and dependent. No such element exists in the ego ideal of most men, and they regard compliance as antagonistic to the ideal of being assertive, masculine, and dominant. The superego of each sex will reinforce, by its prohibitions, the ideals in the ego ideal. What the mother loves in the little girl and values so highly is imitative of herself. This generally includes compliance and dependency. What the mother values and loves in the little boy is more ordinarily related to his functioning as an oedipal object. This includes his strength, independence, fearlessness and manliness. Since the father carries these same traits in his own ego ideal, he will tend to reinforce these differences in the ego ideal of his sons and daughters.

MASOCHISM

Freud's formulations about masochism and sadism (1920b, 1924) evolved along two lines. His initial proposal was that the instincts of sadism and masochism were a complementary pair. Masochism, he thought, involved the turning of aggression upon the self, and was derived from sadism, which is aggression against the object. Freud's second view of masochism was that both sadism and masochism are derivatives of the death instinct. According to this view, masochism is the primary phenomenon and sadism is the secondary phenomenon. Both are conceived of, finally, as defenses against castration anxiety.

In a book edited by Chasseguet-Smirgel (1970), the authors attempt to adhere to the classical model, which relates masochism to the libidinal phases of development. What has been added is some further consideration of the role of object relationships. Chasseguet-Smirgel regards the turning to the father as a way to repair the narcissistic wound inflicted by an omnipotent mother. Torok (1970) attributes masochism to the unresolved relationship with the mother at the anal phase of development. In this phase, the child turns her anal sadism toward her father and her father's penis. Chasseguet-Smirgel, in addition, formulates the existence of a feminine instinct, the instinct of the girl to free herself from her mother. This obviously does not explain why the girl, and not the boy, changes objects.

We have a different formulation. We do not view masochism as the seeking of pain as punishment for unconscious guilt. Rather, masochism has several other determinants. The first is the greater need of a woman to be loved. This grows out of her early adaptation to being the narcissistic extension of her mother. During the early preoedipal phase, the little girl sacrifices her own wishes in order to fulfill her mother's needs. Incorporated into the ego ideal is the concept of subordination to the needs of the loved objects.

In addition, a woman requires a period of increased dependency during parturition and as she nurtures her young. In order to secure care during this period, she is willing to sacrifice other needs.

Girls are also identified with their masochistic mothers. In addition, the woman seeks to repair the defect in her body ego representation by obtaining a penis and a baby. To this end, she again subordinates other needs. She also uses masochism as a mechanism to control what she perceives as the generally more aggressive male. That part of masochism, which is the willingness to temporarily subordinate one's own needs for the sake of another, is intrinsic to the maternal process. It is not pathological.

Orgasm requires the loss of ego boundaries. It is experienced as a temporary fusion. This repeats the state of fusion with the mother in early infancy. This state of fusion is more prolonged in girls than in boys. Therefore, women are more willing to sacrifice for this experience, which they have known longer and is very gratifying to them.

We believe that women almost always have residual difficulties in separating from their mothers. The advent of pregnancy often ameliorates this. The cycle goes on as women have greater difficulty in separating from their children both early in the child's life, and later, when children leave home. The "empty nest syndrome" has been amply described elsewhere. To continue the state of fusion, most women are willing to subordinate other needs, including pleasure, independence, self-assertion and career actualization. Another determinant of masochism is the real sadism of the father, which occurs in some cases.

NARCISSISM

Based on our own clinical experience, we believe that women have an almost ubiquitous defect in self-esteem. This may be qualitative and stable as compared to men, or merely more labile. There are several determinants of narcissism. The narcissistic problems that result in poor self-esteem are related to the early narcissistic injury, due to almost simultaneous loss of the mother during separation-individuation and the observation of the anatomical differences between the sexes. Another determinant of this type of narcissism is identification with the mother who requires a narcissistic object, her small daughter, to repair her own narcissistic defect.

The personality of the father is often a determinant of female narcissistic disorders. If the patient has a narcissistic father, she can either identify with him or be unable to turn to him as a way of separating from her mother. Patients who have rejecting fathers have two problems. First, there is further loss of self-esteem, and second, there is the inability to separate from the mother, which is increased by the father's unavailability. A depressed father has the same effect. Chauvinistic fathers also contribute to problems in self-esteem by encouraging the subservience and inferior role of the female child. Seductive fathers contribute to a different form of narcissism, namely, narcissistic exhibitionism.

We think that the narcissistic investment by women of their entire bodies, clothing, and adornment represents an attempt to repair the loss of the mother through the use of transitional objects, as shown in the clinical case material.

Narcissistic exhibitionism also results from identification with a narcissistic, exhibitionistic mother. Alternately, the failure to be attractive results from either the fear of competition with the mother or the fear of the actualization of the oedipal wishes to the father.

THE EGO

The authors believe that there are differences between men and women in some ego functions. Most women are usually more capable of empathy, intuition and nurturance and are freer in their emotional expressiveness than men. We think that a great number of women are not as capable of clear, sharp, abstract thinking as are men, unless they have a considerable male identification. This identification results from the situation in which the father is seen as good and nurturant, and the mother as bad and rejecting. In our clinical experience, women who are successful in careers have a considerable identification with their fathers, even in those cases where the mother was a successful professional. (Men are more empathic, intuitive and nurturant when they have a considerable female identification.)

Another reason for the decreased abstract thinking ability in women is their diffuse perception of their inner genitals and a less clear focused body representation than that of men. It is our conclusion that the derivative cognitive functions have their anlage in body ego representation. Thinking proceeds from the concrete to the abstract. It seems obvious that the best adaptation for both sexes is for each to have both masculine and feminine characteristics. This would lead to a greater flexibility in functioning and to a greater ability to understand and to relate to each other. Freud did recognize the basic bisexuality (identification with both parents) of every human being.

THE SYMPTOM-FREE SUCCESSFUL WOMAN

The symptom-free successful woman whether working or not, has achieved a feeling of self-actualization and a high degree of separation and individuation. Her penis envy has been transient and not persistent. She does not have to resort to the fantasy of an illusory phallus and, therefore, she does not experience castration anxiety. Her sexual fantasies are oedipal and displaced in nature. She is able to relate warmly to people of both sexes. In her love relationships she is more self-sacrificing than her male counterpart. She is capable of orgasm by masturbation and in heterosexual relationships which, however, may be by clitoral stimulation with or without intercourse. She is generally empathic, intuitive and nurturant. The structure of her superego allows her great flexibility. Her ego ideal has in it the representation of both parents, who are generally seen as benevolent. Her self-esteem is more dependent upon her relationships with others than is a man's, and is also more dependent on relationships than on achievement. She has some degree of narcissistic exhibitionism since she wishes to be desirable to her love objects. When necessary, in a nurturing capacity, she will tend to subordinate her own wishes to those of others. Certainly, every woman who chooses motherhood must be able to do this. Women who are unable, or who choose not to have children of their own, gratify their needs for nurturance in vocational and avocational activities.

CHAPTER 10

Treatment of Women by Women

The formulations that we have presented about what is pathological, and more specifically, about the developmental level of the pathology, have very special relevance for psychoanalytic or psychodynamic treatment of women. They also raise the issue of the gender of the therapist.

PROBLEMS OF THERAPIST GENDER

The Male Analyst

Women increasingly are seeking out female therapists, often after a long and unsuccessful experience in treatment with a male. The failure of treatment may be attributed to a variety of errors. Perhaps the most common is the tendency to undermine ambition and to analyze away frustration based on a real failure of self-actualization. This is an erroneous approach because the theory that ambition is related to unresolved penis envy is incorrect. In cases where unresolved penis envy has caused aggressive and maladaptive competition, analysis should uncover and allow for the working through of the primary narcissistic problem that occurred in the preoedipal mother-child dyad. Failure to come to terms with the anatomical difference between the sexes always reflects preoedipal problems.

Another common clinical error is the infantilization of women by supporting excessive dependency needs, passivity and pathological masochism, instead of analyzing these traits. While a certain amount of seductiveness and narcissistic exhibitionism may be charming, the failure to question heavy reliance on such behavior patterns may prevent these women from making any progress in analysis. The male analyst is especially susceptible to such errors when the seductive female patient entraps him because of his own unresolved oedipal conflicts.

The defensive tendency of some male analysts to inhibit reawakening of their own castration anxiety can pose a similar countertransferential problem. This happens with phallic women patients or with women patients who have the fantasy of an illusory phallus. In addition, we frequently find that the male therapist fails to empathize with the bodily needs of a patient of the opposite sex. Often, they have a preconceived idea of what a woman should be, and thus may concentrate heavily on the analysis of oedipal problems to the exclusion of the more important and deeper preoedipal issues that have deformed the female oedipal complex.

In particular, some male analysts may have a condescending sense of females as frail, scatterbrained and in need of masculine protection and guidance. Because of their own preoedipal relationships with their mothers they maintain a narcissistic investment in this view and are severely threatened by active, successful women.

Many female patients evoke severe separation anxiety in their male analysts as a result of their own unresolved separation anxiety. They cling to their male analysts as mothers, which if unrecognized and not analyzed, may be another cause for anxiety in the male. The difficulty for male analysts to accept and to analyze the maternal transference is a countertransference error in the classical sense. It stems from the analyst's own failure to resolve his castration anxiety, which is reawakened when he is seen by his female patient as having feminine attributes.

But by far the more dangerous countertransference difficulty is reflected in the sexual abuse of female patients by male therapists, a phenomenon which rarely has been reported with female therapists and male patients. This abuse is often rationalized in a variety of ways. In our experience, the male therapist is often psychiatrically ill, with grandiose and omnipotent fantasies. The question that still remains is how his psychopathology failed to be noticed or treated during the therapist's own training and analysis. We believe it is a result of the fact that omnipotent and grandiose fantasies are acceptable when they occur in men. If these fantasies occurred in women, they would be immediately challenged on the basis of having psychodynamic roots in neurotic, unresolved penis envy. A successful analysis depends on the analyst's ability to allow and to analyze transference from every period of development. It requires reasonable comfort within the analyst of either sex with his or her own bisexual identifications.

Many male analysts, however, are as capable of empathic and intuitive understanding of female patients as are women analysts, and many women analysts are unconsciously identified with the same attitudes that would ordinarily be called "chauvinistic" if they occurred in men.

The Female Analyst

Women analysts are not immune to countertransference problems. In our experience, these fall into several categories. There can be considerable resistance to being seen in a masculine role, such as the father or the phallic mother. These transferences often reawaken unresolved penis envy in the female analyst. Another resistance is to the transference in which the female patient treats the female analyst as the oedipal rival, which threatens to reevoke unresolved oedipal problems in the analyst. An additional problem for female analysts may be unconscious rivalry with the female patient, based on the analyst's own unresolved rivalry with her oedipal mother. But, by far the most common counter-transference error in female analysts is the tendency to be too maternal and overprotective of a regressed patient, re-acting as a mother might towards a small child, instead of recognizing or analyzing the regression as a defense against oedipal rivalry. In addition, the female analyst's wish for a child may be actualized by treating the patient as her child.

It is the impression of the authors, who have heard and participated in many case conferences and presentations, that women therapists are generally less resistant to the supervisory interpretation of countertransference errors. We can only speculate on the reasons for this. Interpretations of countertransference are often perceived as criticism. This is true for therapists of both sexes. Whereas women admit to their hypersensitivity to criticism more readily than do men, many men respond by becoming more aggressive. They tend to cling more tenaciously to their rationalizations for countertransference behavior as a way of protecting their bodily integrity and staving off castration anxiety. Women are more often motivated, because of their wish to please and to be loved, to admit the errors that they made.

Women, in general, also seem less threatened by regres-sion. The authors have attended many case conferences where women analysts are less frightened and pessimistic about hysterical, narcissistic and masochistic psychopath-ology. Obsessional patients of both sexes are regarded by men as healthier. This occurs even in cases where the rig-idity in the character structure will present great problems for analysis and often masks borderline features. Hysterical patients are more commonly diagnosed as borderline, even when an assessment of ego functions shows general strength.

Despite countertransferential problems with male analysts, the authors are not necessarily recommending that female patients see female therapists. The strong initial wish of the patient to see a therapist or analyst of a specific sex should be respected and eventually analyzed. It is important to honor the patient's preference regarding the sex of the analyst in order to assure that analysis is initiated. This choice can then be analyzed once the transference neurosis is established.

There is one more problem that must be taken into account in the choice of the analyst by gender. Female analysts often become pregnant, which always poses specific problems within the analytic situation. These problems depend upon the nature of the transference. Most extreme in response are those patients of both sexes who cannot tolerate a pregnancy in their analysts in the course of an analysis. They are patients for whom the fetus is not merely a sibling rival. They have often lost their caretaking objects, and have neither resolved their rage nor their despair over this. The following is an example:

A young woman presented herself for treatment during her medical internship because of mood swings and the fear of cognitive disorganization. She had a very poor relationship with her mother and, in fact, had not seen her parents in many years. She seemed to become more organized and less panicky in the presence of a female analyst whom she saw as a "good mother." When she noticed the analyst's pregnancy she became physically ill with several complaints. She felt overwhelmed by her work and yelled at nurses and female supervisors. She told her analyst that she wished that her baby would die. In fact, the analyst did have a miscarriage. The patient was overtly gleeful and evoked countertransference rage in the analyst. The analyst

handled this in a passive-aggressive way, that is, not clar-
ifying or interpreting the response properly. The patient
remained panicky and continued to function poorly at work.

One year later, when the analyst again became pregnant,
the patient became overtly cruel. This time, the analyst had
worked through some of her own conflicts. She was able
to interpret the patient's fear of abandonment and was able
to help the patient to verbalize these fears. The patient's
understanding of her own separation anxiety enabled her to
be more forthright in then vocalizing her dependency needs.
Prior to this she had been so aggressive that she defeated
the legitimate fulfillment of these needs.

As we presented our theoretical formulations, we have
provided clinical vignettes and even brief case studies. It
might be argued that the material was selected to prove our
points. These vignettes have another failing. They do not
illustrate the variations in treatment conducted by an analyst
who considers preoedipal problems as pivotal for female
psychology, in comparison to an analyst who focuses primarily on oedipal problems. The final section of this book,
therefore, contains the case histories of ten analyses, so that
we may present a series of tapestries of female psychology
rather than just an occasional thread.

CASE STUDIES

Case 1: A woman with hypochondriasis, depression, paranoia and severe penis envy

Debra was one of my early female analytic patients. She
grew up in several diverse environments and was often left
to her own devices as an unplanned, menopausal child of
working parents. She had an academically successful
brother many years her senior who had left the family for

professional training while she was a child. She had been an advantaged, educated young woman who recently arrived in New York for postgraduate training following her marriage to a young man planning to begin professional practice in this area. This marriage was arranged by an aunt and uncle upon whom the patient had become increasingly dependent during the last two years of her college education. The referring analyst anticipated that she would be a difficult patient because of her psychopathology and sense of entitlement.

"Debby" was a 21-year-old, small, pale, dowdy woman appearing old beyond her years. She was carelessly, almost inappropriately dressed in view of her economic status and background. She appeared to be acutely ill, felt depressed and had a variety of physical symptoms. She complained of headaches, palpitations, irritable bowel syndrome, nausea, frequent urination, and most recently, bouts of vomiting which threatened her graduate studies. She was aware of the connection of these symptoms with her recent marriage, her move and the beginning of graduate work. She had a neat psychodynamic formulation of her case in which she saw the major issue as her conflict about independence. She came to treatment because extensive medical evaluation revealed no physical cause for her symptoms. She did not believe in psychiatry and made it clear that she did not trust psychiatrists in general and me in particular. Her demeanor quickly changed from whining and plaintive to critical, demanding and adversarial.

She came to her initial sessions prepared with notes from which she expected me to take a history. She seemed bored by the minute details she had dredged up to make things easy for me. It was clear that she was in charge of the hour and was not to be interfered with. She had some knowledge about psychoanalysis obtained from her analyzed uncle. She considered me obviously untrained and without appreciation

of her superior intelligence. While still face-to-face she insisted on providing the following history.

She was born in the midwest to a family consisting of
mother, father and older brother. Her father, an attorney,
worked as a businessman, his entrepreneurial endeavors
necessitating the family's many moves. It was only in the
course of her college education that she learned that her
father was not allowed to practice law because of a conviction for questionable practices and that he still was involved in shady business dealings. She had idealized this
often absent parent but now acknowledged that he was probably dishonest. Debby's mother was chronically depressed
and had many physical complaints. She had welcomed the
birth of her son but was less than enthusiastic about the
birth of her daughter. Her daughter was perceived as frail,
inadequate and resembling her father's detested family. She
was encouraged by her mother to stay home and at rest. She
taught herself to read by the age of three and recalled herself
as being an unhappy, withdrawn bookworm.

Her continuous memory began at age eight when her
brother returned home briefly while completing his medical
training. He paid attention to her and encouraged her developmental efforts. Despite her obviously superior intelligence she had difficulty in school, which she attributed
to two factors: that a foreign language was spoken at home,
and that she was painfully shy and self-conscious. It became
clear that she was anxious, phobic, withdrawn and almost
friendless.

As she prepared to enter her last year of high school the
family made what was supposed to be their final move to
the west coast. She was sent to boarding school and planned
to meet her parents at their new home when the school year
was over. Upon her arrival she found that her parents had
separated after her mother had had a brief psychiatric hospitalization for severe depression. Her brother died suddenly

of a heart attack several months later. The patient dropped her plans to attend college in the northeast and decided to go to Israel for a year, using the money left to her by her brother. During this year she took a heavy course load using the Hebrew she had learned several years earlier, and became ill. A somewhat older man befriended and cared for her, bringing her treats in her room. She became deeply infatuated with him, cut school and ran around with him in what she described metaphorically as a "drunken state." The two lived on her inheritance while he treated her poorly. She became pregnant and had to arrange for her own abortion. It was not until several years later in analysis that she could recognize that this man had narcissistic and psychopathic character traits similar to her father's.

After the initial face-to-face meetings, arrangements were made for a classical analysis five times a week. Although ostensibly eager to begin, she threw obstacles in the path of treatment which threatened to disrupt it. She arranged a school and work schedule which conflicted with the previously agreed upon treatment hours. She stopped taking medications prescribed by her internist that provided symptomatic relief. She threatened to stop taking her birth control pills as well. She claimed that she found herself unable to pay the agreed upon fee. She resisted any efforts to explore her disruptive behavior. She initially behaved like the injured party. My failure to respond to this tactic produced a fury and a refusal to comply with the basic analytic rule of regular attendance.

Fortunately, I had confronted a similar dilemma with my first female analytic patient. At my supervisor's suggestion I had successfully introduced a nonanalytic technique called a "parameter," which consisted of my insistence on compliance with the basic rules as a condition for psychoanalysis. I knew that this would change the analytic relationship and would produce feelings and fantasies that would later require analysis.

I was not surprised when Debby accepted the terms and brought her first dream. "I was married to another man but I don't know who he was." She would not associate to this dream or the others that followed, which indicated that my assertiveness was equated with masculinity and control. My prior experience with a similar patient had taught me not to depend on a prolonged honeymoon period. Debby became sicker and at times felt so anxious and physically ill that she could not listen to me. She accused me of deliberately trying to make her more ill, yet she continued to come regularly and on time. In her stories about her life she portrayed authority figures as omnipotent and capricious.

She defensively blamed herself for her difficulties rather than those who had treated her badly (her father and boyfriend). Interpretation settled things down somewhat though she continued to present herself as a hopeless wreck. When asked why she had to see and indeed, accept herself this way, she looked back at me smiling and said that as long as she was so sick I would have to take care of her.

She was forced to interact with her mother over some family issues during which her behavior was masochistic and guilt-ridden. Recognition and analysis of the meaning of this behavior allowed her to be less provocative with her mother. To her surprise and chagrin her mother responded reciprocally. She continued to be provocative with me. It took months of work to analyze parts of her tenaciously paranoid transference relationship. When conditions in the consultation room (heat, light) were not precisely to her liking, she insisted that I had deliberately arranged them to annoy her and stubbornly refused to talk to me for the duration of the hour. She would taunt me with the fact that I must be enjoying her discomfort. Her physical symptoms abated, to be replaced by a torrent of unremitting rage directed at me. Unlike my earlier similar patient who had never thought of or referred to me as anything but "that bitch," this patient revealed later that somewhere she knew "this was like a play in which I felt I had to take a role."

After a brief vacation Debby reported violent escalating arguments with her husband. Interpretation of the displacement led her to threaten to be sick all over again. The analysis of this fantasy led to an understanding of her sensitivity to perceived abandonment. We also clarified the meaning of physical illness, which she had used to make her mother stay or return home to care for her. We began to elucidate both her own and her mother's chronic depression. There were hints that her mother might have made a serious suicidal attempt when the patient was in midlatency. The patient explored her relationship with her husband and how her chronic undermining behavior threatened his career advancement. Unconsciously, this was designed to "keep him home." With abatement of this behavior he indeed became less depressed and advanced in his profession while remaining supportive of her. She was able to feel proud of him and not diminished by his success. She had pregnancy fantasies which heralded a shift in the transference paradigm. Becoming very seductive with me, she dreamt of an intimate involvement with a woman she was able to recognize as me. Analysis of this paternal transference proceeded to a regression to her prior maternal transference. She remembered a serious illness in childhood which she had perceived as a punishment for being the bad child who caused parental fights. Indeed, they did fight about her mother's tendency to give into her coercive regressive behavior, while her father felt that a "good smack" would cure her. She realized she had always felt "no good," weak and damaged. Particularly she felt that she had an intellectual defect always standing in her way and currently hampering her academic efforts. The fact that she projected her badness and stupidity onto me allowed her to secretly salvage some feelings of goodness and omnipotence.

One evening the patient, her husband and some friends approached a restaurant where my family and I were having dinner. I almost did not recognize her. She was beautifully attired and made-up and was engaged in laughter and animated conversation. She behaved appropriately when she recognized me, but revealed that she had felt ill at dinner. With great shame several weeks later she told me that she had felt intensely envious of my youngest daughter and self-conscious about being caught ''dressed up,'' admitting that she never came to analytic hours looking attractive. These two revelations proved to my satisfaction that I was not being seen in a classical oedipal transference paradigm as Debby's oedipal father, despite the brief period when I was perceived as a man. Although she had noticed my husband in the restaurant this caused her no difficulty. She was entirely preoccupied with my relationship with my daughter and her need to ''play ugly'' as part of her previously stated desire to force me to care for her as a preoedipal child. At the time I already had conceptualized the relationship between penis envy and poor preoedipal mothering experiences.

She revealed much later that she had been afraid to compete with me since, alongside of her feelings of being inferior and her need to demonstrate it, there was a secret fantasy that she was more attractive and capable than I. She feared that I would ''destroy her'' for these fantasies and that I would become depressed and abandon her. The oedipal rivalry could come only as part of a maturational process and after resolution of the preoedipal problems which had arisen from a disastrous early mother-child relationship. When a more classical oedipal transference began to evolve, Debby equated sex with masculinity which would put her in danger of castration. Her real failures in life, coupled with her unconscious fantasy of my omnipotence protected her fantasied penis.

She began to wear hanging jewelry and fondled it during sessions. This behavior contained masturbatory elements and use of her jewelry as a transitional object. It was her penis and at the same time me. She had long before secretly admired the jewelry I wore. At the same time she began usurping some of her husband's masculine role with finances. He had always been the "accountant in the family." Debby became pregnant, felt masculine and referred to the fetus as "he." She remembered a period of fierce competition with boys in childhood and in fact had a period of great success at a sport generally acknowledged as masculine. She had attributed her father's "success" to his possession of a penis and considered her mother's work only marginal while she sought to avoid identification with her mother's damaged (penisless) state. Dressing attractively she rationalized this by saying, "You can't wear blue jeans with a belly." She still feared that I would take her penis baby away. She dreamt of herself as "a little boy holding onto your apron strings," and began to feel comfortable about sex and discussing it in analysis. She had previously viewed sex as an act in which "something was taken away" from her. Her fantasies of birth were of mutilation, and she had a nightmare about lying on the delivery table "ripped open and bleeding" and the doctor's having trouble "repairing the hole." After an uneventful delivery of a baby boy she again avoided sex and said, "I hate my vagina."

Breast-feeding was experienced as blissful and she had conscious fantasies that her son was part of her body. Weaning was, predictably, a time of great anxiety. She dreaded losing the feeling of genital fullness and general well-being which characterized nursing for her. She also had severe separation anxiety in the form of overconcern for her son's health. She began to make friends with other women. Slowly she came to terms with the idea that they might have something to offer her though they did not have penises either.

Her father became ill and the extent of his business failures had to be confronted. Debby felt distraught since, "If my father can't make it, neither can I. Neither of us have what it takes." She focused on me in her search for a penis. Dreams revealed that she thought I had a penis which I would give to her. She negated this interpretation. Reality again became pivotal for her treatment. She learned from a friend that I had a beautiful home different from my office, which was described to her as very feminine and pretty (flowered wallpaper and a china cabinet). She felt shocked, depressed and had a recurrence of somatic symptoms as her rage was displaced to household help and colleagues. Interpretation enabled her to redirect this rage toward me. She had the transient paranoid fantasy that I had decorated my home to upset her. This was patently absurd to her and could be contrasted with her prior, almost paranoid, delusional beliefs about how I had arranged the conditions of my consulting room.

Two other events helped in the resolution of her secret wish for me to give her the physical gift of a penis; her professional success and her need to retain the hope that there was still something to be gotten from her mother. Her mother was, in fact, a difficult and controlling woman who used physical complaints and depression as a way of manipulating Debby. Nevertheless, Debby contributed to this by being provocative. She insisted on feeding her son foods that her mother and even she herself disapproved. She would not have given him "junk food" in her own home. Interpretation of her behavior provoked her last episode of blind rage at me and flurry of somatic symptoms. Her pseudostupidity also surfaced and now seemed as alien as her paranoid feelings had become.

Real difficulty with scheduling arrangements led to a request that we cut back from five to four sessions a week. My willingness to comply was experienced as my taking from her as her mother had done. Working this through led to her first overt expression of trust in me and her own capability to manage her life. One area of poor functioning was as yet unresolved. This was her displeasure with sex. She now could discuss it in detail. Her displeasure was defensive against the rage of recognition of her castrated state. She dreamt of being physically ill as a child and running to her father as a maternal substitute, not merely as her mother's rival for his love. Her failure to obtain his affection affected her more profoundly than it would a child with a better maternal relationship. She had wanted a penis to repair the damaged void that she felt in relationship to her depressed mother. Her brother's brief return to the family had accomplished this and had temporarily allowed her to function better. She began to mourn her brother's death and to understand the relationship between this event, her affair and her aborted pregnancy. For a long time in her life her own hope for success and happiness was by having a penis and being a man. Any situation that threatened this fantasy brought depression and rage, which when directed at herself resulted in physical symptoms. To resolve these it was necessary to mobilize her rage at her mother in the transference.

Because of my dawning understanding of the dynamics of pathological penis envy I was able to provide a holding environment. It seemed to me that Debby's bitchiness, paranoia, and grandiose omnipotent behavior was a grotesque caricature of the transient behavior of many adolescent girls, which seems to assure the final separation from the mother. There is an attempt to perceive a sense of inner goodness by projecting the sense of badness (because of unacceptable rising sexual and aggressive impulses). The grandiosity and omnipotence in this stage of development is reparative to a sense of vulnerability. For Debby the unrelenting search for a penis also had a reparative aim since her subjective experience of severe bodily and intellectual damage as well as her poor self-esteem could not have been merely the effect of noticing the anatomical differences between the sexes.

What could have propelled her to such overwhelming psychopathology? Minute exploration of her early relationship with her mother revealed a period when the two had stayed in bed together ostensibly because both were ill. Debby was treated as the narcissistic extension of her mother's body. She failed to separate her own intrapsychic self-representation from that of her mother. This was revealed by Debby's ultimate failure to remember which illnesses were hers and which were her mother's. Predictably, her mother was no help in that regard. Specifically, the mother, when asked, could not recall which had been ill when. Debby's search for a penis was a search to repair her damaged body image and the union of her self-representation with that of her internal representation of her mother.

Some years later this patient returned to treatment after the birth of a daughter. Paradoxically, this child seemed to be a stranger to her. She used this sense of strangeness defensively to protect her desire to merge with the child as her mother had with her. Interpretation led to a more comfortable relationship between the two. Still later, the patient called because she sensed her reluctance to send this bright child to full-time nursery school. Although this was not analyzed, I believe that "touching base" with me was necessary before she could let her daughter fully separate from her.

Case 2: A Young Woman with Homosexual Behavior

Diana, an adolescent college student, sought help because of her homosexuality and resultant depression. Along with her clear good looks were clipped hair and a studied carelessness in dress that camouflaged her gender. Her clothing was loose and she wore neither brassiere nor make-up.

Diana reported that she was the eldest of two sisters. Her father was described as a distant and ineffectual man who, nevertheless, did well enough in business to provide generously for his family. Her mother was described as a petite, "hysterical" career woman who had amassed her own fortune. The marital situation of Diana's parents was described as shaky. Her father was said to have his own apartment to which he went when his wife "had a fit and threw him out." The patient's perception of her father was that he was pathetic and her mother was unstable and crazy even after years of psychiatric treatment. Diana remembered that her mother had confided in her about numerous love affairs and, when angry at the father, often manipulated Diana into fighting with him.

Diana had many years of analysis in her hometown to "help me bear the craziness in my home." She spoke of her tendency to lie and to act impulsively, and told of a rape perpetrated on her in the eighth grade by her babysitter's boyfriend. Once she had stolen a friend's book, with which she had been hit by her mother. Despite great embarrassment, she also revealed compulsive, aberrant behavior, namely, that she would sneak out of the house, stuffing her books a few at a time down the sewers until she had rid herself of her entire library. She felt that this behavior was "sick" and had been as incomprehensible to her then as it was in the present.

Diana formed an immediately warm and cordial treatment relationship. This puzzled her because she had described herself as deliberately and habitually distant and paranoid in personal relationships. Trying to be honest, she furnished what she considered to be a detailed history, but she refused to discuss the details of her sexual behavior. Soon after treatment began she became involved with a young heterosexual woman who looked like her mother and who had the analyst's first name. She felt exploited, manipulated and disappointed in this relationship, and dealt with her feeling by abusing the usual campus drugs. She stated flippantly that her parents could not care less about her drug-related behavior, but they were disturbed by her sexual preference. Diana was asked if she could refrain from using drugs to deal with painful feelings and come and talk about them instead.

She arrived at the next session high. Although she intended to conceal, it, I noted it. She was amazed that I could be "in tune" with her, yet was sullen and defiant. I told her that she was expecting to be punished. Surprised, she said that her mother would either not have noticed, or "beat the shit out of" her. She then had a series of stormy sessions in which she was clearly attempting to provoke a power struggle. Correct interpretations about her need to control me led to earnest introspection in the session, but was accompanied by homosexual acting out. When this was analyzed as acting out of the transference, the patient responded by becoming angry. When told that she preferred to make war rather than love in the treatment, she replied that her mother alternated between being unresponsive and seductive. The patient's behavior with her lover caused the lover to behave in the same "push-pull" way.

Meanwhile, the patient did excellent work at school and turned down other activities in order to excel, although she seemed to have no life direction in mind. When asked about this she said she was surprised that I would concern myself with it. Upon beginning to think about the future she chose an area of endeavor that her "disinterested" father had once recommended to her. She became somewhat paranoid about reporting her plans and disclosed the fantasy that she would one day surpass my income. However, she was afraid of retaliation from me for her fantasies and began to react to me as she had to her father. She saw my consultation room as warm, but tacky. (Her father would also have wall-to-wall carpeting, but her mother would have oriental rugs in keeping with her impeccable taste.) She also fantasied that I would lead her toward vocational success, then undermine her at the last minute. This was a pattern in her relationship with her father, who would be supportive and take her to "business lunch," then withdraw from her out of deference to her mother's jealousy and negative remarks. The patient hated him for his subservience. (She did not yet realize that she played a part in stimulating the triangulation.)

In her homosexual relationships she disclosed that she took the role of the "dominant butch." She meant to say that she thought that she was out to be a better man than her father, but she slipped and said, "a better man than my mother." It became clear that she sensed a role reversal in her family. She would later recall that once her mother had abandoned the family for a year, during which time her father cared for her.

In answer to questions about the fragile picture of her mother she had initially presented, she showed me scars from "accidental" wounds. She recalled with some shock and pain that indeed she had once been very seriously wounded, quite deliberately, by her mother. She began to realize that in her homosexual relationships she would much prefer to be the passive and cared-for partner. She became good friends with a man and began to dress and appear softer and more feminine, trading her worn sweatshirts for cashmere sweaters. However, she was enraged with one of my other patients who was clearly a housewife, and ranted on and on about how I could not possibly like this other woman. She reacted with rage to the interpretation that she was behaving like a jealous lover.

During one hour in her second year of treatment, she casually mentioned that her mother had gone to the hospital for some unknown minor gynecological procedure. When I asked if it had been an abortion, Diana was furious and indignant. She felt that I had insulted her mother and wanted to leave the hour prematurely. I pointed out that it was a straightforward question since she had described her mother as sexually very active. She said that I knew that her father was currently out of the house. When I asked, ''What about lovers?'' she acted dumbstruck and said that she did not know if her mother had ever really had lovers. She felt confused about what she actually had been told and what may have been her fantasies. She then rushed into a flurry of sexual activity in which her behavioral and emotional inconsistencies were reminiscent of the relationship with her mother.

During my vacation, Diana called to say that her mother had arranged a summer job interview for her to work for a man with whom the mother was somehow involved. It seemed that the mother also planned to work for him, although it was unrelated to the mother's usual area of work. At this time the patient had been visiting a female friend, her first friendship without sexual overtones. Suddenly she felt negatively toward the friend, without conscious reason. These negative feelings were displaced from her mother. She felt that her mother was confused about who it was that needed a new job, she or the mother, and that she herself had felt confused and helpless in speaking with the mother.

We spent several months dealing with the patient's identity confusion and reality testing difficulties, just like those of her mother. This led to our understanding of her bizarre symptom, the compulsive disposal of all of her books. When she had stolen *one* book from her friend, her mother had repeatedly hit her with each of the books as if she had stolen them all. Diana's confusion in her relationship with her mother extended to confusion of reality in other areas of her life. This related to whether she had been the seducer or the seduced and even invaded her sense of gender identity and choice of sexual object. Thus, shortly after the "rape" while in eighth grade, she began her first homosexual relationship. She had not been raped at all, but had invited the babysitter's male friend to her bedroom. The babysitter and her boyfriend made love in Diana's parents' bed, but she told her parents she had been raped.

While discussing earlier transient homosexual relationships, she began a stable homosexual relationship with a young woman with whom she now lived. She was very jealous of this woman's other nonsexual relationships and experienced terrible separation anxiety when forced to be apart from her. During this period she studied and worked successfully, and became able to relate to both of her parents and to visit home without turmoil. She discovered that if she kept both parents separately and simultaneously abreast of her activities (taking an extra course that required tuition, working at a part-time job, joining a health club), neither would be jealous or upset. She obtained an excellent summer job and began to feel some heterosexual interest. She decided to remain friends with, but leave her homosexual lover, and took a more conveniently located apartment of her own without anxiety. She applied to graduate school. With her evident increasing success, both parents became less concerned with her. She could accept their minimal financial support and decided to do the rest on her own. She reported having a sense of who she was, where she was going, and what was real and possible in her life. She no longer felt panicky about being alone.

As her treatment progressed, she regressed before visits home and, once, before a long trip. She was confused about her feelings toward me, alternately hating me, admiring me, feeling unreal with me, and hating herself. She had never

really achieved a state of constant self or object-represen-
tation. Separations remained a major problem for her. She
revealed that she could not fall asleep alone without the
fantasy of an imaginary companion. Other aspects of her
history that contributed to her identity confusion and diffusion related to false stories about her family that her
mother had told her as a child.

Upon experiencing some financial difficulties, her father
wondered if it was necessary for Diana to continue in treatment and requested an appointment to see me. Diana's
mother became cold and distant and, clearly jealous and
insinuated that Diana did not want her to see me. I therefore
elected to see them both. They were fighting at the time and
could not arrange to come to my office together, so I saw
Diana's mother first. I noted that she knew a great deal
about herself and was honest in admitting her early damaging behavior. Diana's mother had engaged nursemaids
to look after her daughters, but as soon as they developed
any attachment to these women, the women would be fired.
The mother would then attempt to assume the care of her
children by herself. Feeling overwhelmed, she physically
abused them and then would hire help for their care. She
repeated this pattern throughout their early childhood. She
was aware of frequent mood swings and held herself responsible for her daughter's difficulties.

When I saw Diana's father, I asked him whether he had
been aware of the mother's behavior and why he had not
intervened. He told me that he had tried to have the mother
committed for insanity on several occasions, but could not
arrange this. His observation early on had been that if he
showed any attention to his daughters, his wife would become enraged and more irrational. Therefore, he elected to
withdraw from them. He would have left his wife if not for
his fear for his children's safety. He said, "I know that
Diana does not think that I love her. I wish she knew." I

recommended that he tell her. He told me that Diana's mother had not ever left the family for a protracted time. This clearly had been Diana's wish. Diana had said that her mother did not come home with the family from vacation for one year when Diana was eight. In reality, Diana's mother had remained behind for two days because the family's luggage had been lost. Diana's father did effect a reconciliation with her, and she continued to be careful never to neglect her mother. Several months later, while visiting her parents' home, she met an appropriate man with whom she was able to begin a long relationship. She was concurrently making good friendships with heterosexual women.

Diana's relationship with me helped her to become a reliable observer of her behavior within her family. On a visit with her mother she noted, with some shock, that her mother entered her room and came over to her bed with her robe open. She was able to recall that her mother had behaved similarly throughout her life and that she responded to this intrusive, seductive behavior both with feelings of anxiety and sexual arousal. These were similar to feelings she had had with transient homosexual partners who would turn on her, or abandon her, just as her mother had. On one occasion, her mother even insisted that she cancel plans with her new boyfriend in order to meet her at the family's summer cottage. When Diana arrived, her mother was kind to her, but she was expected to do all of the housework and shopping. The night that her father arrived, her mother said, "You can go home now, Diana."

Diana's mother used both her daughter and her husband as phallic extensions and sexualized the mother-daughter relationship. She was not able to maintain object constancy because of the vicissitudes of her own narcissistic needs. Diana was thus put into the position of choosing, first, between her father and her mother, and then, between her boyfriend and mother. She generally chose the latter in an attempt to prevent her mother from disorganizing. Her experience in analysis was the first one with a woman who did not use her in a narcissistic manner, although she had feared this. A working through of her damaged self-representation and her wishes to both reunite with and to destroy her mother led to her ability to select an appropriate man. Her father had not been available by choice, in order to appease her mother and to protect the children. Thus he prevented significant triangulation to decrease the symbiosis between Diana and her mother, which would have led to Diana's oedipal conflict.

The major portion of Diana's analysis was accomplished during the time she made her first heterosexual relationship and slowly learned to be sexually responsive to a man. During this period, she had severe difficulty in maintaining an intrapsychic representation of the analyst. The only way she was able to be orgasmic initially was by visualizing the analyst looking at her in a benign and approving way.

At the end of the analysis, Diana was able to mourn. She disclosed the true nature of the opening transference, which she had concealed. It had been openly homosexual, tinged with the same feelings that she later realized she had had towards her mother. She was able to resolve her guilt about these feelings, realized the nature of her mother's severe illness and learned how to treat her so as to minimize the fluctuating seductiveness and jealous rage. This meant an identification with the analyst's ability to remain stable and reliable in the face of Diana's own early mood swings and difficult behavior.

Case 3: Misdiagnosis of a Young Woman who Appeared Helpless, Depressed and Suicidal

Betsy, a young married woman in her twenties, had had three years of intensive psychotherapy and, most recently, suffered from anxiety and depression not alleviated by high dose medication. She originally had been referred for treatment after becoming engaged while in college, because she had repeatedly cancelled her wedding date. Her parents already had used their influence to help her fiancé gain admission to a prestigious professional school and committed themselves to the full financial support of the couple.

At the urging of her first therapist (an older man) Betsy did marry and begin her professional schooling. But, she was unhappy in her marriage, and although an excellent student, was insecure in school and had considered dropping out. She was very thin but wore bulky clothing to hide her body, of which she was ashamed. She was unable to make the simplest everyday decision without her mother's help, which overtly contrasted to her relationship with the men in her life. She was estranged from her successful and dynamic father, who was fed up with her. In addition, she was very angry with her younger brother who was markedly unsuccessful, but whom she considered to have all the advantages in life. She even felt that she had been given only part of a name, "Betsy," instead of Elizabeth, which revealed the extent to which she felt cheated by her mother. Even her one friend, a fellow student with whom she studied, was weary of her constant complaints.

Betsy forced her husband to cook and to manage the household, then treated him with derision. She felt that he was her intellectual, social and cultural inferior, despite her parents' attempts to buy him proper attire and introduce him to the finer things in life. Furthermore, she despised his compliance to their wishes. Despite being anorgasmic, she flatly refused to discuss sex with her first therapist because she did not want to hear "all that nonsense about penis envy."

In her initial diagnostic interviews she revealed that she had been manipulative with her initial therapist, even telling him that she had suicidal ruminations in an attempt to get his special attention. She became frightened, however, when he began to consider that she be hospitalized. She had specifically sought treatment with a female analyst whom she heard about through acquaintances. The qualities that attracted her were the analyst's reputation for being "sharp" and presumably looking as though she had just walked out of a chic New York store.

After careful diagnostic evaluation, the patient's psychopathology was assessed to be well within the neurotic range. She was offered analysis and asked to gradually discontinue her medications. She initially was quite frightened by this request. In contemplating her decision she stood in front of the window of her skyscraper apartment and, for the first time, genuinely considered jumping. However, she responded to the analyst's invitation to try to understand why she had to make herself so sick. She correctly perceived that the analyst did not think that she needed hospitalization, but that she would listen with interest and concern to the "silly complaints" dismissed by Betsy's family and former therapist.

During the first year of her analysis the work centered entirely around two themes. The first was why she had to be so infantile and sabotage her academic success. The second was why she had reduced her husband to the status of a maid, whom she then despised. It turned out that her regression and success phobia were a kind of no contest defense. If nothing was expected of her, then she need never be exposed as a phony. She was presenting herself as damaged in one way, so that no one might find out that she saw herself as damaged in other ways. Specifically, she kept her weight down and covered her body because she was ashamed of not being sexy and feminine.

She claimed to like her boyish figure but could not reconcile this with the severe panic at having her very long hair trimmed. When, at her mother's insistence, she had a badly needed haircut, she cried hysterically for two days. She then had a dream related to the gift with which her mother had bribed her to get the new hairstyle. She dreamt that the gift had come damaged. Her associations were to the erector set her brother had received one Christmas, when all she had received were dolls. She then told a story of which she had been very ashamed. She retaliated against her brother one holiday by eating all of his candy as well as all of hers. Interpretations centered around her perception that her brother was given special things which she could not acquire either through eating or dieting, or by the way she dressed or kept her hair.

In time, she would not always allow her mother to select dresses for her but was, as yet, unable to completely make her own choices. She gradually did cut her hair to a fashionable length, though with much anxiety and grief. With regard to her behavior with her husband, she began to realize that under the guise of her own impotence to manage household affairs, she had made him the housewife. She secretly gloated over this and, at the same time, despised his castrated state. This interpretation followed a dream in which she had made a dinner that was a failure and then angrily ripped off her apron. Her associations were to her husband's appearance in an apron that had been bought for her. Her reaction was that, if not for his beard and short hair, "You'd think he was a woman." She had always despised his beard, ostensibly because it wasn't "clean-cut looking." She preferred the "college jocks." She wondered if she didn't resent her husband's masculinity and if, in fact, she had not chosen a man who could be rendered "female."

Her school career went extraordinarily well and she was less regressed at home, but she still relied upon her mother, demanding that her mother come from some distance to pick up her clothes for altering or dry cleaning. She also demanded many gifts from her family and became conscious of "holding onto money." The gifts, of course, never satisfied her.

The second phase of her analysis, during which she worked professionally and began to make friends, was occupied with the theme of penis envy and competition. It was recognized first as the cause of her sibling rivalry and this led to a repair of the relationship with her brother. She now treated the analyst as she had her father and showed off her achievements as she always had attempted to do with him. She remembered a pleasurable period in which she had worked in her father's office on weekends, until her brother reached the age when he devoted his time to the brother's school athletic activities.

At this point, she asked if the analyst had a briefcase. Failing to coerce her mother into providing her with one, she spent several tortured days combing the stores and settled for a case which she considered less than adequate. But then she added an expensive pocketbook to it, both of which were parked ostentatiously in front of the analyst in the consultation room. Interpretations about this behavior were acknowledged, but were not really effective until her father neglected to appear to witness a very important professional milestone in her career. Her response was immediate and surprising to her. She bought the first article of clothing that she had ever purchased without her mother, a pin-striped suit. She was delighted and really considered herself to be quite stunning and feminine. She came in to report with chagrin that one of her colleagues had said, "Well, that's one way to be the best dressed man here." This was a potent interpretation. She became depressed and unsure of herself.

Betsy's first analyst had encouraged her to settle short of her potential, that is, to accept her castrated, damaged state. In the face of this, she had become seriously regressed. She would not allow any analysis of her obvious penis envy.

With a female analyst who paid attention to her difficulties in achievement and in separating from her mother, she was able to analyze (and therefore prepare to give up) her penis envy. Analysis revealed that she saw having a penis as a way of engaging her mother. The symbolic substitute for the phallus (clothing, pocketbooks, briefcases and money) were initially coerced from her mother as a substitute for love. Therefore, the phallus was also seen as a breast or nurturing source, a way of completing mother and/or herself as well as a way of competing with father and brother for her mother.

After the multiple meanings of her penis envy were analyzed through the review of her past behavior, it became clear that she needed to maintain a union with the mother of her early childhood (by remaining infantile). Upon visiting her parents' home, she took back an old transitional object (a teddy bear) to sleep with. Her husband became angry at this and, for the first time, made some sharp observations about her avoidance of becoming an adult sexual woman. He was tired of dealing with her as a baby. She suppressed any analytic discussion of the weekend because she was afraid that I would take the toy from her, and because she was beginning some sexual activity in her marriage.

The marital sexual relationship was unsatisfactory to her and she soon developed a crush on a colleague, a ''macho'' man, whose name she often confused with her father's. Her greatest fear about beginning a love affair centered around the conviction that the analyst-mother would be angry and envious. This marked the beginning of an oedipal transference relationship. She struggled with great shame and anxiety, during one hour, to tell the analyst that she had the fleeting notion that she was becoming the more attractive of the pair. She had a dream about a dress that she had had as a little girl. She hated the dress. She fantasied that her

mother discouraged her from pretty, more grown-up clothing and that she had kept her looking plain and childish.
She noted that the man to whom she was attracted admired
bright colors and sexy-looking clothes. Very tentatively and
with the approval of a friend, she bought some clothes which
she considered sexy. Indeed, she was correct. Her mother's
response was extremely negative. The patient's preoccupation with finding the right apparel, and her need for more,
persisted as the analysis proceeded through the vicissitudes
of the oedipal conflict. The patient separated from her husband, legally changed her name to Elizabeth, and began a
love affair in which she was orgasmic in intercourse for the
first time. She gave up her teddy bear and reported a curious
phenomenon, namely, that she talked to her lover's penis.
[Galenson (1973) had reported the use of the penis as a
transitional object for oedipal phase boys.]

The new sexual relationship was chaotic because Betsy
had chosen a man like, yet very unlike, her father. She
made tremendous maternal demands on her lover. When
these were unmet, in a rage she stabbed her teddy bear.
When she complained to her mother about the vicissitudes
of this relationship, her mother said, "You should have kept
the husband that we bought for you." During this period
of time, in which the preoedipal maternal transference was
being acted out by the patient both with her boyfriend and
mother, she came to terms with her mother's intrusiveness
and limitations. She began to take pride in her own cooking
and in the activities her mother did so well, which she had
previously avoided.

The transference shifted after interpretations that the
patient was treating the analyst as an ally against her preoedipal mother. The analyst then received some telephone
calls from the patient, which were related to pseudo-emer-
gencies in which she felt overwhelmed. The analyst was
accused of being no help at all, and in a rage, was attacked

"for being a fraud who had no penis either" and who could not give one to the patient. In fact, Betsy felt that the analyst could not give her anything else as well.

Through the interpretation of transference fantasies and dreams, Betsy recovered some data that had been repressed and which related to her mother's childhood experience of early parental loss. The mother was remembered as someone who relied on her husband as a maternal figure, was chronically depressed when the patient was small, and was angry at the patient for the advantages that the patient had which the mother herself was denied as a child. The patient experienced a profound withdrawal of her mother's love as soon as she was not completely helpless. Instead, she was to be rewarded for behavior affirming the mother's demand that she be pretty, quiet and good. In contrast, the patient's brother was pressured to succeed athletically and academically and was clearly the more valued child.

For the patient, having a penis meant being a school and work achiever and being entitled to independence. Being female meant dedication to snaring and holding a man. She had the fantasy of an illusory phallus, but lived with the fear that she would be discovered lacking. Additionally, she feared that she would be unable to attract a strong, bright, successful man. She had angrily bowed to pressure to marry the man that her parents bought for her, further evidence of her inadequacy.

When the narcissistic injury that resulted from her poor relationship with her preoedipal mother was analyzed, the patient was able to choose a man who was both dynamic and maternal. She perceived his penis as both her baby and her bottle. She was able to give up her obsession to get to the top of her profession, a task which required sacrifice of a multitude of avocational activities acquired in the course of her analysis and which she had come to enjoy. Ultimately, she developed the desire for a child and the conviction that she could adequately nurture it.

Case 4: A Woman with a Real Physical Disability

Amanda, a 32-year-old, slender, young-looking woman, was awkward and poorly dressed. She was referred by a friend after a death in her family, was quite depressed, and felt that she could not cope at work or with her husband and three children. After a short period in psychotherapy her depression was relieved as she became aware of her guilt due to anger at the person who died. She then requested analysis to deal with her marital and sexual problems and to reveal her developing fantasies about me, which she could not discuss face-to-face. Because of her experience with me in psychotherapy, referral to another analyst was recommended, but the patient sharply refused.

Amanda was born to a politically active family, members of a minority group. She was the second of two children, with a brother ten years older than herself. Her mother had been a wealthy woman and quite bright, and the patient perceived her as sweet but unable to control her children's fights. She perceived her father as a bombastic, all-knowing tyrant, who never practiced the profession for which he was trained. He worked until he lost his job and then became a businessman. She described her brother as "exactly" like her father. She was raised by maids while her mother worked and her father travelled. During her latency she recalled sharing rooms with her parents or with her brother.

She remembered herself as a shy, awkward child with frequent temper tantrums and envy of her brother's brightness. She met the son of a beloved mother-substitute and married him after several years of courtship, when she was 19 years old. Her husband, ten years her senior, was a pedantic, obsessional attorney who travelled during their early marriage, which precipitated quarrels over her loneliness. He then worked closer to home while she attended college and graduate school. Although she finished her courses, she was inexplicably unable to complete her thesis. During the period of her schooling and shortly thereafter she had three children and several other pregnancies. She worked part-time and continuously while raising the children with the aid of maids. For the past eight years at one job she was considered to be a creative, helpful, albeit easily angered, member of the staff. She had an active social life and many friends.

Amanda started her analysis eagerly, presenting herself as a flighty, melodramatic coquette with superficial obsessional defenses, including intellectualization, reaction formation against aggressive and sexual feelings, and concerns over being controlled. As these were explored, they rapidly gave way to expression of her great need to be appreciated and admired and her long-standing history of feelings of inadequacy. At the same time, her inflated self-image was revealed in her behavior. Happily talking to patients in the waiting room, she rationalized this as due to her maternal feelings. Actually the analysis of her behavior revealed that she felt entitled to intrude upon their privacy to receive attention. She would also intrude into a friend's marriage and provoke fights, looking for individual and exclusive attention from either partner. These represented displacements from her wish to be very special to me and to receive my exclusive attention, which I interpreted to her.

Superficially charming, Amanda tried to coldly control me with "fascinating" stories that had grandiose themes of specialness. One was about how she dressed poorly to show that clothes did not make her pretty, since her prettiness showed through without appropriate attire. Her excessive "giving" behavior to her husband, children and friends, as well as her attempt to be my special patient, were told with a thinly veiled hauteur, revealing a strong defense against aggressive wishes. She complained about the isolation of the couch, where she felt like a "dummy" when she could not understand my simplest interventions directed toward increasing her ability to view her own feelings and attitudes in the past and present. She compared her not hearing me to her behavior when her "self-centered" husband would lecture her repetitively, while she felt enclosed in glass. This also repeated feelings of isolation and intimidation by her father. She sometimes felt I was not in the room, and I frequently felt excluded.

An early dream of a whale with an oar in its mouth revealed Amanda's underlying wishes for fusion, oral incorporation and phallic incorporation as defenses against her oral aggression. She associated to a baby looking for a mother and alluded to her sexual feelings for me. She slipped in her associations saying "maidenhead" for masthead and also felt that she was "floundering" and "at sea" on the couch. I supported her during this period of her isolation and deprivation by interpreting her search for a good mother in me. Shortly thereafter, there gradually emerged a pronounced idealization of me as a fairy godmother with a wand, who stayed in my office all night and waited for her to come to sessions. She fantasied that she was my special patient and perceived only two of my other patients, both crippled (one with crutches, one blind). This picture of me would alternate with one as a cold and haughty, greedy lady who was only interested in her as a case. This devaluation would occur whenever she was slightly disappointed by me in a real or in a fantasied way, such as when she thought that I had smiled at another patient and not at her. Her idealization was interpreted as a projection of her grandiosity, which she delegated to me and then took back into herself. This made her feel special. I also interpreted her devaluation of me as a projection and reintrojection of another old self-image and as an attempt to tear me down to avoid any dependency on me. It was also a defense against any awareness of her envy and hatred, which she expressed outside of treatment. She kept telling me that I was "bad," and that I occasionally felt inadequate showed the strength of her conviction and persuasiveness.

Idealization prevailed, but Amanda neither thought of nor missed me between hours. During weekends and separations she felt bored and restless, and when exploration of these feelings revealed shallowness, she became more anxious. She dreamt of me as a judge with a big wig. She would associate with confusion to a picture (on the wall) of a mother and child nuzzling, not sure whether they were biting or kissing. This reflected the state of her transference. After periods of devaluation, she was fearful that I would abandon her. Unempathic to her husband, she flaunted her relationship with me to him, attempting to get him angry and thus make him force her to leave the analysis. When I interpreted this as a displacement of her own anger and disappointment in me, and her own wishes to get rid of me whenever I did not match her picture of me as an ideal mother, this behavior slowly ceased.

Concurrently, Amanda projected her own sadistic superego onto me with expectations that I would rage at her for not being an ideal patient. A slip, "clitoral" for "critical" clobbering, something she expected, alluded again to sexual fantasies which she could not discuss. She defensively threw herself into hard work, having identified with me as a hard worker. Thus she fled from an object relationship to work on her thesis with which she had great difficulty. As the problem was discussed she related a history from childhood to the present of being treated as a clowning youngster. Her mother had thought such behavior was "cute."

Amanda said that her mother was perfect and that life with her was rosy. She could only admit that her mother might not have been a good mother when the patient was small. She also noticed that her mother had not related to her grandchildren when they were toddlers. However, Amanda maintained the idealization of her mother. She also had a long history of attaching herself to dominant women teachers with whom she would become the "pet." She would discard them when they disappointed her. With her idealization of them she would also feel small and incompetent. This reaction was also reminiscent of her relationship to her father, who thought that she was very bright and lectured on topics that overwhelmed her, never listening to her replies.

As Amanda became more able to observe herself, her anxiety increased. I agreed to her request that I see her five times weekly, instead of four. Feeling safer with me, she became able to speak of her sexual fantasies. She dreamt of me or of herself with a penis, dozed in my waiting room dreamily thinking of sitting on my lap and nursing or crawling about my rug near my feet. She was frightened during sex, at which time she visualized her husband as an angry gorilla. As yet unable to explore this, she felt that interpretations of her projected rage onto him were somewhat helpful in decreasing her anxiety. She experienced wishes for me with a penis, holding her and getting into her.

At this time there was a regression in Amanda's speech, which resembled baby-talk and had a strange, almost primary process quality. While I did not feel a lack of empathy, I felt bored and puzzled. I speculated that she struggled to cover up a problem that remained to be discovered. She did this by creating a lot of emotional commotion to distract me. She saw herself as center stage in social and work situations and acted out roles to entertain me and to prevent me from seeing her real sense of defectiveness. Additional evidence was her delight and talent in interactions with brain-damaged children who easily regressed to primary process modes. She also identified with my crippled patients and dreamt of telling lies and fairy tales.

Amanda tried to make her defects appear as purely psychological to hide the fact that they might have a more organic reality. I gently confronted her with what I felt was her unconscious, unplanned, automatized kind of distortion and attempt to distract. I wondered if she had this problem with others. She assumed that I was saying that she was schizophrenic and that she spoke in a "word salad" and had a fantasy that I had "banged" her over the head. When I asked if she had ever banged her head, her history of head-banging and signs of early minimal brain damage emerged. This was further underlined by memories of severe hyperactivity in childhood, which may have explained her hyperactive and flighty associations as an adult. Her parents had been unaware of her cognitive disability. I noted that her hyperactive, "cute" language, which we came to call "pseudosalad," was being used defensively to avoid acknowledgement of the possible congenital defect or learning disorder.

Thus, Amanda began life with a narcissistic distortion in her self-image because she had a basic fault in her cognitive and perceptual processes. She envisioned herself as "dumb" with a "hole in her head" long before she perceived the anatomical difference between the sexes. Therefore, her wish for a penis (almost conscious) was to make her feel complete and bright. This is the reverse of the usual woman, who perceives the difference between the sexes and her own "inferior" genital apparatus first, then shows a wish for a penis as a compensation for her "inferiority." Such women can feel inadequate intellectually as a result of their own penis envy. By contrast, this patient had a true inadequacy with which she had to cope before analysis of her preoedipal and oedipal problems could proceed.

Amanda gradually recalled a history of dyslexia, scoliosis, convergence difficulty and severe motor incoordination. With some intellectual appreciation of her plight, she began to do what she had instructed her students to do: use a tape recorder, editor and typist. She was quite capable of helping her students to compensate, and by changing her approach, was finally able to complete her own thesis. Although the change in her presentation during the sessions was slow, she commented proudly that outside of the analysis her friends noticed she no longer spoke "baby talk" and saw her as a mature, interesting woman.

Envious of my "perfection," Amanda was now able to listen to my interpretation of her alternating idealization and devaluation of me. This partially defended her against hatred and envy of me and the fears that I would mistreat and exploit her as she felt her parents had. She experienced herself as dependent and anxious. She dreamt of having a "manhole cover," which revealed a conscious wish for a penis to repair a sense of inner emptiness she had experienced since childhood. With some minor surgery leading to transient urinary difficulty, she experienced severe castration, separation and annihilation anxiety. Exploration of these fears revealed her previous inability to tell me of the destructive hostility and aggression she felt toward men. She had thrown her son against a wall when he wanted to be fed, and when she was too busy had jammed food angrily into him. Rage towards men surfaced and castrating, destructive wishes were openly expressed. These interfered with her being orgasmic in intercourse when she had archaic fantasies that her husband's penis would come out of her mouth or damage her. I interpreted her own wishes for phallic incorporation and her fears of biting rage.

Amanda's rage turned to me with fantasies that I preferred men to her. This interfered with her wish to possess me completely as she had wished to possess her mother. Within this context a masculine identification emerged. I interpreted and reconstructed that she had perceived her mother as unable to help her, but that she saw her mother as understanding her father and her brother. She had identified with her father and then had a fantasy of filling the hole in her head (not primarily the one in her pelvis) with a penis. Fearful of full recognition of this defect, she regressed again to flight in her associations.

As she began to trust me more and see me as separate, Amanda revealed a picture of herself as a destructive shark and to feel guilty and depressed over her past behavior to her son and to me. Separation anxiety emerged, as well as intense curiosity about me which resembled a more classical transference neurosis. Her curiosity about me was displaced to friends and fantasies about their having intercourse. She recalled seeing her parents "copulating violently" in early life, while she felt excited and wet the bed. In her sexual fantasies she identified with a man. This early stimulation, I said, was too much for her to process. It had led to a confusion in her sexual identity and to an idealization and identification with her father and his phallus. In time, the more I interpreted, the more her cognitive ability increased.

When Amanda changed jobs suddenly and I noted she did this without discussion, she began to recognize her wish for a "magical transformation and rebirth" with me. She experienced shame and depression. She began to flirt with married men on weekends, which I interpreted as a flight from her homosexual feelings for me following a dream of a mermaid turned into a woman who was penetrated through all orifices, again indicating her preoccupation with gaining an illusory phallus. At the same time, she became more interested in sports and started to improve her coordination. Increasing honesty led her to tell me that she had lied about her income. We spoke of how she had hidden this from me, feeling that I would milk her dry. We both agreed to an increase in fee, upon which she dreamt that I squeezed her breasts, extracting coffee. A close friend had given her a coffee machine that was costly, which she refused. Her projected and warded off intense oral and homosexual wishes were thus interpreted.

Amanda continued to rage at men who possessed the "repair" for her defect and envied women for their intelligence, but diverted us from talk of her own disability. I realized that she intellectually appreciated her plight but that she was not emotionally convinced of it. When she wished to give me a copy of her thesis, I introduced a parameter (later to be analyzed) by accepting a "raw" copy. It revealed mirror-writing, phonic spelling, reversal, dysgraphia, conceptual errors, contiguity of concepts in time rather than by content, and perseveration. When we discussed this she slowly developed a conviction about her deficit. The following reconstruction was made: Her faulty self-image was the result of her first learning that she was "dumb" and later that she was a girl. Reparative fantasies of an illusory phallus appeared, along with castrating wishes and castration anxiety. She had turned to women, upon whom she projected a phallus, and used them to defend her against shame and humiliation as well as fear of exposure during her school years. She had perceived her father and brother as clever, further strengthening her perception that it was better to be male.

Amanda then told me of her envy of both her husband's and my abilities. In her anamnesis, a picture emerged of her parents as cold and her father as intensely aggressive. Although her mother functioned well on the surface, her indifference led to Amanda's intense oral frustration and aggression. As progress occurred in the analysis, there was a mobilization of oedipal issues. Amanda noted differences between herself and me and fantasied meeting my husband and flirting with him. She also reported that she saw her husband as more separate and was now able to get him to edit her work. He frightened her less as her projection of rage onto him decreased. Fearful of competing with me, she defended against this by a fantasy of becoming a therapist. She was able to understand this behavior as a flight from seeing herself clearly and as an avoidance of her rivalry.

With improvement in Amanda's dress she became quite attractive, and even wondered how I had been able to tolerate her previous behavior. More able to tolerate guilt and depression, she was capable of increasing tenderness toward her husband and attained orgasm in intercourse for the first time. She called this period a "watermark," immediately recognizing it as an aphasic expression for "hallmark." Issues of competition with her mother for her father and with me for my husband and male patients were primary. She felt more sure of herself, considered changing jobs and did return to school for additional graduate work. She now felt that seeing me four times weekly would suffice, since her difficult schedule did not allow her to come the additional day.

Amanda had had many pregnancies and wished to have another. This wish represented a very early wish to have a baby in order to fuse with her mother and feel complete. This was a preoedipal wish which later had oedipal features. The wish for a baby was so strong that it had been enacted many times. During her pregnancies, Amanda felt full and "safe" and had many fantasies of herself as a baby with a good mother.

One year later, Amanda tried to precipitate a premature termination because her teachers began to recognize her defect and she felt humiliated. She wanted to leave analysis before having to confront the fact that it could not repair

her basic neurological fault, only her faulty adaptation to
it. Her teachers noted her grandiose standards and her inability to appreciate her real accomplishments. Unable to
escape having to work harder than others, she began to
accept this and to provide more cognitive structure for herself, such as slower reading, outlining, and using a dic-
tionary. She felt better able to learn and be reconciled to
her "ordinariness." Less anxiously concerned with competition and impressing authority, there was a decrease in
her grandiosity. She was even able to feel pride in her work,
sexuality and relationships. When her husband was hospitalized she handled his illness without melodrama, while
her mother "wailed." This, in fact, led her to see her
mother's cyclic depressions and "bitchiness" as well as a
warmer side of her father revealed in his supportiveness.
Although neither parent had been able to give her the early
guidelines that she had desperately needed, she was now
resigned to a reasonable relationship with them. Her associations led to my feeling that she had introjected me as
"a good enough mother" and had traversed rapprochement.

The patient again brought up the issue of termination
which we discussed. She was no longer impulsive and decided on a date six months in advance, to which I agreed.
During this period she felt sad about leaving and happy that
she could now be on her own. There was a fleeting return
of grandiose symptoms and a discussion of her wish to
return now and then, acknowledging that her defect and
perhaps her wishes for grandiosity would never completely
disappear. She realized that she would not be a "perfect"
termination case because of her craving for attachment, and
understood that this was intensified by her mother's depression and use of her as an appendage. Shortly before termination, although still angry that I could not cure her, she
concluded from a dream, "Oh, Mom, you haven't cooked

all that I wanted, but it will have to be good enough and now I can cook by myself."

Case 5: A Male Analyst, Female Supervisory Assistance, and a Patient With Severe Early Trauma and Loss[1]

Julie, a pretty, bright, 24-year-old actress, came to treatment depressed and concerned about her erratic sexual behavior over the past three years. She felt that she had managed her life well until then. She had graduated from college early and had planned to enter law school. During this time she had her first sexual affair, and she became pregnant. Depression followed an abortion and lifted when she began to date again. She initially felt safe with her boyfriend but her depression returned. She had guilty thoughts about premarital sex and her abortion. Concurrently, she was accepted to law school. She felt ambivalent about this and convinced herself to reject law as a threat to her femininity. It was at this point that she entered treatment.

Julie was the third of four children, her three brothers eight years older, five years older, and two years younger than herself. She viewed the older two as successful men, but saw the youngest brother as a very dependent underachiever who was "spoiled" by their mother. By the time the patient was seven years old her father was an alcoholic who alternated between helpless dependency and a state of angry and jealous hatefulness. Her mother was perceived as an immature, ineffectual individual who could not deal with her husband. The patient felt safe and protected only during summer and vacation visits with her maternal grandparents. There she had a country life that included a room

[1] We are grateful to our male colleages for making this case material available to us.

of her own and many dogs to play with. This and the love that she received made these times special.

When Julie was thirteen years old, her father became so ill that the family was forced to live with his mother in a mountain community. She felt uprooted, cheated, and angry with her father, siding with her mother and brothers against him. Following a family argument, he died of alcoholic liver disease. At the time she felt relieved and had no tears for him (and only later experienced considerable guilt about her feelings). Her mother worked and her grandparents assisted the family financially. She attended a girl's school and then a university, was an excellent student and considered her school days to be happy and successful.

Julie's initial treatment attitude was relief at the opportunity for catharsis. It was difficult for her to discuss her abortion, and she became tearful and hyperemotional. Her initial relationship to the analyst was openly affectionate, as had been her earliest feelings for her father. Her first dream was: "I was in a long line with too many people everywhere. The girls had a special line. I was nervous and too scared to go into the next room. I watched and they came out of the other door. They all had hysterectomies. I felt relieved." Her associations all concerned femininity.

Julie's male analyst was soon cast in the role of her oldest, demanding and controlling brother. When he did not criticize her, she became self-critical and berated herself for not going to law school and for her love affair. After an unsuccessful attempt to regain acceptance to law school, she settled into treatment. Initially she attempted to handle all feelings about the analyst by convincing herself that he was a neutral professional. Her ambivalent feelings were displaced to her boyfriend. Any attempt at interpretation was met with intellectualization and further displacement.

Soon thereafter Julie became more assertive with her boyfriend and began to enjoy their relationship. She had an active dream and fantasy life, which did not preclude discussion of several areas of her real past and present life. She clearly identified with her brother and felt angry with her father, despite little memory of him other than the last two or three years of his life. She was angry with her clinging and dependent mother, and recognized that her mother also was an alcoholic. She idealized her maternal grandparents and recalled the grief that she had felt at her grandfather's death.

Julie had repetitive dreams whose setting was a bathroom, as well as dreams of being in bed with her boyfriend while her father was in the background. Other dreams were of dogs running and hunting in the fields. Occasionally she was able to identify the analyst in her dreams. As she and her boyfriend discussed marriage, their relationship became strained. She became critical of him, found herself less interested in him and less frequently orgasmic. She compared him to the analyst, whom she saw now in a very positive, idealized way. She began to hint of erotic transference feelings, and dreams of horses became more prevalent.

A severe illness in the analyst briefly interrupted treatment. Julie deliberately had chosen a young therapist for fear of people "dying and leaving." Over the next few months she terminated her love affair. Although she felt guilty and depressed, her work performance improved. She made some necessary changes there and began to deal with her employer in an adult, straightforward way. For the first time she realized how sad her role had been. She connected this directly to her father's death, reevoked in the context of the analyst's illness.

She began to see her mother more often and felt less dread at this. At this time she had the first of four "sharks dreams." She was on a swinging vine over a moat filled with menacing sharks. This led to analysis of some aspects of her castration anxiety and fear of being a castrating woman. She then dreamt that she was watching a girl sit on the lap of a man who was not her husband. He had just died. Everybody was sad that such a young girl would be a widow. The man had died of cancer, which was discovered to be a brain tumor. The direct flight into oedipal discussions was understood as a defense against her feelings toward the analyst. Shortly thereafter, a missed session was blamed on the analyst and associations to her anger dealt with penis envy. The next shark dream followed. Three rows of sharks represented her three brothers. She was unable to cross a moat at her grandmother's house and only her youngest brother could make it. Her associations were still about penis envy and castration anxiety. She expressed considerable anger toward her brother because of his dependent and clinging nature. The fourth shark dream came later, after recovery of childhood memories in which she was being chased around the house. This was analyzed as a residue of the memories of sex play with her brothers.

Two months later Julie fell desperately in love with a handsome and strong city fireman. He was a war veteran who raised dogs. After a few dates they became sexually involved and almost inseparable. She idealized him and felt herself being completely swept away. He was equally taken with her and moved into her apartment after a few weeks. They soon began planning marriage, and both families met and were informed of this. As she contemplated marriage, she said that she could not concentrate on her analysis. Most of the sessions were filled with stories about the romance. This continued until shortly before summer vacation. By then, the couple had been living together for two months and she was beginning to find herself critical of him.

During this period of acting out, the analysis was in danger. Any attempt to help Julie to see this was met with intellectualization and displacement. After she began to bring up the "small complaints" it was much easier for the analyst to believe that the acting out could be worked through. On return from the summer break complaints became louder. She no longer had time for herself. Her boyfriend was lazy and unmotivated to make more money. He was also inconsiderate and demanding of her sexually, paying little attention to her needs. He was frequently depressed and missed work, and, on several occasions got drunk and verbally abusive. She became tired of all the demands and felt that the romance was slipping away. She hinted at vaginismus but would not discuss her sexual behavior in detail. She wanted to ask her lover to leave but became fearful of physical abuse and her feeling of being overwhelmed with guilt. Finally, she was able to work out these feelings and tearfully asked him to leave. Once asked, he left quietly.

During and after these events, Julie was able to see the acting out nature of her behavior. The choice of a fireman had to do with her need for protection from her father-analyst's violence, only to have him become sadistic in the relationship. He was no longer a savior and protector, but a dangerous and dreaded object. She had begun thinking of him as either violent or helpless. She now actively remembered similar feelings about her father and recognized that this might be the source of her attraction. She recalled some early good times with her father and first became aware that something was wrong when, at age seven, she noticed that he would lie on the couch and cry. The fireman had been a defense against the return of the repressed, and once he was gone many memories were recovered quickly.

At the anniversary of her father's death, Julie felt depressed and disclosed the fantasy that she had caused her father's death, and that she wished to leave analysis before the analyst could leave her. The ramifications of the analyst's illness were not understood by him (or by his male supervisor), except in terms of the loss of the father. However, a female analyst who looked at the process notes suggested, rather, that the difficulty in analysis and acting out of the patient had to be understood in terms of the relationship to the mother. Julie's mother had abandoned her just as her analyst had. This had occurred just after the mother's miscarriage, which the patient had witnessed. The importance of this maternal abandonment had *not* been understood by either male analyst or male supervisor.

Once the love affair following the analyst's illness was understood as an attempt to replace Julie's analyst-mother, the patient recalled a fantasy just after her father's death that she would have to sleep alone forever. She recalled her idealization of her father as a young child and how shattered she was because of his alcoholism. The idealization was excessive because he was also her primary caretaker, a role which her mother had relinquished.

Julie was aware of her fearfulness of men. She dreamt about intercourse related to the bathroom and watching what might fall out of her vagina. This was a transference dream in which she recognized the analyst and her concerns about pregnancy and abortion. She recalled witnessing her mother's miscarriage, which had taken place in the bathroom when the patient was between 1 year and 2½ years of age and led to Julie's preoedipal wish to have a baby. Her later masochism and depression were viewed as the result of her failure to actualize this fantasy.

Julie then began to discuss masturbation as well as bathroom behavior, followed by many sessions filled with reminiscences about other family members. Meanwhile, she avoided relationships with men. A dream about her parents doing something "scary" led to the early memory of her father having a "seizure or something" in the bed with her mother. This was a primal scene screen memory. The mother's abortion and her own wish for a baby marked the entrance into Julie's oedipal conflict. Julie recalled that later, when she had witnessed her father's behavior with her mother, she had fantasied that her mother's and her own miscarriage had followed physical abuse. The analyst's countertransference problem at this time related to this avoidance of closeness as a defense against his own preoedipal wishes.

Julie began to discuss termination as a defense against her increasing preoccupation with the analyst. She disclosed that she had sexual fantasies involving the analyst, which had gone away at the time of his illness. They had resurfaced again only to be quelled by her love affair with the fireman. The longing for mother was compensated by turning to a paternal object. As the time for Christmas separation approached, Julie became increasingly anxious. She was angry at her mother and resentful of the relationship between her mother and grandmother. She began to think of her mother as unreliable and stated that she had always felt that way. The analyst was now leaving her just as her mother had left her after her mother had had the miscarriage. Julie thus dated her depression to age two, related to her mother's loss of her baby. It was her mother, not her father, who had deprived her of a baby. She thought a great deal about the analyst and had erotic fantasies while on the couch. She felt angry and complained that this was making it impossible for her to date without feeling guilty. She experienced headaches when on a date and tried to analyze away the pain. Either the patient or the analyst, or both, were actively fighting closeness because of previous preoedipal disappointment. She then had a homosexual dream and stated that she was "tired of talking about daddy; mother is important, too." This was followed by a series of sexual dreams. They led to the disclosure of the specifics of her sexual behavior, which she had viewed as bad and dirty.

Dogs then became a big topic as Julie began to look into buying several hunting dogs of her own. Many sessions began with dog stories, which eventually was analyzed again as resistance. It became clear that the dog was to be a replacement for the analyst as well as for the greatly desired baby.

Dreams revealed a shift from paternal to maternal transference, in which the analyst was her mother who became unreliable after her miscarriage. She also realized how furious she was with her mother whenever she felt the least bit dependent upon her. She was proud of her financial independence and that she managed her money well. She became interested in sex and dating again, and talked of motherhood and wanting a baby. Simultaneously, she over-fed her dog and caused an orthopedic problem. The analysis of this behavior led to her own fear of starvation in the analytic situation. It also reached directly into her desire for perfection and her intolerance of mistakes. She discussed both her fears of losing her mother and her fears of termination. Menstrual blood in her dreams was related to her mother's miscarriage. A vivid dream about a "dead rat in the toilet" brought forth memories and feelings about this traumatic event of early childhood. A symptom of faintness at the sight of blood related to hostile feelings toward the analyst for his illness, and earlier towards her mother for the miscarriage. She then recalled that her father had died shortly after her mother had left him.

The first dream after the setting of a termination date had to do with Julie's "incurable emotional lameness." This was followed by attempts to deny the meaning of termination. She became more tearful in the sessions and complained of headaches and depression. Separation anxiety could be easily seen. Another dream had to do with her work schedule. Her employer had not given her the exact number of hours she had requested and she was fussing. Then there were many sessions about separation, her mother's miscarriage and her own abortion. More sexual and bathroom dreams, as well as a fantasy of intercourse with the analyst after termination, were expressed. Shortly before the summer she revealed that "some of the old stuff has come back." She was feeling inferior at work and not using her talent. She had a fear of letting people get to know her and a fear of closeness. She felt all alone in the world and questioned her choice of career. Also, the old boyfriend who had impregnated her was coming back to town, and Julie was afraid that she would return to him. She remembered masochistic behavior in that relationship, the price she thought she would have to pay for having a baby. This constituted a repetition of her fantasies about her mother's sexual behavior and subsequent abortion and were interpreted as such.

Following this, Julie felt better and looked forward to vacation. She experienced a good month and returned reluctantly to the analysis. She had begun dating again, which she enjoyed. She was seeing one man more and more frequently and realized the pleasure in dating someone with similar interests and goals. She soon had a dream about her "black unconscious," analyzed as a return of her fear of craziness. Her fears were quickly allayed.

Gradually Julie began to experience the analyst as a more real person and talked with ease about his personality and the treatment process. It became easier to discuss the effect of his prior illness. She revealed a fantasy that she had stuck a large hypodermic syringe into her analyst's heart, which was seen as identification with her father, just as the patient had perceived her father to stick his penis into mother, thereby damaging her. Her transference to the analyst at that time was similar to the analyst as mother. Julie experienced pleasure over her gains in analysis and said that she felt like a woman for the first time in her life. She felt at peace with her feelings about her father and was doing well with her mother and brothers. She was making realistic plans for her career. Her relationship with her employer was solid, and she let herself fall in love with her new boyfriend without desperate feelings of the past.

Postscript

The above is the history of an analysis that stalled because of acting out, which occurred despite attempts to analyze the conflict in terms of the patient's wishes for her father. Both the male analyst and his male supervisor had believed that these wishes were precipitously and painfully reawakened in the context of the analyst's severe illness. However, a female analyst reviewing the case material realized that the maternal aspect of the patient's relationship to the analyst had been neglected. The patient, whose oedipal struggle was profound, had turned to her father as both an oedipal and a maternal object, after abandonment by her mother. This occurred in the context of her mother's abortion, which the patient had witnessed when she was a preoedipal child between one-and-one-half and two years of age. It was only after the maternal transference was acknowledged and analyzed that the patient was able to resolve her problems.

Case 6: Death of the Mother and the Wish for a Baby as a Replacement

Barbara, a married housewife in her early thirties with a two-year-old son, sought treatment for depression and her inability to stop smoking and to lose weight. She became depressed when she began to contemplate a second pregnancy, not wanting to become pregnant while overweight. She also feared that smoking would damage the fetus. The obesity and smoking thus stopped her from trying to conceive and, although she wanted to overcome these symptoms, was unable to do so. Overtly angry at her husband for pursuing graduate education, she felt abandoned by him. The two had been mutually dependent until he embarked upon his graduate studies, which kept him away from home for long hours. Barbara was unable to allow her son to attend nursery school because she found it difficult to separate from him.

Barbara, a menopausal baby, had two significantly older brothers from whom she felt estranged. After a long struggle with illness, her mother had died when Barbara was sixteen years old. Thereafter, Barbara took care of her father, whom she resented, while her brothers "lived their own lives." Eventually she married a childhood sweetheart, a very maternal man, who had lost his own mother as an adolescent. She had an intense relationship with a maternal aunt and envied the attention that this aunt lavished upon her own children.

As Barbara's story unfolded, it became clear that she was almost completely isolated from social contacts. She devoted herself exclusively to the care of her son, toward whom she felt both love and resentment. He was beginning to become independent and to be left to play with other children in a neighborhood playground within sight of the house. He insisted on calling Barbara by her first name, as he might call a playmate (which indeed she was). Barbara's husband was annoyed with her. She neglected her appearance and refused to go out because she was afraid of leaving her son with a babysitter. Furthermore, her husband found her boring because she had no interests except in their son. Her husband had begun to work longer hours than necessary, and apparently this was related to his feelings about their relationship.

In the opening phase of treatment Barbara was pleasant

but aloof. When the analyst noted this, she explained she did not allow herself any close relationships because "you always lose." As she detailed the frustrations of her daily life, the analyst pointed out how hard she was working to keep her son close by and dependent. She was also confronted with the reality of her husband's need for a social life and for some time alone without their son. At this she became quite angry at the analyst. She accused the analyst of being just like her father and her aunt who were not appreciative of her "sacrifices" and rebuked her on many occasions. She felt as if her father had used her after her mother's death, while her brothers and her aunt "got off free," much like her husband today. Her perception of herself as a martyr continued, despite interpretation by the analyst, until one of her brothers volunteered to hold a party for her father. Although he could afford this and his children were grown, Barbara insisted that, busy as she was with her son, she would have the party. She had a variety of rationalizations for this.

Barbara's problem might have been conceptualized in oedipal terms or interpreted as envy of her brothers, father and husband (penis envy). Her closeness to her son might have been seen as her need to hold onto her penis-baby. Recognizing the importance of the maternal loss during adolescence, the analyst had begun to conceptualize Barbara's problem in another way. Her symptoms and complaints were understood as her yearning for maternal care. Initial confirmation occurred after the party. Barbara was furious that no one had brought food. Careful questioning revealed that she had made it clear that nothing was to be served that she herself had not provided. She also complained that her wealthy aunt had not brought anything for her son. Exploration revealed that, before her son's birth, Barbara had been promised a layette by her aunt. She had nevertheless arranged to get one, in advance, by herself.

She also revealed that after her mother's death, her aunt had outfitted her with clothes. This aunt had made the arrangements for her wedding, yet even that did not seem enough. At this point, Barbara broke down in tears. "She wasn't my mother. How dare she take my mother's place." Barbara's needy but rejecting behavior led the analyst to a further formulation about her. This dependent but rejecting behavior is the behavior of a child during rapprochement. At this point in the analysis, nothing was known about Barbara's early life; yet it was clear that the loss of her mother during adolescence left her at a point where she had not completed separation-individuation.

Barbara now began to notice the analyst's clothing, berating her for the expense and the vanity of it. (Barbara's aunt was described as beautiful and vain.) She wished that she too might look attractive, but when asked why she didn't bother with her appearance, she said that her mother had been dumpy and unconcerned with how she looked. Barbara revealed that for many years she had been ashamed of her mother, who was an immigrant. Her maternal grandmother had been lost in the Holocaust when her mother was still a child. Her mother had been a chain smoker.

Barbara learned from a mutual friend that the analyst had children but continued to work. She then berated the analyst for this neglect. When it was suggested that the intensity of her anger bespoke a deeper, perhaps earlier problem, she mentioned that her mother had gone to work when Barbara was five years old. Barbara had been a "key child" (carrying the house key on a chain around her neck). She had to come home after school to start dinner, while her brothers had been free to go about their business. While expressing a wish to be slender like the analyst, she also felt an irresistible impulse to "grab all the food in sight." She related this to the childhood experience of her brothers racing home starved, and grabbing all the food for themselves. As a child, Barbara had a habit of stealing and hoarding food. She also stole items from stores. The doll's clothes and makeup that she stole represented transitional objects.

With analysis of her repetition of solutions from childhood, Barbara was able to put herself on a diet and to allow her son more freedom. She found a male teenage babysitter for him. She purchased new clothing. Yet the positive response of friends to this left her angry and depressed. Her smoking increased and she stated flatly that she was killing herself. Analysis revealed that the patient's mother had, in reality, smoked herself to death.

After a visit to her mother's grave, the patient came to session having lost her voice. This hysterical symptom was traced to the wish to scream at her mother at the graveside. The name that she used to refer to her mother in this session was her mother's given name, not the Americanized version by which she had been known. Analysis of this parapraxis revealed the fantasy that the child she wished to conceive would be a daughter and be given her mother's European name. Barbara's former obesity, present chain-smoking and her marital problems all served to avoid the conception of this desired, yet hated female baby, who was to be a reincarnation of her mother. Barbara was able to remember that her own conception had not been a menopausal accident, as previously indicated, but that her mother had repeatedly tried to have a daughter after her sons were born. Barbara now admitted that as a child she had been well loved by her mother and well cared for in terms of what the family could afford to provide. She began to understand that her hostility toward her mother had colored the image of the remembered mother and that she had always felt that she had not gotten enough. Actually, her mother had made her too dependent for too long, and had then left her. The first abandonment was before separation-individuation had been completed, when her mother went to work. The second abandonment occurred in adolescence, when her mother died before separation-individuation could be reworked.

The oedipal period had been delayed in this child for two reasons. First, her mother had kept her too close. Second, her father and brothers virtually ignored her presence in the household. They were resentful of the extra burdens experienced by the mother due to Barbara's birth and the added time taken in attending to her. Barbara recalled activities which she had shared with her mother and had angrily abandoned when her mother went to work. At this point in her analysis she began to cultivate some interests of her own. She took up a craft that had some of the elements of the cooking she had enjoyed with her mother. She put her son in school part-time and soon began to teach the craft that she had learned. She stopped smoking, yet became obsessed that the materials she used in her craft were toxic and would harm the fetus. This was interpreted as her fear that she would harm her baby much as she had wished to hurt her mother. She confirmed that during adolescence she had wished to be rid of her European mother, whose place she felt competent to take. She hoped to thus create a relationship with her more Americanized father and brothers. She never succeeded in forming a relationship with her father. In early adolescence she found a boyfriend (who later became her husband), who served as her oedipal object. Upon finding him she began a reconciliation with her mother, which was interrupted by her mother's protracted illness. She recognized, in the seeds of this adolescent relationship, a rekindling of the relationship that she had had with her mother before the mother's return to work. Her behavior toward the analyst-mother became less hostile.

On the anniversary of her mother's death, she went to religious services. She also visited her estranged family for the first time in years. She began to mourn. At the end of

the mourning period she became pregnant with the child she
had been wishing to conceive. She dreamt about an infant
daughter who called her Barbara. She then realized that, by
encouraging her son to do this, she had attempted to restore
her relationship with her mother by reversing roles. The
reversal did not succeed. She had displaced the anger toward
her mother onto her husband and had to take care of herself
by becoming her own mother, obese, sloppily dressed, and
a smoker. Barbara recalled fantasies of having a baby when
she was three years old (preoedipal). She spent some time
in the analysis considering how she might bring up her
daughter differently, that is, without first smothering and
then abandoning her. Her early fantasies about having a
baby involved keeping the baby close to her. These were
the early fantasies that she had enacted with her son.

Although very attached emotionally to the analyst, she
now missed appointments and threatened to terminate her
treatment precipitously. This was analyzed as a repetition
of her experiences with her mother. After she had recognized
how threatened she had been by genuine attachments which
brought the threat of loss, she was able to continue in analysis until a termination date was mutually agreed upon. This
date was set far in advance of termination so that Barbara
would be able to remain emotionally invested in the analyst
and to mourn the separation from her. Her baby daughter
was born and was given her mother's name as planned,
coupled with a more modern name which Barbara equated
with independence, freedom and joy.

On follow-up two and one-half years later, Barbara felt
that she had filled the gap left by the loss of her mother.
She was eagerly anticipating that her bright and independent
daughter would go off to nursery school in the spring.

Case 7: Sexual Promiscuity as the Result of Repeated Witnessing of Parental Intercourse

Jennifer, a young-looking, unmarried 30-year-old copy
editor and former dancer with an advanced degree, was

referred for analysis by her older lover. He felt that she had difficulties in sustaining their relationship. She had a history of one- to two-year affairs with men, at which time she would feel rejected and then abandon them. She was aware of her difficulties in relating to men and of her emotional overreactivity with them in love relationships and at work.

Jennifer was the only child of the "town scholar and beauty" who married a "rake." Her father was five years her mother's junior. She was raised as a strict religious fundamentalist. Her mother was publicly shy and reticent but privately depressed, rigidly controlling and unresponsive. Her father, a travelling salesman, had a violent temper and had had several affairs. She dimly recalled a "happy" childhood until the age of two and one-half, when she and her mother began to follow her father from army camp to camp until she was four. He would join the two of them in a one-room apartment on weekends. He then was overseas until she was eight. Travelling continued, however, since her mother had various teaching positions and completed a doctoral degree. At age ten, when her continuous memory began, the patient recalled her parents' constant quarrels over religion and her father's women. Her mother attempted to control her father completely.

Jennifer's adolescence was punctuated by yearly moves as her father changed jobs. During this time she quarrelled with her mother about control, and she felt quite lonely. With mixed relief and sadness, she left home after high school to study in a university where she received undergraduate and graduate degrees. She then taught dancing and began a variety of affairs. In her early twenties she gave birth to a baby, whom she gave up for adoption. In every affair she experienced anger, hurt, dissatisfaction and depression.

Jennifer presented herself for analysis as a dramatic, attractive, feminine woman who dressed to appear at least ten years younger than her age. A pseudovivacious and lively quality masked a distinct tone of sadness. She commented upon how little she remembered. My diagnostic impression was of an hysterical defensive organization that included hyperemotionality and impulsive action. Her sadness reminded me of a child lonely and grieving for her mother. Since she began treatment with me two months before vacation during the summer, her first few sessions were conducted face-to-face.

The patient felt happy that she was being seen by a woman, who would better "understand" her. She had previously been in treatment with a male analyst who had left the vicinity. She regarded her transfer to a different therapist as a graduation. Initially Jennifer denied any feeling of loss. In her first dream she slid from slot to slot in a stadium, feeling that the new slot would catch her. Her associations were to basketball games she attended with her parents and to foxholes under fire. In response to queries directed to her associations, she stated that she wanted protection, but that she feared being overwhelmed by her own destructive and merging impulses. ("I will get close, maybe angry, and then be dropped.") I judged from her first dream that she had been afraid that her first analyst would attack her; however, it would take her many years of treatment and the development of an oedipal configuration in the transference to confirm this impression.

Before the summer separation she cried, saying that she felt alone and unprotected. This, I realized, may have been a displacement of feelings to me for the loss of her first analyst, but there was a rapid emergence of a fantasy of a woman analyst as mother. As I sat in my chair I constantly had the feeling of having a toddler on my lap.

After the summer vacation Jennifer started analysis on the couch. A polite and distant style alternated with attempts to be a charming and dramatic little girl. My interventions were met with enormous resistance against understanding the meanings of her experiences and thoughts. When I noted that her tears were connected to feelings of loss she replied, "I don't understand that." She reported a dream of an orphan child, emaciated and sick, who was brought into a room and tied to a metal bar. A sadistic nurse came to torture the child. She felt that she was both child and nurse and associated to her anger at her boyfriend's fear of emotional involvement. Thus she displaced her own fear and anger. She also recounted a history of seeing her parents as cruel beneath their benign surfaces. Asked if she felt that the dream had to do with the analysis or me, she denied either possibility. The surrender to analysis represented a surrender to a cruel mother who abandoned her and whom she feared. She also told the dream as if it were someone else's dream. At this point she was unable to treat her dreams in a personal way and they tended to be seen as little stories.

She flooded sessions with vague and constant chatter and acted out by missing sessions, coming late and unilaterally scheduling vacations. Exploration of these behaviors resulted in an episode of depersonalization on the couch, which was related to a similar episode that day when she had looked in the mirror and seen herself as "too young." Her anxiety was allayed by the interpretation that she felt like a little girl with me, as she had with her mother, and that she was scared.

The depersonalization disappeared and Jennifer's acting out slowly decreased. All my interventions were directed to increasing the patient's ability to observe her feelings and to her fears of free association. She dreamt that she was small and that a large object threatened to engulf her. In associating she noted that I looked like her mother, sitting as if she were sewing. She talked about women with large breasts and seemed to want to be smaller and younger, a small child clutching at me. She remembered that she loved to chatter to her mother as mother listened, but without response.

She became less quarrelsome in analysis and with her lover but complained that he did not talk to her enough. I interpreted her wish for my response, and she began to talk of her work and home situations in which a constant longing for a mother was evident. She connected fears of being left alone with a history of solitary activity and sadness in early childhood. My countertransference fantasies were of cuddling a small child in my arms, which suggested to me the repetition of an intense preoedipal maternal tie. These feelings were displaced to her boyfriend. She reported that *his* divorce was devastating and that *he* could not trust another woman. I told her of her own fears of distrust and devastation, whereupon she recalled her mother's frequent courses to which she was taken along and "abandoned" in waiting rooms and parks. There she would read books or count the ants on the sidewalk while her mother worked.

Wanting an exclusive relationship, Jennifer was jealous of her lover's daughter and women friends. She dreamt that she kept part of him in a box when they separated but was insulted that he called this "penis envy." Although it represented the fantasy of an illusory phallus, I interpreted her need to keep him with her. When she spoke of her imaginary conversations with me, I was able to extend the interpretation to how she kept me with her and used what turned out to be a penis, in her box, as a symbolic tie to her mother. This was confirmed by a dream of being in bed with her lover who turned into her mother.

Jennifer complained of feeling fat, ugly and depressed, the result of frustration of her dependency wishes for her lover as a mother. In part she was defending against her dependent wishes for me by displacing them to him. She perceived her fantasy of being physically close and fusing with me as homosexual, when, in fact it represented the wish to be nursed. She said that she felt anxious, although it was not apparent. Feeling that she wanted "more" from me, Jennifer developed somatic symptoms (headaches, diarrhea and vomiting), which were analyzed as displaced anger at not being gratified. She dreamt of being unable to get through locked doors, viewed by her as inability to get in touch with herself. She felt as though she were in a cocoon and had to control me, which replicated her early omnipotent wishes for control of her mother who could never express any loving feeling.

With exploration of these feelings, a transference neurosis gradually emerged. Jennifer's outer life felt better and now she had problems in analysis. She expressed open longings for me as a good mother and dreamt of lying with her lover on a velvet couch (my analytic couch was velvet) not wanting him to see that she had left "something" lying around. She spoke of her love for me but she could not associate to the bowel movements (which were what she had left). She then spoke of her multiple, sexual relationships in the past. The bowel movements represented beginning humiliation, leaving gifts, and fear of retaliation for her promiscuity. She spoke of her mother and of fears that dreams like this meant that she was crazy.

When I reconstructed that she had been afraid that her mother was crazy, she revealed that her mother had had a psychotic depression when Jennifer was a young adult. Mother had acted peculiarly even before then, did not permit dancing but had given her dancing lessons, and had allowed her to sit on "the pot" with a male stranger who was shaving, then reprimanded her. This memory suggested early overstimulation and exhibitionism. Her anger at me, whom she now saw as requesting absolute dependency, paralleled her anger at her mother for the same. It was also displaced to her lover who made her a "handmaiden." She became rigid with rage on the couch, which I interpreted.

With this she relaxed, fell silent, then remembered not being able to talk to her parents and practice-kissing with girl friends. I noted that she had the desire to kiss me. A sudden derepression occurred leading to memories of sleeping with her mother and an early phobia of a man in her room. She added that she thought her previous chatter had been used to avoid closeness.

With an increasing positive transference, Jennifer was able to reveal her adolescent masturbatory history. A college psychiatrist had told her that masturbation was "fun" and had misunderstood her wish to stop this compulsive activity. Her fantasies of herself had been as femme-fatale and adored beauty from afar, or the rescuer of her people. She feared that I was a prude like her mother. Her mother had told her, when she was six, that masturbation was adultery. She thought then, "but I've done it already." Feeling that this was evidence of early masturbatory activity, probably with incestuous fantasies, I interpreted that she had probably masturbated earlier, perhaps during the period of sharing a room with her parents. At this she became reflective and slowly recalled many primal scene experiences where she lay tensely under the covers, screening her eyes and feeling overexcited and frightened. She also felt that masturbation would drain her of her "seeds." This was noted by me to be a male fantasy, but not yet interpreted. Jennifer also feared that masturbating would drive her crazy and that it was bad, and had projected the latter condemnation onto me.

Amenorrheic for two months, Jennifer feared that she was pregnant. She told her lover, who accused her of black-mailing him into marriage. Furious with him she wanted to hit him, which I reconstructed as her wish to hit her father for his lack of attention. She remembered that her father had hit her mother, and that her mother had abandoned Jennifer when her father returned. Many dreams of snakes sinking their fangs into her and not letting go revealed her symbiotic attachment to a phallic mother, who had actually defended her against poisonous snakes at home. She dreamt that a woman who resembled me urged her to walk by the snakes and look at them emerging from their skins. But now she felt that she was more open and less frightened.

Over the next few months, with a decreasing fear of speaking about sex, further anamnesis revealed that Jennifer's mother had accused her of having an affair with her father. Her father had told her that her mother had probably been raped by her own father, which the patient could now understand as her mother's projection. She again flooded sessions with words and wanted to "pee" on the couch. She remembered her fury at night when her mother was with her father, and would wet the bed in anger at her mother. When she felt that I was not being supportive, I interpreted her rage and feelings of abandonment by her mother and fear of retaliation of her own intense and frightening attraction to her father.

Brave enough now to criticize my clothes, Jennifer only transiently experienced nausea. This defended her anger at me and fear that I too would retaliate. Themes of being different from me emerged. She feared that I would demand that she imitate me as her mother had demanded. Jennifer also "confessed" that she had censored many associations because of her fantasy that I would destroy her relationship with her lover. Interpretation of this as a repeat performance and as a projection of her own wishes led to a slip, "Secrets From a Marriage," for "Scenes from a Marriage." This revealed secret thoughts about her current relationship with her lover and also early thoughts and feelings about her father. She had isolated herself in her early years and had lived a romantic, secret fantasy that partially denied and assuaged her loneliness. Jennifer reported a screen memory at the age of eight. During a tonsillectomy she recalled a good smell and jumping off the table, after anesthesia, to hit the doctor. She recollected that during surgery she "dreamed" of a line of marching mummies. Here Jennifer had apparently reversed painful reality. (The smell was bad and she was agitated before surgery.) As a child she was frightened of death, abandonment and any loss of control, and in the present situation surrender to the analytic process caused her great anxiety.

Interventions were now directed to Jennifer's pervasive phobia of being alone, a defense against her traumatic past. She reported a screen memory of crawling, at age two, to a neighbor lady whose husband had "sleeping sickness and rages." This led to associations to her violent father who came between her and her mother. A full delineation of her previous extensive promiscuity revealed an identification with a phallic mother. To this, she now added a masculine identification with a father who had displaced her in mother's bed. He had also denied her the seductive presence of a man with whom she could have practiced her emerging femininity, and a man with whom she could have triangulated and thus decreased her symbiotic attachment to her mother.

Seeing me as phallic mother and oedipal father, Jennifer dreamt of a mournful meal with Dr. Zhivago. I noted that she saw herself as my mistress. She associated to always being the "other woman" and recalled watching her father's fights and her own fights with girls. Over the next few months she experienced a return of memory of a period of tomboy behavior between the ages of eight and ten, which her father had fostered by taking her hunting and playing football. He later publicly shamed her for dating and called her a "whore."

In the transference Jennifer alternated between images of me as an oedipal father and as a phallic mother with whom she identified. A dream of looking down from a firetower led to exploration of her confusion about sexual roles. Her homosexual transference was dealt with as a regressive avoidance of men, and she acted like a man to avoid them. Dream themes of being chased by scary men led to memories of her fear of her father and to wishes to kiss his nose, which he claimed was dirty. She suddenly left her lover when he "refused" to marry her. (This was only understood later as an acting out of her fearful fantasy. She had disavowed, and had never told me until just prior to termination phase, that he had brought a ring back for her from the Orient.)

Jennifer began to experience shame because of her homosexual transference. She saw men as "making things into shit," and displaced genital for excretory functions. She tried to give me business advice, and "fathered" her friends and cross-examined her interviewers while she was looking for a job. She disliked one of my male patients but felt close to a woman patient she had seen for several years. Her phallic identification was continuously interpreted as an avoidance of men. She began to associate analysis to loss of a tooth space and to feelings of castration as a woman. Increased castration anxiety led to an increase in her masturbation, which supported her illusion of a phantom phallus. She feared that I would replace her with a male patient, although she had felt special and chosen before. She now became curious about me and fantasied that I was married to a weak, ineffectual and nonthreatening man.

As Jennifer began to understand her defensive masculine identification, she was able to acknowledge her wishes to be her father's "other" woman. Now that she felt that she had destroyed her own relationships with men, she feared that I, as an oedipal mother, would disapprove of her jealousy of men and her penis envy. She also wanted every man to be aroused by her, the punishment for which would be my rivalry. Depressed and guilty at her state of incompleteness, she recalled feeling neither that her father loved her, nor that she had loved her son. Before giving this son up for adoption, she had thought to bring it to her mother to raise. She remembered wishes to have a child when she watched the ants (preoedipal). With remorse, Jennifer spoke of her son and felt that she had to atone by leaving him money in her will. She then permitted herself to find an executive job, to buy her own home and to mother herself.

However, severe guilt about the loss of her child ensued. This precipitated a regression. Dream images of pulling blood from her vagina led to feelings of disgust and derogation. A dream of carrying a crystal statue with a broken tail that could never be repaired finally led to her giving up the fantasy of an illusory phallus. She felt depressed that she would never have a baby or family and said that she was currently leading a nunlike existence, that her sexuality was frozen. She dreamt that I had a castle, but that she was full of poisonous mushrooms. With interpretations that she felt evil, there was a full affective outpouring of how inferior she felt compared to me. She continued to work through how ''bad'' she felt for giving up her baby. She mourned this loss and dreamt of ''fallen'' women, feeling that no man would want her. Early masturbatory fantasies of having father's baby recalled guilt-laden memories of genital experimentation with boys and seeing her father naked.

Jennifer then lost weight and shyly told me that many men now found her attractive, which frightened her. She no longer attempted to convert men to Romeo-fathers. This represented a progression. Anamnesis revealed that she could now recall women friends of her father, who had liked him. She became jealous of me and my fantasied children. Teaching herself speech in order to get a better job was also done to become ''educated'' as I was. She remembered her mother's great ambition and that she had been a well-liked educator. It was at this time that she also told me of the ring her lover bought her, and I realized that she had fled from her oedipal rivalry in the transference by acting out.

Jennifer was again involved in a relationship with loss of her previous full orgasmic ability. With exploration of this she became aware of her castrating wishes and her use of defensive maneuvers with men. Either she would submit, leading to shaming the man, or reduce him to a castrated state by doing everything for him while remaining frigid. She dreamt of ripping a dog away from a man. I interpreted her treatment of men as a fetish, the dog representing the penis that she longed for. She remembered having played with her lover's penis and fondly calling it by a pet name. Clearly, she had never understood men and was blinded by the penis and by identification with her mother and other women contemptuous of men. The result of this interpretation was the slow ripening of her ability to relate to her new boyfriend and the return of her orgasmic ability. She was promoted to a position where she taught and had client contact in which she was now no longer provocative. She took chances and asserted herself, and viewed her own previous pseudoenthusiasm as a cover for her feelings of emptiness. Feeling full was now related to being truly curious about people and their motivations, unlike her mother, and in identification with me. She admired men who defied powerful women. She said that she guessed she had used me as a model to judge and evaluate herself constructively, thus had unfrozen the introject of a nonloving mother.

Thinking one day of meeting my husband, Jennifer recalled how her father had rescued a widow who was on fire on her front lawn. This was followed by a dream of her bursting into a flame, which allowed the interpretation of open oedipal rivalry. Anamnesis revealed that she had felt as a child that she would burn in the fires of hell, with excitement and with retribution. Her ability to openly discuss this indicated the decrease in her anxiety. She teased me about playing with "King Kong" and was more able to make use of metaphor. She told me, "Neurosis is seeing today through yesterday's glasses. I don't need glasses." This was also a comment on her beauty and on my wearing glasses. She felt that she was my equal, and with this she raised the issue of termination. After several sessions, a termination date was agreed upon.

During the termination phase Jennifer reviewed her analysis, felt sad and surprised at her gains, which included decreased anxiety, ability to handle pressure, decrease in omniscient and omnipotent wishes, and ability to share with both sexes, single and married. There were some mild symptoms that recurred, including fear of men and fear of aloneness. Her perceptions of me became more realistic. No longer did she see me as the "beauty" and "the scholar." She was grateful for what she had received and recognized how much she had had to learn. She realized the change in her self-observation from her last dream, in which she drove away with her lover, telling him why he did not get along with his mother and waving goodbye to her own mother. Knowing that this represented a goodbye to me, she was nevertheless cognizant that the dream was about analysis and about her ability to truly communicate with men. She left smiling and tearful, saying that one day she would let me know how she is.

Case 8: A Patient Whose Father Was Her Maternal Object

Lydia, a boyish-looking, unmarried medical student in her early thirties, sought an analysis because of difficulty in making commitments to men. She dated older, unavailable men and severed relationships with them when they became too close. She was referred for treatment by a relative she regarded as a mother-substitute. She saw her problems as related to the death of her father with whom she had been close and to the infantile relationship that she had with a domineering mother.

Lydia was the child of a middle-class, first-generation American family and had three brothers considerably older than herself. Her parents frowned on women being "too smart." She described her mother as a domineering, superficial, unempathic and alternately intrusive and rejecting housewife who favored the patient's older brother. Her mother had told her that her birth was "an accident." Lydia, her father's favorite, remembered him vaguely as a silent and handsome, quietly angry man who travelled extensively in business. She could speak of him only with tears, and after his death felt shame at being fatherless and frightened that her mother would die. She could not remember any affection between her parents. However, she and her next older brother were mildly affectionate and he had tried to help her with her schoolwork. The patient shared a room with her mother after her brothers left home to marry. Unlike the patient, the three brothers were trained in a skill, were in business, and had children.

Shortly after college, Lydia moved away from her mother's home to live with friends for a few years, then moved into her own apartment. Unsatisfied with her paraprofessional work, she completed premedical courses and began medical school. In contrast to the way she presented her history initially, once analysis proper began she revealed a typical obsessive character organization, with isolation of affect, preoccupation with control of thinking and behavior, reaction formation with undoing, and a superficial intellectualization. She saw me as a critical and controlling mother who disapproved of her. She tried to involve me in answering questions and in providing magical solutions, made many critical remarks and avoided expressions of affection.

Exploration of the tense brevity of her communications revealed that she substituted lonely hard work to win approval by performance and to avoid interaction, intimacy and exposure. She had many memories of her mother telling her when to eat and to sleep, going through her possessions and eavesdropping, and currently demanding daily phone calls and knowledge of the patient's whereabouts. Lydia acceded to these demands with silent fury because she feared hurting her mother. Explorations of her expectations that I would act similarly increased her ability to verbalize freely.

Lydia was shy in class, work and social situations. In an attempt to avoid feelings of isolation she would peep at me frequently as I sat behind her. Her quiet tears represented an inhibited cry for help. She displaced her concerns about me to teachers, whom she saw as controlling and uncaring because they allowed her to do everything without collaboration.

Her first dream, a retrospective one, was of hearing noises in her parents' bedroom, ignoring them, only later to enter and find her mother dead. Lydia denied her curiosity and rage. She became active at school, where she demanded full attention. She refused dates. She tried to please me and spoke of the fear that I would leave her, viewing herself as my assigned case (an accident for me as she was for her mother). Her compliant transference defended against an emerging power struggle. She reported a dream where a doctor was driving a car very fast, while she and her fellow students were making fun of another student who resembled me. This reflected her fear that we were going too fast in the analysis and that too much would be asked of her. Lydia then imagined that her angry thoughts about me would be revealed and that I would retaliate in anger, and continued to have obsessional thoughts that a car would hit her. She herself loved fast action activities. She understood that the cars in her dreams represented the analytic "trip." I interpreted her dissatisfaction with me for not giving her enough, fast enough, and also her fear of a head-on collision with me.

Afraid of dependency and passivity, Lydia tried to control the analysis. Dreams during this period were of losing control of the car and not being in the driver's seat. With interpretation she became anxious about her affectionate feelings towards me, which she experienced as homosexual. She began to lie down before I reached my chair and reacted to separations from me with anxiety and depression. She sobbed about wanting closeness and spoke of being unable to obtain care. Her fears of separation were interpreted and she then expressed her anger at my "withholding." A dream of taking a friend's tennis racket, having a key to her apartment and wanting to wear her shoes revealed her wishes for and fears of closeness with me and her images of me as a phallic woman. These represented negative oedipal and phallic female (preoedipal) defenses against oedipal fears.

It is typical of many female analysands who are in treatment with women to begin their analyses with a defense against a deep longing for the preoedipal mother. This mother is frequently perceived as phallic. If the mother is perceived as inconsistent and unavailable the patient may develop a transference that is experienced as homosexual, since mother is not considered safe and perceptions of her are sexualized.

Lydia became afraid that someone would enter my office while she was there, and that a man would break into her apartment. With interpretation of her condensed fears of her intrusive mother and the male, she began openly to speak of her sexuality. The power struggle with me decreased and she attempted to identify with me, establishing a homoerotic relationship to ward off increasing oedipal rivalry. Superficial, shifting sexual involvements with men masochistically defended her against trusting a man. This was dealt with on two levels; first, the fear of the abandoning man, and second, the fear of the sexual man. I conceptualized that this patient's neediness for men had to be related to her poor early relationship with her preoedipal mother, which accentuated the need for a man as a father and as a mother.

Lydia wondered if I would approve of her relationships with married men. She began to connect me with her mother and to express feelings of isolation, loneliness, starvation and abandonment. Dreams suggesting masturbatory activity (gymnastics and bicycle riding) emerged. There was a strong erotization and masculinization of me in dreams. She recalled that she had masturbated in adolescence, fearing that masturbation would lead to pregnancy. Although she did not remember the actual context of her fantasies, I interpreted them as her fear and wish for a baby. These adolescent fantasies were a reenactment of those that occurred during masturbation in the oedipal period.

Lydia first displaced the erotic transference by running to married men, and then regressed defensively to preoccupation with separation issues and somatization, including nausea and stomachaches. Dreams with walls caved in and bones turned to jelly suggested that early separations were felt as catastrophic. She felt needy and continued to overeat. After I interpreted her regression as a flight from the erotic transference and her wishes for me as a preoedipal mother she became more directly able to confront her transference wishes and to examine her competitive fears. At this time she became less afraid of examinations at school.

Lydia then dreamt of inviting a man resembling me into her garden. She told her mother that she was in analysis, thus seeking a rapprochement and her mother's availability during our summer separation. Her promiscuity decreased and she began an affair with a teacher, after learning that he was leaving to work elsewhere. Envious of my "pretty" clothes, she began to dress in a more feminine way. I was now viewed as warm and sympathetic and different from her mother. She also began to experience morning nausea and fantasied having a child. Associations were to her relationship with her mother and her vicarious wishes for infantile care and attention (preoedipal). In addition she reported violent nightmares and was relieved that I was not overwhelmed by this "crazy" material. Phobias of leeches and of being bitten emerged. She had been previously unaware of these. She associated them to an early memory of her stern, forbidding father, with a lit cigarette in his mouth, asking her to jump to him in the water. She also recalled standing in front of him, intimidated, while he lectured to her and she had nothing to say. This paralleled her feeling of intimidation on the couch.

Lydia wanted to give me a book of erotic poetry written by a woman, but feared that I would see this as phallic. She then spoke of her own identification with males and of her envy of them. She felt that men had received more from her mother, yet she also looked for a father in her mother. She recalled being fed, cared for and toileted by her father before his frequent trips began. These recollections suggested that Lydia's father had been the main maternal object as well as her oedipal object.

An early history of confusion over sexual identity emerged when she expressed envy and competitive feelings toward a male patient. Issues of phallic repair (illusory phallus) alternated with a self-image of a masochistic, denigrated, subservient woman. She was amenorrheic at this time. Told by her gynecologist that this was psychosomatic, she quoted the analyst of the aforementioned poetess, "When you learn to be a woman and accept it, you'll get your period." She slowly began to menstruate regularly.

Increasing fears of a rapist breaking into Lydia's apartment and her rage at current paternal surrogates were interpreted as a projection and as a wish. This led to her recall of an early history of rape fantasies and of her father coming home late, causing her mother to think he was an intruder. This was interpreted as Lydia's own wishes and temptations for her father. Marked sexual curiosity about me emerged as her previously utilized work, activity, multiple involvements and phallic identification were less successful defenses against a paternal oedipal transference. Curious about my husband, she wanted to meet and flirt with him. She recalled that her mother had had a lover when the patient was a teenager. When her maternal uncle had attempted to kiss her at camp, she had not trusted her mother enough to tell her of the incident and she could not face the guilty temptation that she had experienced. She felt that men were violent, which protected her expression of rage at father's abandonment. She had acted out her wishes with married men. Her promiscuity represented a wish for a preoedipal mother in a man and her maternal father, as well as punishing behavior toward men. After interpretation of this she produced several incestuous dreams, and all of her promiscuity stopped. She then feared that I would get sick with a heart attack and leave her. Her father had died of a heart attack, and she remembered that she had fantasied that her father had had love affairs when he travelled.

I had some difficulty seeing myself simultaneously in the role of male lover and as the preoedipal receptacle for Lydia's strong wishes to eat me up, crawl inside of me and to have me as a sexual parent. These countertransference problems were in response to her overwhelming neediness, a result of her having only one parent, whom she experienced as unable to understand her needs. Her mother was also abandoning, first leaving her to the care of her father, then leaving after father's death, and finally using the patient as an extension of herself when she insisted that the patient share her bed. Lydia's oedipal situation had become complicated at her father's death when she was eight. This further propelled her regression back to her preoedipal mother and into a confused and "sticky" separation-individuation problem.

As Lydia's abilities to speak in and out of the analysis and to be assertive increased, she was able to complete a research paper that was accepted by her school. Her self-esteem increased and she dreamt of having her hair cut in a thinly disguised version of mine. She was afraid that I would object to her looking prettier. Fear of her sexual feelings was interpreted as fear of the loss of her mother, whom she had experienced as unavilable before and during the oedipal period. Dreams then became triadic, with two women competing for a man. She felt more competitive with women and more feminine and engaging with men. She shifted constantly in the analysis between wanting a phallic mother and needing a loving, maternal father.

Interpretation of these transferences led to further de-repression. The patient who had not been able to recall the content of masturbatory fantasies now did. Her primary fantasy had been one of lying with a boy near a pool, watched by everybody. I noted that it was she who had wished to watch me and my husband, and I reconstructed that she had heard or seen her mother and father in bed as a child. This was affirmed in her memories of sharing their bedroom during the early years of her life.

She fantasied again that I would not want her to have a man. This was interpreted in terms of her difficulty in competing with her mother, who used her as a phallic extension and was not only her rival but her only dependency object since the father was absent. She became depressed at the anniversary of her father's death and recalled that no one had helped her to mourn. This became related to her demanding, needy attitudes to me. She dreamt of a man finding his long-lost wife and leaving her, while she took the wife's place in a rowboat. Associations led her to a woman teacher's husband, an abandoning boyfriend and to her father. More able to feel guilt and depression over her past "incestuous" behavior, she feared now that I would be jealous of her success. She stopped externalizing her problems and wishes for promiscuity, and her defensive, superficial busy talk disappeared.

Subsequent dreams of removing bloody tampons led her to recall her revulsion at menstruation and to an image of me as helping her to pull out an illusory phallus that she thought she had. An image of herself as a damaged and dirty woman emerged. Issues of bisexuality were interpreted as confusion about sex and identity, having had only one parent. Her multidetermined promiscuity was interpreted both as wanting to act like her father in order to keep him with her and as avoidance of intimacy with men for fear of the loss of her phallicly perceived mother. Dreams revealed wishes to incorporate the phallus orally and vaginally in order to repair her ugly, castrated, starving self-image. At this point she graduated from medical school and was offered a position in a distant city. I interpreted that she wished to run from her temptations for me as a loving parent. I neither told her to stay nor to go, but only that she was attempting to put me in the role of a bad parent. She elected to stay at a position in the city in order to continue with her analysis.

Lydia met her future husband and was finally able to visit her father's grave and to cry. She dreamt of having her boyfriend's, her father's, and my baby. She revealed that she had wished that her father were alive and that her mother were dead, having held her mother responsible for her father's death. Her mother had rejected her father's gifts and affection and had filled the house with relatives. Lydia feared a nongiving, intrusive, grabbing man whose strength she wanted. This was her mother's picture of men. Frank castration anxiety appeared in dreams of losing teeth and of electrolysis. Because of her mother's binding, unempathic attitudes, she experienced an upsurge of homosexual anxiety with me as her relationship with her lover grew.

Increasingly successful at work, Lydia was given many accolades. Her love relationship deepened and fantasies about women revealed her protection of her rivalry. She could not understand a dream that her mother had washed and shrunk her slacks to a little "girl-boy" size, since she saw me as helping her to grow up to be a woman. Gradually, with interpretation, she saw this as her own fear and wish. Her relationship with her lover became more mutually giving, and she began to live with him and to be able to talk to her mother, and feared losing both of them. She experienced a transient loss of full orgasmic ability, regained only with fantasies of married men.

Worried that her mother and I would become sick if Lydia were close to a man, she remembered her mother's severe depression after her father had died. She also had jumped nude on her father, while he was in bed shortly before his death. Guilty that her wishes led to his death, she dreamt of cars with hoods torn off and of clams that bit, revealing vagina dentata fantasies. She felt that her mother had killed her father by neglect, and feared that she had done the same with her sexual wishes. Struggling with rage in dreams, behaviorally she was more friendly. One day she was quite empathic when I was ill, and expressed the wish to take care of me. At this time her choice of medicine as a career was analyzed as a wish to rescue both her dead father and to cure her depressed mother.

In bed with her lover, she dreamt of sleeping with her father. This led to a regression to preoedipal issues and to her attempt to maternalize her lover. Upon deciding to marry him, she became slightly depressed. Analysis of this revealed her fear that I would not stay with her and the memory that her mother had left her for several weeks shortly after her father's death. She was married and her mother, indeed, left for an extended trip. My countertransference feelings of jealousy signaled the emergence of a positive oedipal configuration.

After more than one year of marriage to her supportive and firm husband, and following success in her work, Lydia dreamt that a psychiatrist smiled and said goodbye. She began to think of termination, which mobilized her ambivalent feelings about having a baby. She told me that she had looked me up in a directory a year previously, knew that I had children, and was envious. She wondered if she could be a better mother than her own mother and as good a mother as she had fantasied I was. She used these issues to try to convince me that she was not ready for motherhood or termination.

Becoming sad, she experienced a rapidly kaleidoscoping series of wishes for and fears of an engulfing mother as well as a jealous rivalry with fatherly men. She also reexperienced a mild success phobia with feelings of failing self-assertion simultaneous to murderous fantasies toward me and her mother. She feared that having a child would drain her dry and that her husband would be jealous of the child. Recalling her mother's preoccupations with her sons, she felt that her mother's neglect of her father included the neglect of herself. Upon deciding to become pregnant, she felt that it was time to terminate analysis six months later, at the time of my vacation. She was now, not coincidentally, the same age as her mother had been when her mother had given birth to her. There was a definite sense of separateness from her mother and from me, indicating separation-individuation had been traversed, and she had more positive images of both of us.

Lydia then became angry at being "evicted," although she had decided to leave. She feared punishment for her wishes for oedipal victory, which was reflected in dreams of dropping apples, caring for babies poorly and having miscarriages. She described symptomatic acts of ruining things at work. Just as termination approached she became pregnant. Severe anxiety that her baby would be malformed led to her request to delay termination. I agreed, since I felt that analysis would be invaluable in leading to her better understanding and resolution of the condensation of preoedipal and oedipal issues that she presented. I thought privately that she needed me as a good mother while she was pregnant. We agreed that she would continue her analysis through her pregnancy and for a few months longer. Lydia's fear of a deformed baby reflected two central issues: a view of the baby as draining, which represented a projection of her own oral rage at her mother and in early life; and a guilty wish for punishment for her promiscuity and wishes for her father and his penis. The baby was, in part, a substitute for giving me up. She saw her cephalo-pelvic disproportion as a punishment for oedipal wishes and the Cesearian section she would require as a reparation.

Regressions and progressions during this pregnancy were understood vividly by the patient and by me. Wishes for this baby were also wishes for a phallic repair. Lydia's penis envy was a solution for dealing with issues of separation and merger as well as a defense against wishes for her father's child. Wishes for narcissistic self-sufficiency emerged, since she had experienced neither parent as completely reliable and loving. As these were interpreted, the patient experienced a great deal of anger with me as a nonloving mother and a grateful wish to give to me as a loving father. Lydia and her husband enjoyed their sexuality more fully, although she feared that he would suffocate her with his affection. When she learned through amniocentesis that she would have a boy, she was initially disappointed. She had wished for a girl to replay her relationship with her mother in a more satisfactory way. She also revealed that she had always wanted twins. Exploration of this fantasy led to memories of a male cousin that had lived with her family immediately after her birth. Her father had not wanted this, but her mother had insisted on taking her dead relative's child into the house. Her mother had been depressed at the loss of most of her family during the Holocaust. The taking in of her cousin was something her father had not wanted which led to a deterioration in the parental relationship and to her father's travelling. Her cousin, in adult life, was psychotic, which added to Lydia's fearfulness that her child would be deformed.

Because of sufficient confidence in me and in her mother, Lydia became able to relate to both of us with more warmth. Hatred and death wishes toward her mother were then more tolerable. Her mother had told her that her father actually did spoil her and that the mother did not intervene. She fantasied that I was divorced and that I was having an affair with my office mate. Her dreams and associations revealed that she wanted this man, who resembled her father and that she wished I was dead. With interpretation of this and of her early rage projected onto the fetus, her fears of a deformed baby slowly dissipated.

Close to the anniversary date of her father's death Lydia gave birth to a boy. She called to say that she felt ecstatic. Two months later she returned to analysis and to work, after she had found a "good enough" babysitter. Her concerns about a substitute caretaker led to her sudden recollection that she had had a baby nurse for three years. Her father had wished her mother to retain this nurse and her mother had refused. Her relationship with her own baby felt gratifying and pleasurable. She managed to decrease her husband's concerns over their son taking her attention away from him. She felt ready to set a termination date a few months hence. This period was marked by sadness and worries about being less assertive, but these were evanescent. She dreamt of her child losing a leg and of being her employer's baby, both of which she herself recognized as recapitulations of her wish for me as a good mother and her fears of castration.

Case 9: Anorexia Nervosa as a Result of Maternal Invasiveness

Tova, a 21-year-old undergraduate student, physically and emotionally resembled a 16-year-old. She was seen in emergency consultation after having been taken to a gynecologist because of her amenorrhea. The gynecologist, who found her emaciated and cachectic, sent her for a psychiatric consultation with a presumptive diagnosis of "anorexia nervosa."

Despite the fact that she looked so malnourished, Tova was an exceptionally beautiful young woman who felt that she was overweight. She stated that she was unconcerned about the occurrence of her period, but that it was of great importance to her mother. Her father and her two brothers were rabbis, and she had been seeing a young orthodox man in professional training, whom her family were urging her to marry. However, she could not be married if she was not menstruating, and therefore, considered to be infertile. Her own response was one of indifference.

As we were on the brink of her high holy days and Tova begged not to be hospitalized, we worked out an arrangement that she eat at least a subsistence diet and start on antidepressant medication for her profound sleep disturbance. Under great pressure the family agreed that the analyst could remain in touch with the situation by telephone, which they otherwise would not answer on the holy days. The family almost put their injunction against the use of the phone ahead of their concern for the patient's critical medical condition. The parents also had great reluctance about the patient entering treatment but were under great pressure from the mother's gynecologist, who was the mother's former obstetrician. This physician was an older, religious woman whom they deeply respected and so they agreed to their daughter's treatment.

At first Tova could give only a sparse history. Her illness began after a rugged summer at a camp for special children, where she had felt that it was her duty to work. She painted a very rosy picture of all of her family and was unable to see herself as either depressed or emotionally ill. A contract was made to stabilize her weight and to take her medication, and the mother agreed to stop harassing Tova about her eating if these conditions were met. Her father refused to appear for a family meeting. One brother, who was trained in psychology, phoned, did not deny the extent of his sister's illness, and spoke openly of how his mother ruled everyone with an iron hand. Particularly, he told me that the patient had been sent to a girl's Hebrew academy against her wishes and to her great unhappiness. She had been pressured into a particular undergraduate program that her mother herself had hoped to complete, but which she had failed to do.

When this conversation was repeated to the patient, she confirmed the picture after a stony silence. Tova also admitted to doing her schoolwork in a compulsive manner, often going for two days without sleep. She presented this behavior as if it were voluntary, but it was obvious that her compulsive behavior and insomnia were out of her conscious control. Although Tova seemed unaware of it, the only area of her life in which she exerted any control was in her choice not to eat.

The first inkling of discontent that Tova furnished spontaneously was in relationship to the birth of a niece. Both of her sisters-in-law, averse to birth control, had been producing a baby a year. Her ''good-willed'' mother had gone to help out and then had a terrible fight with her daughter-in-law because she had undertaken to clean and rearrange her daughter-in-law's entire house. The patient then revealed that her mother still cleaned her room, washed her clothing and went through, not only her dresser drawers, but her pocketbook as well. However, Tova seemed very blind to the effect that her mother's behavior had on her.

As denial about her mother's intrusiveness diminished, Tova became irritable with her boyfriend and broke off their relationship. When her mother berated her, she answered, "If you love him, then *you* marry him." The patient then became clinically depressed and blamed herself for being a bad and a selfish person. For quite a while she was unable to see that the complaints that she directed to herself represented ones directed to the mother inside her. She wore religious insignias in great profusion in an attempt at repentance, undertook a difficult and unpleasant volunteer job and redoubled her religiosity. For the first time, her mother recognized Tova's behavior as abnormal, upon which she was hustled off to her brother's family for a weekend. While there she felt compelled to enslave herself with child care. She avoided going to the Sabbath service by hiding in a closet and later pretended that she had been to the service. This episode led her to recognize that she was irrational and out of control.

Tova's hostility toward her mother began to be displaced onto her school instructors, to the point where she was threatened with having to leave the program. As long as it was not her decision and something that was beyond her control, she did not feel guilty. In fact, she felt somewhat gleeful when her willful behavior of rebellion began. She dressed more casually and expressed her annoyance more openly in treatment, became sloppy in her room, ate when she pleased and began to come and go without her mother's permission. She learned to drive the family car and used it to go to work on Sunday, deliberately leaving the gas tank empty. She changed her program at school and expressed the wish to move out of her parents' home. Since the family was made aware of her grave diagnosis, and since she was obviously improved physically and emotionally, they agreed to allow her to do this. She then moved into an apartment with two orthodox women and joined a progressive young orthodox congregation. Although her mother continued to call Tova constantly, she was able to keep her mother out of her life.

Tova had lapses in her orthodoxy, which she revealed only to me. Later she became convinced that I, the analyst-mother, would chastize her. In many overt physical ways, in haircut and style of dress, she was becoming more and more like me, a repetition of the manner in which she had become a duplicate of her mother. She became secretive with me and met interpretations with covert hostility.

Tova began to experiment with psychodrama, which she imagined was in defiance of me. She then became involved in a play, lying to her parents about her evening activities. She did not complete her courses in the programs that she had chosen and kept this a secret from both her parents and from me. But she did tell me that she had begun to date men who were not orthodox. As she became more sexually involved she was asked about birth control, which she immediately obtained assuming that she had my permission to do so. One of the women with whom she lived objected to her behavior and soon became the displaced object of her rage. She acted against this woman in ways to force her to break religious laws, for example, shutting off the lights on the Sabbath so that this woman would commit a forbidden act by turning them on.

This ushered in a honeymoon period in Tova's treatment in which she made constructive efforts on her own behalf, and she saw me as encouraging. After some overt battles with her mother, the two seemed to reach a truce on all subjects but the holidays. The patient regularly became depressed at holidays because of the family's insistence that she spend all her holiday time with them. Not only did she see this as invasion of her privacy but she now celebrated in a manner quite different from theirs. Although she had agreed to remain on maintenance medication, increasing her dose as needed, she stopped several times. This was analyzed in terms of the way she had treated her mother and refused to take her food. However, she was no longer anorectic, her menstrual periods had returned, and in general she was doing well. She completed her courses and contemplated changing from a dutiful job to one in which she experienced pleasure.

Despite these gains, on the eve of one of the major holidays which fell on a weekend, Tova telephoned me from a subway station. She had refused her family's holiday invitation and had not made alternative plans. She felt lonely and guilty and was overwhelmed with the desire to jump in front of a train. I told her to go home, pack her clothing and come to my office. I considered hospitalization, but no bed was available at the hospital where I had admitting privileges. To hospitalize her elsewhere would have meant an abandonment and a rejection. In an unusual departure from classical practice, I decided to take the patient with me to my own home. The patient barely protested. In some way she wanted and expected this solution. She revealed later that she indeed would have attempted suicide had an alternate solution been proposed.

Tova's behavior was multidetermined. First, she expected that her own mother would be mortified and disgraced, and second, she wished unconsciously to intrude on my life, critically assessing my failure of orthodoxy as her mother had done with her. She wished to be my child over the weekend. She tested the limits to see if she could refuse to go to the synagogue and if she could leave my family and read in her room. She attempted to stay up all night and to study as well as to refuse meals. She found a noncritical atmosphere and thus was able to join with my children in games and celebration. After the holiday she immediately told her mother exactly what she had done. To her amazement, her mother sent a letter of unconditional gratitude to me.

Tova soon took a job that she enjoyed and made plans to move in with a nonorthodox friend. She began to date men more distant from her background, which now brought her genuine pleasure. She then insisted on calling me by my first name in an attempt to consider herself my peer, rather than to be my child. A year after termination of her treatment, she wrote a card which expressed her gratitude for having learned "not to be a clone." She noted that she was engaged in many activities and had managed to end an unhappy romance. She was also contemplating graduate school.

The omission of any material about Tova's father in the case history reflects the fact that he refused to be involved, seldom ever spoke to her directly, and was absent a great deal from the family, both because of his work and his stringent religious pursuits. She mentioned him rarely and dreams were of one older brother perceived as the paternal object. He denied her the presence of a protective male figure who might have decreased the invasiveness of her overtly intrusive mother (Abelin, 1971). He was not available as an object to love and to become involved with. This was never analyzed in her almost five years of treatment.

Some years after termination of treatment and travel abroad, I received a note from the patient. It is important in that it indicates Tova's awareness of a new integration in the mother-child relationship: "Your warmth and support and positiveness helps me through some dire straits. Your showing me the love, yet respect for a child's independence that a parent can possess, was a revelation to me. I had no idea that a parent could act or feel that way toward a child. You have helped me to become a whole, good, sensitive individual as opposed to a clone of my mom, someone born to live out her dreams.''

Case 10: The Search for a Baby in an Adolescent Girl with a History of Maternal Abandonment and Paternal Seduction

Ginger, a 16-year-old vivacious and flamboyant young lady, was brought to treatment by her parents. They had not agreed to her requests to see a psychiatrist because they felt that she was not "crazy." However, Ginger had consciously arranged for them to find her in bed with her boyfriend, since she knew that her mother would consider this to be a sign of deranged behavior. At that point her mother agreed that Ginger needed help. Beneath the daughter's facade of histrionic good humor lay a sad and silent depression.

The first session was conducted with Ginger and both parents. Her mother related the patient's early history, while the patient looked at her with rage and flirted with her seductive father. The patient's mother stated, "Sex will damage my daughter if she has it before she is married," but could not explain her comment. Despite the fact that the mother had been in psychoanalytic psychotherapy for five years, she admitted to never understanding her "little girl." The patient's father identified that the patient had acted out as a way of forcing treatment. He acknowledged that her behavior signaled internal problems which he could not understand and for which she required professional help. Ginger's mother immediately challenged him by saying,

"I know more about my daughter than she knows about herself."

Ginger began therapy showing great enthusiasm and an immediate and expressed wish for me to be an understanding and good mother. Her first dream, early in treatment, actually laid out the course of her treatment. It was in three parts: (1) "I was fighting with tigers who became pussy cats that I petted, and then they turned into paper tigers; [2] The scene changed and there was a computer outside of my bedroom. One man dressed as a detective in a white trench coat and brimmed hat, and another in a black trench coat and brimmed hat, were both pushing my buttons; [3] Suddenly someone gave me a large green gem, which enabled me to become a child again. I was running around the livingroom, happy, with other little children about five and six years old. We were all in pajamas with gloves and covered feet."

Ginger's immediate associations were to the color green, the color of her mother's eyes and to her wishes to have a good relationship with her mother and to be a child again, as if by magic. She could not understand or even associate to the ideas of "patting a pussy" or to men pushing her buttons. She related a history of how she used her boyfriend as a maternal substitute, calling him on the phone and speaking for hours when she was lonely and demanding to be held, saying that holding was better than the "sex" that he preferred.

Treatment began with an initial power struggle over "who is boss." As this was investigated, Ginger slowly developed a deep and lasting attachment to me as a "good mother" who would allow her to have thoughts and feelings of her own, yet not allow her to "try things before I'm ready." An analysis of this transference revealed that her mother had been a relatively warm and empathic woman until Ginger's brother was born when Ginger was two years old. At that time she sensed her mother's depression. (Only later did she relate it to her maternal grandmother's illness.) Largely ignored by her mother, who was quite angry with Ginger for voicing envy of her brother, she turned to her father and paternal grandmother. She was her father's favorite, and he was both her playmate and ally. Ginger remembered that she and her brother became a pair, and that she mothered him constantly. Later, when her mother became pregnant and miscarried, Ginger had behaved as if this baby were to be her own, naming the child with a girl's name that resembled her own and her father's.

As treatment progressed, warm feelings to me were at first expressed and then defended against by displacement to two girlfriends. In addition, feelings of closeness brought with them homosexual anxiety. This was displaced to a gym teacher at her school who, indeed, was a homosexual, and of whom the patient was quite afraid. Ginger continued to date her first boyfriend, maternalizing him, chattering to him on the phone for hours, insisting on cuddling and giving in to sexuality only because he wished it. She idealized this "older" man (by four years). It slowly became evident that he was sociopathic and incapable of telling the truth. In addition, he showed severe paranoid trends. As this became obvious to Ginger, she commented on his likeness to her father.

When Ginger and her boyfriend separated she experienced difficulty in getting away from him, and turned to the use of marijuana and cocaine in an attempt to help deal with feelings of depression and identity confusion. She experienced me as "foggy." She began to overeat, to be excessively preoccupied with her weight although she was not heavy, and experienced deprivation between sessions. She recalled being a chubby child and always looking like a freak to her mother, who had wanted a child, she thought, as fragile and with the same hair color as the mother. She had memories of being dressed as a boy and had a "stubborn streak" at the ages of three to five, when she would throw off the rubbers and sweaters that her mother always made her wear. With interpretation of her fears of and longings for me she began to slowly control her diet and use of illicit drugs. Always a writer, she was able again to write many short stories and poems. She was dating. Upon graduation from high school she decided to attend a college close to home in order to stay in analysis.

While in college Ginger again experienced homosexual anxiety with a group of women who were actively homosexual and, because of this, lived at the school for only one year. She became involved with a maternal man who was bisexual, a relationship again more for holding than for sexual relations. At one point, to test me, she brought him with her to treatment, wondering if I would throw him out like "an old shoe." This behavior was multidetermined, since she was also wondering if I, unlike her mother, would accept her choice of any friend. During this stormy period of her treatment, with many periods of testing and passive-aggressive behavior, the patient was doing well socially and in her work. She slowly began to reveal her sexual history, at first in notes to me and then in speech.

Ginger had been exposed to early sexuality and nudity in her home, taking baths with her father and brother and watching her father urinate. She had tried to urinate standing up and masturbated from latency, using the water faucet of the bathtub to stimulate her clitoris. Her early pregnancy fantasy had to do with urination: "A man peed inside of you." She and her brother had shared a room and been involved together in sexual play, about which her parents had been oblivious. Her father would frequently say, "Tell your mother I'm going to tickle you to death." She would then run to tell her mother, who absentmindedly replied, "That's nice, dear."

Ginger experienced rage and depression at my absences, at which time she turned to drugs. This was interpreted on two levels: the rage at her mother's unavailability, physically and mentally; and the anger at her father for his inconsistent stimulation and withdrawal. Many dreams of me as an elderly woman with red hair that turned white led to her recall of her early relationship with her paternal grandmother, whose favorite she was. She looked like this grandmother and was her ideal of a child, which the grandmother had transferred from her only son, the patient's father.

She and her mother had been involved in a power struggle as siblings for the grandmother's attention. Indeed, her grandmother had required shock treatment after her son was married, but was the main mothering figure when Ginger's mother had a postpartum depression. Both her grandmother and mother were perceived as very well-dressed, feminine, "tinkling" creatures, while she felt heavy and malformed. Analysis of this as a separation-individuation problem relating to her need to maintain a separate identity led to complete control of her dieting and her giving up of drugs.

Ginger was now dating another man with whom she became involved in sadomasochistic activity. When she discussed this with her father he wished to join her in it. This was horrifying to Ginger and led to her early memories of seeing him as huge and violent as well as her fears of and wishes for his brutal attack. The relationship with this man was short-lived. When Ginger graduated from college, she moved to her own apartment because she and her mother were involved in a power struggle and because she did not wish to be the mediator between her parents when they quarrelled. Although this led to a brief depression and feelings of aloneness, she adjusted to it rather rapidly.

Shortly thereafter, she met a somewhat older businessman with whom she lived for one year. He was involved with his ex-wife and later with another woman, and had a two-year-old little girl. The patient experienced great maternal feelings to this child, and this relationship led to the recall of many similar feelings towards her brother and memories of good and bad times with her father. The relationship, however, did not last. During her training for an advanced degree, and in the middle of a beginning oedipal transference to me, her grandmother was diagnosed as having terminal cancer. The patient was bereft: the man she was living with was quite annoyed at her inability to give to him when she was depressed; her mother immediately left to travel; her father became extensively involved in business; and her brother was at college. Therefore, the care of her grandmother was left more or less to her, and she was able to empathically care for her.

A long period of mourning ensued after her grandmother's death. Her parents developed an open marriage, leading rapidly to divorce. Ginger became involved in a fight with her mother over whether her mother would inherit her grandmother's jewels, which were left to her brother and herself. She saw her father as relatively ineffectual in helping her. In the end, her mother "stole" several items not rightfully belonging to her and then accused Ginger of stealing her silver. During this turmoil, Ginger did not regress, but rather became more able to handle her external reality and relate to me as an adult. Her father then told her of her mother's frigidity and his long history of affairs. While all of this turmoil continued, Ginger began to write her first book, which seemed to serve as a sublimation, enabling her to be a participant and observer of the crisis around her. During this period she actively identified with me and found herself to be the "stabilizer" of her brother. A long period of sexual abstinence followed. She received an advanced degree, did more free-lance work and continued to write her book. She became increasingly aware of her father's erratic and eccentric behavior, dress, manner and self-absorption.

Ginger fantasized that I had a son just older than she and that she wished to meet and marry him. This led to her recall of romantic fantasies about her brother. Her active fantasies frightened her, since she feared my rivalry. She was becoming more beautifully dressed and also feared my envy. She was dating and looking for a man who was able to be firm and understanding, and commented that this would be difficult for her since her father had been so sadistic. Her mother, who had been in therapy when the patient was nine, had become severely depressed when her therapist died. She was again in treatment, this time with a woman psychiatrist. The patient was able to recall mother's extensive "crazy attachment" to this therapist, and her instantaneous attachment to many friends and to the grandmother. In these attachments her mother would copy "wholesale" all features of the person with whom she was involved. With this insight of the as-if quality of her mother, the patient felt sad and attempted a rapprochement with her, which partially succeeded. They were able to talk of the arts and of literature.

During termination phase Ginger worked through her previous inability to maintain distance from her father, who had tried to control her life. She was busy searching for a man who had the best features of both parents.

This patient's entrance into the oedipal conflict seemed to be the classical entrance of becoming aware of the anatomical distinction between the sexes, turning to her father and jealously enraged at her mother. She had wished for her father's baby in identification with her mother, who was then pregnant. However, this occurred during the rapprochement period at the crossroads of separation-individuation. The patient was caught in a longing for her unavailable mother and a turning to her father as both a preoedipal and oedipal object. This case represented a three-generational maternal problem, since Ginger's mother had herself been deprived of a good mother and was constantly on a search for one, finally found in the paternal grandmother towards whom both Ginger and her mother behaved like siblings.

Glossary

ACTING OUT
: The behavior occurring in the course of analytic treatment is an enactment (usually outside of the analysis), rather than a verbalization in the analysis, of feelings and fantasies arising in the transference.

ACTING UP
: Many kinds of generalized, impulsive, pathological, antisocial and dangerous behaviors.

ADOLESCENCE
: The period beginning with pubescence, usually ages 10 to 12, lasting to 20+ years of age, during which the individual must deal with resurgent strong sexual drives, the reexacerbation of the oedipal conflict, the achievement of self-certainty, the establishment of a vocational role, the establishment of a sexual identity, and the definition of moral, ethical and political ideals.

AFFECT
: A subjectively experienced feeling state.

ANAL PHASE   A developmental phase from age
                                  18 to 30 months, when toileting
                                  functions are primarily invested
                                  as sources of pleasure. During
                                  this period the child struggles to
                                  establish autonomy and control
                                  of both these functions and of
                                  general motoric activities.

ANAMNESIS   The recall of early childhood
                                  experiences; the patient's per-
                                  sonal history as given by the
                                  patient.

ANOREXIA   A disease primarily, but not ex-
NERVOSA   clusively, of adolescent girls and
                                  young women who starve them-
                                  selves. They have a severe dis-
                                  turbance in body image.
                                  Starvation leads to other phys-
                                  iological complications, such as
                                  loss of menses, growth of body
                                  hair, and eventually, to circu-
                                  latory collapse.

ANXIETY   A feeling of distress, worry or
                                  fear, often accompanied by
                                  physiological manifestations,
                                  such as rapid heart beat and
                                  breathing, sweating, tremulous-
                                  ness, nausea, diarrhea and faint-
                                  ness. It is the signal that
                                  something internal is wrong.

ASCETICISM	The repudiation of all instinctual gratification.
BODY IMAGE	The mental representation of the body.
CASTRATION ANXIETY	Anxiety about loss of the phallus. It is a result of the child's wish to castrate the father and his fear of talion punishment. Castration anxiety also occurs in girls with an illusory or fantasied phallus.
CATHARSIS	The opportunity to ventilate things causing worry, shame, guilt or anxiety in a nonjudgmental atmosphere.
CHARACTER	A constellation of traits that makes each individual recognizable. A repetitive pattern of adaptation to life.
CHARACTER DISORDER	A rigid, inflexible set of traits and ways of dealing with life that avoids the subjective feeling of anxiety, often at the expense of annoying and disturbing other people.
COMPULSION	The involuntary repetition of symbolic behaviors whose unconscious meaning is not understood.

CONFLICTS

These occur either between the individual's wishes and the demands of reality or between or within the various agencies of the mind (Id, Ego and Superego).

CORE GENDER IDENTITY

The individual's sense of his own sex.

COUNTERPHOBIA

The impulsive courting of what one unconsciously fears.

COUNTER-TRANSFERENCE

The classical view which recognizes those responses of the analyst that occur because of incomplete resolution of his own infantile conflicts. The total view includes all responses of the analyst that are used to understand the patient.

DEFENSES

A series of unconscious intra-psychic maneuvers, set in motion to deal with conflict.

DENIAL

A primitive defense mechanism in which the ego avoids becoming aware of some painful aspect of external reality. It interferes with adequate knowledge of reality.

DEPERSONALIZA-TION

A feeling of unreality about the self. The loss of a sense of wholeness and cohesion of the self.

DEPRESSION

A feeling of hopelessness and helplessness.

DEREALIZATION

A state in which the world seems unreal or uncanny.

DISPLACEMENT

The unconscious investment of a person or thing as a substitute for the original person toward whom important thoughts, feelings and fantasies are unconsciously directed. This is part of dream work and is an unconscious defense mechanism.

DREAMS

Universal productions of the mind which occur during sleep. The understanding of these productions provides information about the unconscious.

EGO

A series of mental functions that are stable over time. It is the agency of the mind that mediates between the other agencies of the mind (Id, Superego) and between the internal world and external reality. It is a "structure" in the sense that it is a stable set of functions.

EGO IDEAL

The internal representation of

the self as the self would like to be.

EGO SPLITTING

The division of the self and others into parts which separate good from bad attributes, such as the good mother and the bad mother, rather than the mother who combines both qualities.

EMPATHY

The ability to perceive and be sensitive to the emotional experience of another. A temporary and partial identification with another.

FANTASY

Wishful belief.

FIXATION

The failure to have negotiated a developmental stage and its problems and to have gone onto the more mature aims and objects.

"GOOD ENOUGH MOTHERING"

The process wherein a mother fosters independence, yet allows some dependence, provides some frustration, but neither neglects nor overwhelms the child.

GUILT

The feeling of remorse wherein the individual feels that he or she has done something bad or wrong.

HOLDING ENVIRONMENT	An environment created by the mother which allows the child to experience optimum but not overwhelming frustration in a secure and protective setting.
ID	The portion of the mind which is the repository of infantile unconscious wishes.
IDENTIFICATION	The process of becoming a realistic likeness of a parent or other important person, generally partial and not total.
ILLUSORY PENIS	See "Castration Anxiety."
INSIGHT	The subjective experiential knowledge acquired before or during an analysis which leads to self-understanding.
INTELLECTUALIZA- TION	The unconscious binding of instinctual drives in intellectual activities or verbalization.
INTERNALIZATION	The assimilation of standards of behavior, feelings and goals from external example into the internal mental apparatus.
INTERPRETATION	Making the unconscious conscious.
INTROJECTION	The unconscious assimilation of

the mental representation of another into the mental representation of the self.

ISOLATION OF AFFECT

An unconscious disconnection of ideas and feelings originally associated with them.

LATENCY

The period of life from about five years to eleven years of age when the child devotes most of his energy to work, play, peer relationships and the acquisition of the skills of his culture.

MASOCHISM

A turning of aggression upon the self.

MASTURBATION

Sexual play with the self, including genital self-stimulation.

NARCISSISM

Normal narcissism is treating of the self as one might treat a beloved one; a focusing on the self. Abnormal narcissism includes feelings of grandiosity, omnipotence and automatic entitlement.

OBSESSION

Unwanted recurrent thoughts.

OBJECT RELATIONS

Dyadic relationships.

OEDIPUS COMPLEX

A period occurring between two and one-half and four years of age (Oedipal phase) in which the male child competes with his father for his mother as the sexual object. For females it is a period of competition with the mother for the father as the sexual object.

ORAL PHASE

Occurs during the first 18 months of life. The mouth, tongue and skin are primarily invested as organs of pleasure. The aim is to suck and to be held. The object is the mother.

PARAMETER

A departure from classical analytic technique (interpretive) that can be eventually analyzed.

PENIS ENVY

The envy of having a penis, to which may be attributed nonsexual qualities such as general strength, success and independence.

PHOBIA

The unwanted fear of certain objects or situations which are symbolic.

PRIMARY PROCESS

A kind of cognition that operates according to the pleasure principle. It allows for coexistent opposites. It has no negatives or qualifiers. It is simple and concrete. Tactile, visual and olfactory modes take precedence over auditory and visual modes. Time is distorted.

PROJECTION   The unconscious attribution, to the external world or to an external object, of a painful idea or impulse in the self.

PROJECTIVE IDENTIFICATION   The insertion of one's own affects or perceptions into the therapist or other object who then identifies with those affects or perceptions.

PSYCHOSIS   A state of psychological decompensation marked by disturbance in rational thinking and extreme affective lability or flatness of affect. There is difficulty in distinguishing reality from fantasy. Aggressive and sexual impulses are often uncontrolled. Specific symptoms vary according to diagnostic category.

RAPPROCHEMENT   A subphase of development occurring between 15 and 24 months of age, in which there is a growing awareness of others and a need to recognize and relate to them, accompanied by a further separation from the mother. It is characterized by the practicing of separation and reunion. If properly resolved the child has a constant mental representation of the mother, which allows physical separation for increasing periods of time without anxiety or grief.

RATIONALIZATION — A plausible reason given for an act, feeling or fantasy, which is not the real reason, but merely a substitute for the actual unconscious motivation.

REACTION FORMATION — The defense mechanism, which is unconscious, of replacement in consciousness of a painful feeling or idea by its opposite.

RECONSTRUCTION — The analyst's attempt to correlate, understand, conceptualize and present to the patient earlier experiences that cannot be remembered, but which the patient's productions indicate must have occurred.

REGRESSION — The return to early stages of development that produce less anxiety.

REGRESSION IN THE SERVICE OF THE EGO — Play or creative work outlets for the controlled expression of primitive instincts, both sexual and aggressive.

REPRESSION

The unconscious defense mechanism of forgetting, the cornerstone of all the defense mechanisms; the unconscious withholding from awareness of an idea or feeling.

RESISTANCE

The often unconscious avoidance of free association in psychoanalysis by changing subjects, forgetting and producing a variety of interferences during the psychoanalytic process.

SADISM

Aggression or symbolic castration in which the perpetrator or sadist reassures himself (or herself) that he(she) is the castrator, not the castrated.

SCREEN MEMORY

Usually a false or distorted memory, or an actual memory that serves to symbolically disguise an infantile conflict.

SELF

A mental configuration that mirrors the individual's characteristics, potential abilities and mental or physical limitations.

SELF-
    REPRESENTATION

The mental model of the self.

SEPARATION
    ANXIETY

The anxiety that accompanies physical separation from the

caretaking individual, usually the mother.

SEPARATION-
INDIVIDUATION

The process that takes place between mother and child from age 6 to 24 months. It ends with the recognition of separateness of the self and the caretaking object, and the separation of the mental representations of self and object. If successful, the child emerges with a cohesive mental representation of all aspects of the self and of all aspects of other individuals.

SOMATIC
SYMPTOMS

(Psychosomatic symptoms, somatization) Physical, medical symptoms in which the body or a body organ expresses repressed conflicts and affects.

SPLITTING

See "Ego Splitting."

SUBLIMATION

The highest level of the unconscious defense mechanisms. The energies of the instinctual drives are funnelled into socially acceptable behaviors, such as creativity, work and play, which serve adaptation and the needs of the community.

SUPEREGO

That part of the mental apparatus commonly called the conscience. It contains the prohibitions against direct preemptory expressions of instincts. Its beginnings are from parental injunctions. With the ending of the oedipal phase it is massively internalized.

SYMBIOTIC PHASE

A stage of development occurring from 2 to 6 months of age in which the mother acts as a stimulus barrier to relieve the infant's tension states. The baby smiles in the presence of the good (tension-relieving) mother's face. The infant has not yet formed the "me" and the "not-me" perception. The mental separation from the mother is only beginning.

SYMBOLIZATION

A process whereby an idea or object stands in place of what is of primary interest and importance and which represents the latter. It is part of dream work and symptom formation.

SYMPTOM

A symbolic representation of conflict, which is a compromise formation consisting of unconscious impulses and defenses against them.

THERAPEUTIC ALLIANCE

The alliance between the analyst's analyzing ego and the reasonable, self-observing portion of the patient's ego.

TRANSFERENCE

The process by which the patient repeats with the analyst, his or her relationship to infantile caretaking figures, and the modifications that have since occurred in relating to these objects or their later substitutes.

TRANSFERENCE NEUROSIS

The repetition of *all* unconscious conflicts of the patient with the analyst, during the course of an analysis, which parallels the patient's infantile neurosis.

TRANSITIONAL OBJECTS

Soft, cuddly, overused and overworn objects, such as blankets and stuffed toys to which the child clings. These represent both the child and the mother and serve as a symbolic tie to the mother.

UNCONSCIOUS

The descriptive unconscious is that portion of the mental functioning outside of awareness. The dynamic unconscious is that part of the unconscious that is kept out of awareness by work, because of its relationship to conflict.

UNDOING

A two-stage act which symbolically and unconsciously repre-

sents the expression of a sexual
or aggressive impulse followed
by its reversal.

WORKING
THROUGH

The continuing application of
analytic work to overcome resistance persisting after the initial interpretation of repressed
conflict.

References

Abelin, E. (1971), The role of the father in the separation-individuation process. In: *Separation-Individuation: Essays in Honor of Margaret S. Mahler*, ed. J.B. McDevitt & C.F. Settlage. New York: International Universities Press, pp. 229–251.

Abraham, K. (1925), Character formation on the genital level of the libido. *Selected Papers on Psychoanalysis*. London: Hogarth Press, pp. 407–417.

Ananth, J. (1978), Hysterectomy and depression. *Obstet. & Gynecol.*, 52:724–730.

Benedek, T. (1968), Discussion of Mary Jane Sherfey: The evolution and nature of female sexuality in relation to psychoanalytic theory. *J. Amer. Psychoanal. Assn.*, 16:244–448.

Berlin, F., Bergey, G., & Money, J. (1982), Periodic psychosis of puberty: A case report. *Am. J. Psychiat.*, 139:119–120.

Bernstein, A. (1975), *Tell It Like It is: A Manual for Instruction of Adolescents.* (Manuscript).

—— Warner, G.M. (1981), *An Introduction to Contemporary Psychoanalysis.* New York: Jason Aronson.

—— —— (1983), Three cases of the onset of anorexia nervosa after prolonged use of the Milwaukee brace. (In press.)

Bibring, G., Dwyer, T., Huntington, D., & Valenstein, A. (1961), A study of the psychological process in pregnancy and of the earliest mother/child relationship. *The Psychoanalytic Study of the Child*, 16:9–24. New York: International Universities Press.

Blum, H. (1976), Masochism, the ego ideal and the psychology of women. *J. Amer. Psychoanal. Assn.*, 24:157–191.

Bonaparte, M. (1953), Passivity, masochism and frigidity. *Internat. J. Psycho-Anal.*, 16:325–333.

—— (1963), *Female Sexuality.* New York: International Universities Press.

Breuer, J. & Freud, S. (1892), Studies on Hysteria, *Standard Edition*, 1:1–319. London: Hogarth Press, 1966.

Bruch, H. (1978), *The Gilded Cage. The Enigma of Anorexia Nervosa.* Cambridge: Harvard University Press.

293

Brunswick, R. (1940), The preoedipal phase of libido development. *Psychoanal. Quart.*, 9:293–319.

Chasseguet-Smirgel, J., Ed. (1970), *Female Sexuality: New Psychoanalytic Views*. Ann Arbor: University of Michigan Press.

Chertok, L., Bonnaud, M., Borelli, M., Donnet, J., & Revault D'Allones, C. (1969), *Motherhood and Personality*. Philadelphia: Lippincott.

Chodorow, N. (1978), *The Reproduction of Mothering: Psychoanalysis and the Sociology of Gender*. Berkeley: University of California Press.

Clower, V. (1975), Significance of masturbation in female sexual development and function. In: *Masturbation: From Infancy to Senescence*, ed. I. Marcus & J.J. Francis. New York: International Universities Press, pp. 107–143.

——— (1976), Theoretical implications in current views of masturbation in latency girls. *J. Amer. Psychoanal. Assn.*, 24:109–125.

Deutsch, H. (1925), The psychology of women in relation to the functions of reproduction. *Internat. J. Psycho-Anal.*, 6:405–418.

——— (1930), The significance of masochism in the mental life of women. *Internat. J. Psycho-Anal.*, 1:48–60.

——— (1944), *The Psychology of Women*, Vol. 1. New York: Grune & Stratton.

——— (1945), *The Psychology of Women*, Vol. 2. New York: Grune & Stratton.

——— (1960), Frigidity in women. In: *Neurosis and Character Types*. New York: International Universities Press, pp. 358–362.

——— (1961), Panel: Frigidity in Women, reporter B.F. Moore. *J. Amer. Psychoanal. Assn.*, 9:571–584.

Developments in sexual research (1982), *Sexual Medicine Today*, 14–15. : American Medical Association.

Drellich, M.B. & Bieber, I. (1958), Psychological importance of the uterus and its functions. *J. Nerv. Ment. Dis.*, pp. 126–322.

Erikson, E. (1950),

——— (1959), Identity and the Life Cycle. *Psychological Issues,* Monogr. 1. New York: International Universities Press.

——— (1968), Womanhood and the inner space. In: *Identity, Youth and Crisis*. New York: Norton, pp. 261–295.

Freud, A. (1966), *The Ego and the Mechanisms of Defense*. New York: International Universities Press.

Freud, S. (1905a), Three essays on the theory of sexuality. *Standard Edition*, 7:125–353. London: Hogarth Press, 1962.

——— (1905b), Fragment of an analysis of a case of hysteria. *Standard Edition*, 7:3–125. London: Hogarth Press, 1962.

——— (1909), The analysis of a phobia in a five-year-old boy. *Standard Edition*, 10:5–149. London: Hogarth Press, 1955.

——— (1912a), Contributions to a discussion on masturbation. *Standard Edition*, 12:293–294. London: Hogarth Press, 1958.

——— (1912b), Totem and taboo. *Standard Edition*, 13:1–165. London: Hogarth Press, 1955.

———— (1915), Papers on technique. Observations on transference love. *Standard Edition*, 12:157–175. London: Hogarth Press, 1963.

———— (1917), Introductory lectures on psychoanalysis. *Standard Edition*, 16:241–496. London: Hogarth Press, 1957.

———— (1919), A child is being beaten. *Standard Edition*, 17:175–205. London: Hogarth Press, 1969.

———— (1920a), The psychogenesis of a case of homosexuality in a woman. *Standard Edition*, 18:145–172. London: Hogarth Press, 1955.

———— (1920b), Beyond the pleasure principle. *Standard Edition*, 18:1–74. London: Hogarth Press, 1955.

———— (1923a), The infantile genital organization. *Standard Edition*, 19:139–145. London: Hogarth Press, 1961.

———— (1923b), The ego and the id. *Standard Edition*, 19:3–66. London: Hogarth Press, 1961.

———— (1924), The economic problem of masochism. *Standard Edition*, 19:155–170. London: Hogarth Press, 1961.

———— (1925a), The dissolution of the oedipus complex. *Standard Edition*, 19:173–182. London: Hogarth Press, 1961.

———— (1925b), Some psychical consequences of the anatomical distinction between the sexes. *Standard Edition*, 19:253–260. London: Hogarth Press, 1961.

———— (1926a), Inhibitions, symptoms and anxiety. *Standard Edition*, 20:77–174. London: Hogarth Press, 1959.

———— (1926b), The question of lay analysis. *Standard Edition*, 20:177–258. London: Hogarth Press, 1959.

———— (1930), Civilization and its discontents. *Standard Edition*, 21:57–145. London: Hogarth Press, 1961.

———— (1931), Female sexuality. *Standard Edition*, 21:223–243. London: Hogarth Press, 1961.

———— (1933a), Femininity. *Standard Edition*, 22:112–135. London: Hogarth Press, 1964.

———— (1933b), New introductory lectures on psychoanalysis. *Standard Edition*, 22:5–182. London: Hogarth Press, 1964.

———— (1937), Analysis terminable and interminable. *Standard Edition*, 22:209–253. London: Hogarth Press, 1964.

———— (1940), An outline of psychoanalysis. *Standard Edition*, 23:139–207. London: Hogarth Press, 1964.

Friday, N. (1973), *My Secret Garden: Women's Sexual Fantasies*. New York: Pocket Books.

Galenson, E. (1971a), A consideration of the nature of thought in childhood play. In: *Separation-Individuation: Essays in Honor of Margaret S. Mahler*, ed. J.B. McDevitt & C.F. Settlage. New York: International Universities Press, pp. 41–59.

———— (1971b), The impact of early sexual discovery on mood, defensive organization and symbolization. *The Psychoanalytic Study of the Child*, 26:195–216. New York: Quadrangle Books.

————— (1973), A research investigation of sexual behavior and symbolic functioning during the second year of life. Sixth Symposium on Sexuality and
Psychoanalysis Revisited. Society of Medical Psycho-Analysis, New
York, March, 1973.
————— Blau, S., & Vogel, S. (1975), Disturbance in sexual identity beginning
at eighteen months of age. *Internat. Rev. Psychoanal.*, 2:389–393.
————— Miller, R. (1976), The choice of symbols. *J. Amer. Acad. Child Psychiat.*, 5:85–96.
————— Roiphe, H. (1974), The emergence of genital awareness during the
second year of life. In: *Sex Differences in Behavior*, eds. R.C. Friedman,
R.M. Richard & R.L. Vandewicli. New York: Wiley, pp. 223–231.
————— ————— (1976), Some suggested revisions concerning early female
development. *J. Amer. Psychoanal. Assn.*, 24:29–57.
Green, R. (1976), Human sexuality: Research and treatment frontiers. In:
American Handbook of Psychiatry, Vol. 6, 2nd Ed., ed. S. Arieti. New
York: Basic Books, pp. 665–691.
Greenacre, P. (1948), Anatomical structure and superego development. In:
Trauma, Growth and Personality. New York: International Universities
Press, pp. 149–164.
————— (1950), Special problems of early female sexual development. In:
Trauma, Growth and Personality. New York: International Universities
Press, pp. 237–258.
————— (1952), Some factors producing different types of genital and pregenital
emotional organization. In: *Trauma, Growth and Personality*. New York:
International Universities Press, pp. 293–302.
————— (1953a), Penis awe and its relation to penis envy. In *Emotional Growth*,
ed. M. Lowenstein. New York: International Universities Press, 1971,
pp. 31–49.
————— (1953b), Certain relationships between fetishism and faulty development of the body image. In: *Emotional Growth*. New York: International
Universities Press, 1971, pp. 9–30.
Harlow, H. (1962), The effect of learning conditions on behavior. *Bull. Menninger Clinic*, 26:213–224.
————— Harlow, N. (1966), Learning to love. *American Scientist*, 54:244–272.
Horney, K. (1924), On the genesis of the castration complex in women. In:
Feminine Psychology, ed. H. Kelman. New York: Norton, 1967, pp.
32–53.
————— (1926), The flight from womanhood: The masculinity complex in
women as viewed by men and women. In: *Feminine Psychology*, ed. H.
Kelman. New York: Norton, 1967, pp. 54–70.
————— (1932), The dread of women. *Internat. J. Psycho-Anal.*, 13:348–361.
————— (1933a), The problem of feminine masochism. In: *Feminine Psychology*, ed. H. Kelman. New York: Norton, 1967, pp. 214–233.
————— (1933b), The denial of the vagina: A contribution to genital anxiety
specific to women. In: *Feminine Psychology*, ed. H. Kelman. New York:
Norton, 1967, pp. 147–151.

Jacobson, E. (1950), Development of the wish for a child in boys. *The Psychoanalytic Study of the Child*, 5:139–152. New York: International Universities Press.
——— (1964), *The Self and the Object World*. New York: International Universities Press.
Jamison, K., Wellisch, D., & Pasnau, M. (1978), Psychosocial aspects of mastectomy: I. The woman's perspective. *Amer. J. Psychiat.*, 135:432–436.
Jessner, L., Weigert, E., & Fay, J. (1970), The development of parental attitudes during pregnancy. In: *Parenthood*, ed. E. Anthony & T. Benedek. Boston: Little Brown, pp. 209–244.
Johnson, M. (1963), Sex role learning in the nuclear family. *Child Development*, 34:319–334.
Jones, E. (1927), The early development of female sexuality. *Internat. J. Psycho-Anal.*, 8:459–472.
——— (1933), The phallic phase. *Internat. J. Psycho-Anal.*, 14:1–33.
——— (1935), Early female sexuality. *Internat. J. Psycho-Anal.*, 16:263–273.
——— (1955), *The Life and Work of Sigmund Freud*, Vol. 2. New York: Basic Books.
Karme, L. (1981), Penis envy. *J. Amer. Psychoanal. Assn.*, 29:427–446.
Keiser, S. (1956), Female sexuality. *J. Amer. Psychoanal. Assn.*, 4:563–574.
Kestenberg, J. (1956a), Vicissitudes of female sexuality. *J. Amer. Psychoanal. Assn.*, 4:453–576.
——— (1956b), On the development of maternal feelings in early childhood. *The Psychoanalytic Study of the Child*, 11:275–291. New York: International Universities Press.
——— (1968), Outside and inside, male and female. *J. Amer. Psychoanal. Assn.*, 16:457–520.
——— (1975), *Children and Parents*. Psychoanalytic Studies in Development. New York: Aronson.
Kinsey, A., Pomeroy, W., Martin, C., & Gebhard, P. (1953), *Sexual Behavior in the Human Female*. Philadelphia: Saunders.
Kleeman, J. (1971a), The establishment of core gender identity in normal girls. a. Introduction. b. Development of the ego capacity to differentiate. *Arch. Sex. Behav.*, 1:117–129.
——— (1971b), II. How meanings are conveyed between parent and child in the first three years. *Arch. Sex. Behav.*, 1:103–129.
——— (1975), Genital self-stimulation in infant and toddler girls. In: *Masturbation: From Infancy to Senescence*, ed. I. Marcus & J.J. Francis. New York: International Universities Press, pp. 77–106.
Klein, M. (1928), Early stages of the oedipus conflict. *Internat. J. Psycho-Anal.*, 9:167–180.
——— (1932), *Psychoanalysis of Children*. London: Hogarth Press.
Kohlberg, L. (1966), A cognitive-developmental analysis of children's sex role concepts and attitudes. In: *The Development of Sex Differences*, ed. E. Maccoby. Stanford: Stanford University Press, pp. 82–173.

Korner, A. (1973), Sex differences in newborns with special reference to differences in the organization of oral behavior. *J. Child Psychol. & Psychiat.*, 14:19–29.

Lampl de Groot, J. (1928), The evolution of the oedipal complex in women. *Internat. J. Psycho-Anal.*, 9:332–345.

Lerner, H. (1974a), The hysterical personality: A "woman's" disease. *Compr. Psychiat.*, 15:157–164.

———— (1974b), Early origins of envy and devaluation of women. Implication for sex role stereotypes. *Bull. Menninger Clinic*, 38:538–553.

Lewis, F.M. (1978), Psychosocial adjustment to breast cancer: A review of selected literature. *Internat. J. Psychiat. Med.*, 1:1–17.

Mahler, M. (1963), Thoughts on the development of the individual. *The Psychoanalytic Study of the Child*, 18:307–332. New York: International Universities Press.

———— (1967), On human symbiosis and the vicissitudes of individualism. *J. Amer. Psychoanal. Assn.*, 25:740–763.

———— Furer, M. (1963), Certain aspects of the separation-individuation phase. *Psychoanal. Quart.*, 32:1–14.

———— Perriere, K. (1965), Mother child interaction during separation-individuation. *Psychoanal. Quart.*, 34:483–498.

Martin, R., Roberts, W., & Clayton, P. (1980), Psychiatric status after hysterectomy: A one-year prospective follow-up. *J. Amer. Med. Assn.*, 244:350–353.

Masters, W. & Johnson, V. (1960), The sexual response cycle of the human female: Gross anatomic considerations. *West. J. Surg. Obstet. Gynecol.*, 68:57–72.

———— (1966), *Human Sexual Response*. Boston: Little, Brown.

Money, J. & Erhardt, A. (1972), *Man and Woman, Boy and Girl*. Baltimore: Johns Hopkins University Press.

Moore, B.E. (1968), Psychoanalytic reflections on the implications of recent physiological studies of female orgasm. *J. Amer. Psychoanal. Assn.*, 16:569–587.

Moulton, R. (1977), Some effects of the new feminism. *Amer. J. Psychiat.*, 134:1–6.

Murphy, L. (1962), *The Widening Circle of Childhood*. New York: Basic Books.

Parens, H. (1971), A contribution of separation-individuation in the development of psychic structure. In: *Separation-Individuation: Essays in Honor of Margaret S. Mahler*, ed. J.B. McDevitt & C.F. Settlage. New York: International Universities Press, pp. 100–112.

———— Pollock, L., Stern, J., & Kramer, S. (1977), On the girl's entry into the oedipus complex. In: *Female Psychology: Contemporary Psychoanalytic Views*, ed. H. Blum. New York: International Universities Press, pp. 79–107.

Penney, A. (1981), *How to Make Love to a Man*. New York: Crown.

Person, E. (1982), Women working: Fears of failure, deviance and success. *J. Amer. Acad. Psychoanal.*, 10:67–84.

——— & Ovesey, L. (1974), The transsexual syndrome in males. *Amer. J. Psychother.*, 28:4–20.

Pfefferbaum, B. (1977), A comprehensive program of psychosocial care for mastectomy patients. *Internat. J. Psychiat. Med.*, 1:63–72.

Polivy, J. (1974), Psychological reactions to hysterectomy: A critical review. *Amer. J. Obstet. Gynecol.*, 118:417–426.

Ritvo, S. (1977), Adolescent to woman. In: *Female Psychology: Contemporary Psychoanalytic Views*, ed. H. Blum. New York: International Universities Press, pp. 127–137.

Roiphe, H. (1968), On an early genital phase: With an addendum on Genesis. *The Psychoanalytic Study of the Child*, 23:348–365. New York: International Universities Press.

——— & Galenson, E. (1972), Early genital activity and the castration complex. *Psychoanal. Quart.*, 42:334–337.

——— ——— (1973), Object loss and early sexual development. *Psychoanal. Quart.*, 42:73–90.

Schafer, R. (1974), Problems in Freud's psychology of women. *J. Amer. Psychoanal. Assn.*, 22:459–485.

Sherfey, M.J. (1966), The evolution and nature of female sexuality in relation to psychoanalytic theory. *J. Amer. Psychoanal. Assn.*, 14:28–128.

——— (1973), *The Nature and Evolution of Female Sexuality*. New York: Random/Village.

Sloan, D. (1978), The emotional and psychosexual aspects of hysterectomy. *Amer. J. Obstet. Gynecol.*, 131:598–605.

Stoller, R. (1964), A contribution to the study of gender identity. *Internat. J. Psycho-Anal.*, 45:220–226.

——— (1965), The sense of maleness. *Psychoanal. Quart.*, 34:207–218.

——— (1968a), The sense of femaleness. *Psychoanal. Quart.*, 37:42–55.

——— (1968b), *Sex and Gender*, Vol. 1. New York: Science House.

——— (1972), Etiological factors in female transsexualism: A first approximation. *Arch. Sex. Behav.*, 2:47–64.

——— (1975), *Sex and Gender*, Vol. 2. London: Hogarth Press.

——— (1976), Primary femininity. *J. Amer. Psychoanal. Assn.*, 25:59–78.

Thompson, C. (1942), Cultural pressures in the psychology of women. *Psychiat.*, 4:331–339.

Torok, M. (1970), The significance of penis envy in women. In: *Female Sexuality: New Psychoanalytic Views*, ed. J. Chasseguet-Smirgel. Ann Arbor: Michigan University Press, pp. 135–170.

Warner, G.M. (1967–1969), Eleven grandmothers with postpartum reactions. (Manuscript.)

——— (1970), Psychiatric treatment in a school of nursing. *Arch. Gen. Psychiat.*, 22:338–343.

——— & Lahn, M. (1970), A case of female transsexualism. *Psychiat. Quart.*, 44:476–487.

Wellisch, D., Jamison, K., & Pasnau, R. (1978), Psychosocial aspects of mastectomy. II. The man's perspective. *Amer. J. Psychiat.*, 135:543–546.

Winnicott, D. W. (1965), The theory of parent-infant relationship. *Internat. J. Psycho-Anal.*, 4:235–236.

Witkin, M.H. (1982), Sex after mastectomy. *Med. Aspects Human Sexuality*, 16:50–59.

Zussman, L., Zussman, S., Sunley, R., & Bjornson, E. (1981), Sexual response after hysterectomy-oophorectomy: Recent studies and reconsideration of psychogenesis. *Amer. J. Obstet. Gynecol.*, 140:725–729.

Name Index

Abelin, E., 268
Abraham, K., 159
Ananth, J., 162

Benedek, T., 9
Bergey, G., 139
Berlin, F., 139
Bernstein, A., 66, 94, 111
Bibring, G., 159
Bieber, I., 166
Blau, S., 31
Bjornson, E., 166
Blum, H., 39-41
Bonaparte, M., 5, 6, 7, 10-11
Bonnaud, M., 21
Borelli, M., 21
Breuer, J., 1, 76
Bruch, H., 115
Brunswick, R., 14

Chassegeut-Smirgel, J., 175
Chertok, L., 21
Chodorow, N., 43, 53, 148, 151
Clayton, P., 165
Clower, V., 39-41

Deutsch, H., 5, 7, 8-10, 11, 14, 20-21, 143, 159
Donnet, J., 21
Drellich, M.B., 166
Dwyer, T., 159

Erhardt, A., 34-36
Erikson, E., 19, 39, 111-112, 151, 157

Fay, J., 21
Freud, A., 95
Freud, S., 1-8, 9, 10, 11, 12, 13, 15, 16, 27, 28, 29, 30, 32, 33, 38, 39, 40, 45, 46, 47, 48, 49, 50-52, 54, 76, 77, 103, 104, 105, 106, 109, 122-123, 143, 175, 178
Friday, M., 121
Furer, M., 21, 22

Galenson, E., 30-32, 103, 117, 210
Green, R., 18
Greenacre, P., 16-18

Harlow & Harlow, H. & N., 15
Horney, K., 7, 11-13
Huntington, D., 159

Jacobsen, E., 24-25, 29
Jamison, K., 162
Jessner, L., 21
Johnson, M., 143
Johnson, V., 9, 27-29, 143
Jones, E., 8, 13, 50, 77

Karme, L., 49-50
Keiser, S., 17
Kestenberg, J., 19-22, 143
Kinsey, A., 27
Kleeman, J., 36-39
Klein, M., 14-15
Korner, A., 18
Kramer, S., 32

Lahn, M., 34
Lampl de Groot, J., 14
Lerner, H., 18
Lewis, F.M., 162

Mahler, M., 21, 22-24, 25, 80

Martin, R., 165
Masters, W., 9, 27-29
Miller, R., 31
Money, J., 34-36, 139
Moore, B.E., 9
Moulton, R., 150
Murphy, L., 18

Ovesey, L., 34

Parens, H., 32-33
Pasnau, R., 162
Penney, A., 127
Perriere, K., 22
Person, E., 34, 53-54, 133, 134, 151
Pfefferbaum, B., 161
Polivy, J., 165

Revault D'Allones, C., 21
Ritvo, S., 21

Roberts, W., 165

Roiphe, H., 30-32, 80, 103, 177

Schafer, R., 45-49, 77
Sherfey, M. J., 28, 29
Sloan, D., 165
Stern, J., 32
Stoller, R., 33-34, 37, 38
Sunley, R., 166

Thompson, C., 7, 13-14
Torok, M., 175

Valenstein, A., 159
Vogel, S., 31

Warner, G.M., 34, 66, 94-95, 159
Weigert, E., 21
Wellisch, D., 162
Winnicott, D. W., 22, 147
Witkin, M.H., 162

Zussman & Zussman, L. & S., 166

Subject Index

Abortion, 152-155, 224
  case report, 224
  oedipal conflict and separation-individuation and, 152-155
Abstract thinking, 178
Acting out, 277
Acting up, 277
Adolescence, 111-116, 277
  anorexia nervosa, in, 114-115
  ego ideal in, 42-43
  fantasies in, 121-132, see also Masturbation fantasies
  heterosexual love object in, establishment of relationship with, 113-114
  masturbation fantasies in, 121-132; see also Masturbation fantasies
  menstruation in, 112-113
  pathology of, 114-116
  Ritvo on, 41-43
  separation-individuation problem in, 115-116
  sexual behavior in, 42
  wish for baby in, 269-276
Adoption, giving child up for, 248
Affect, 277
Amenorrhea, 142
Anal awareness, 30
Anal penetration
  as masturbation method, 118-119
  masturbation fantasy of, 124
Anal phase, 278
Anamnesis, 278
Anatomical difference between sexes, discovery of, see Genital awareness
"Anatomy is destiny", 13
Anorexia nervosa, 114-115, 278
  amenorrhea and, 142
  case report, 263-269

Anxiety, 278
Asceticism, 279
Attendance in psychoanalysis, 189
Attractiveness/physical appearance, 192, 193

Baby, wish for, 143; see also Pregnancy
  in adolescent girl, 269-276
  case report, 232-238
  death of mother and, 232-238
  Kestenberg on, 20-21
  oedipal considerations in, 96-103
Birth, fantasies of, 193
Body image, 30, 279
  in adolescence, 111
  repair of perception, 107
  severe trauma and, 82-88
Breast cancer/mastectomy, 161-165; see also Mastectomy
Breast development, early, 138
Breastfeeding/nursing, 164-165

Case reports, 186-276
  anorexia nervosa, 263-269
  death of mother, 232-238
  depression, 186-196
  father as maternal object, 250-263
  female supervisory assistance, 223-232
  homosexual behavior, 196-204
  hypochondriasis, 186-196
  loss, early, 223-232
  male analyst, 223-232
  maternal abandonment, 269-276
  maternal invasiveness, 263-269
  minimal brain damage, 212-223
  misdiagnosis of woman appearing helpless, depressed and suicidal, 204-212

paranoia, 186-198
parental intercourse, repeated wit-
    nessing of, 238-250
paternal seductiveness, 69-276
penis envy, 186-189, 208-209
physical disability, 212-223
severe early trauma, 223-232
sexual promiscuity, 238-250
wish for baby, 232-238, 269-276
Castration, fear of/castration anxiety,
    3, 279; see also Illusory penis
fear of maternal loss and, 70-73
girl's awareness of, 32
Greenacre on, 16
Horney on, 11
in male, 11
menstruation and, 141-142
morality and, 46
Castration shock, 80
severe trauma and, 82-88
Catharsis, 279
Cathartic method, 1
Character, 279
Character disorder, 279
Chauvinistic fathers, 177
Childrearing, full-time work and, 149-
    150
Children, desire for, 151; see also
    Baby, wish for
Clitoris, 9, 10, 105
Masters and Johnson on, 28
masturbation and, 106, 210
orgasm and, 28, 29
Cognitive function, 178
Collaboration of women psychiatrists,
    151-152
Competition, fear of, 54
Compulsion, 279
Conflicts, 280
"Consolation prize" theory, 143
Core gender identity, 79, 280
definition of, 33
Kleeman on, 37
Counterphobia, 280
Countertransference, 5, 280
in pregnancy, 146-147
problems in, case report of, 256
Cultural experience, influence of, 12

Daughter as narcissistic extension of
    self, 148
Daughter-in-law, 160
Death
of father, 225, 227
of mother, 92-94, 232-238
Defenses, 280
Denial, 280
Depersonalization, 280-281
Desire for children, 151; see also
    Baby, wish for
Depressed father, 177
Depression
case report, 186-196, 204-212
hysterectomy and, 165-166, 167,
    168
misdiagnosed, 204-212
Derealization, 281
Development in first year of life, 14
Direct observation, see Research and
    direct observation
Disability, oedipal considerations in,
    94-96
Displacement, 281
Disruptive behavior in psychoanaly-
    sis, 189
Dreams, 281
Dysmenorrhea, 141

Ego, 47, 178, 281
Ego ideal, 4-5, 173-175, 281-282
in adolescence, 42-43
of boys, 174-175
Ego development, morality and, 47
Ego splitting, 282
Ejaculation, female, fantasy of, 131-
    132
Empathy, 282
Empty nest syndrome, 157, 176

Fantasy/fantasies, 282
of birth, 193
of illusory penis, 103-104
of impregnating mother, 106
in latency, 126-127
masturbation, 121-132; see also
    Masturbation fantasies
oedipal, 103-104, 106

of pregnancy, 272
preoedipal, 54-70; see also Preoe-
    dipal reparative fantasies
Father
    death of, 225-227
    as maternal object, 250-263
    narcissistic daughters and person-
        ality of, 177
    superego of daughter and relation-
        ship to, 171-172
Fear of competition, 54
Fear of loss of love, 54
Fear of men, 228
Fear of women, men's, 11
Feeling of empty inner space, 19-20
Fellatio fantasies, 122
Female analyst, 183-186; see also
    Treatment of women by women
Female development
    oedipal considerations, see Oedipal
        consideration
    preoedipal considerations, see
        Preoedipal considerations
Female genitalia
    awareness of, see Genital aware-
        ness
    vagueness of, 80-81
Female psychology, historical review
    of, see Historical review of fe-
    male psychology
Female supervisory assistance, 223-
    232
Feminine sexuality, see Sexuality,
    feminine
Feminine traits, Deutsch on, 8-9; see
    also Femininity
Femininity; see also Gender identity
    Blum on, 41
    Deutsch on, 8-9
    Freud on, 38, 48
    Jones on, 13
    masochism and, 41
    menstruation and, 141-142
    penis envy and, 41
    primary, 33-34, 53
Femme fatale fantasy, 131
Fixation, 282
Freud's contemporaries, 6, 7, 8

Bonaparte, 5, 6, 7, 10-11
Deutsch, 5, 7, 8-10, 11-14
Greenacre, 16-18
Horney, 7, 11-13
Jacobsen, 24-25
Jones, 8, 13
Klein, 14-15
Freudian theory, historical review of,
    1-8
    summary of, 7-8
Frigidity
    Bonaparte on, 10
    definition of, 117
    Deutsch on treatment of, 9-10

Gender identity, 34; see also Core
    gender identity; Femininity
    aberrations of, 34-36
    feminine, 35
    Freud on, 38
    learning and 36-39
Gender of therapist, 181-186
Generativity, 151
Genital awareness, 2, 16, 31, 79-80,
    106
    in boys, 18
    Greenacre on, 16, 17-18
Genital development, comparison of
    girls and boys, 31
Genital phase, early, 30
Genitalia, female; see Female geni-
    talia
Genetically-aberrant children, 34-36
Good enough mothering, 148-149,
    282
Grandmotherhood, 158-160
Guilt, 282

Handling of girls and boys, 18, 53
Hatred of women, men's, 11
Helpless women, case report of, 204-
    212
Heterosexual adjustment, masturba-
    tion and, 117, 133
Heterosexual love object, 113-114
Historical review of female psychol-
    ogy, 1-25
    Freud, 1-3

Freud's contemporaries, 5-14; *see also* Freud's contemporaries
Greenacre, 16-18
Jacobson, 24-25
Kestenberg, 19-22
later contribution from psychoanalysis, 15-25; *see also* Psychoanalysis
Mahler, 21, 22-24, 25
Holding environment, 283
Homosexual anxiety, case report of, 271, 272
Homosexual behavior
case report of, 196-204
in latency girls, 110
Homosexual transference, 257
Homosexuality, 3
in women, 6-7
Hormonally-aberrant children, 34-36
Hypnosis, 1
Hypochondriasis, case report of, 186-196
Hysterectomy, 165-169
depression and, 165-166, 167, 168
Hysterical features, 45

Id, 283
Ideal mother, 41
Identification, 283
Jacobson on, 24-25
Illusory penis, fantasy of, 57-62, 103-104, 283; *see also* Castration anxiety
Incest taboo, 12
Incestuous wishes, 126, 259
Infantile sexuality, theory of, 2
Inferiority of women, socioeconomic, 13-14
Insight, 283
Intellectualization, 283
Internalization, 283
Interpretation, 283
Introjection, 283-284
Isolation of affect, 284

Kinsey report, 27, 28

Latency, 109-111, 284

Clower and Blum on, 39-41
dreams and daydreams of, 110
fantasy in, 110
femininity and masochism in, 41
masturbation in, 39-40, 109-110
masturbation fantasies in, 126-127
superego in, 40-41, 109
Learning and gender identity, 36-39
Learning disability, case report, 212-223
Loss; *see also* Loss of love
case of early severe, 223-232
of child, 248
of mother, *see* Maternal loss
Loss of love
fear of, 54
morality and, 46

Male analyst, 181-183, 223-232
case report, 223-232
Marital function after mastectomy, 162
Masochism, 175-177, 284
Blum on, 41
Bonaparte on, 10
Deutsch on, 8-9
femininity and, 41
Freud on, 8
Kestenberg on, 20
orgasm and, 176
separation from mother and, 176-177
Thompson on, 13, 14
Masochistic features, 123-124
Mastectomy, 161-165
marital and sexual functioning after, 162
sexual desirability after, 162-163
Masturbation, 284; *see also* Masturbation fantasies; Masturbation methods
in boys, 38-39
case report, 244
clitoral, 106, 120
Freud on, 3, 109-110
heterosexual adjustment and, 117, 133
in infancy, 117
Kinsey on, 27, 28

Kleeman on, 38
in latency, 39-40
patients who have never, 121
postoedipal, 116-136
vibrator, 116, 120
Masturbation fantasies, 121-132
adult, 127-132
anal penetration, 124
animal fantasies, 131
being in male role, 124-125
being watched, 128
case report, 257
commonest adult female, 127-132
fellatio fantasies, 122
femme fatale fantasy, 131
group fantasies, 130
machine fantasies, 130-131
masochistic fantasies, 123-124
in oedipal phase, 125-126
oral gratification, 122
prostitution fantasy, 128-130
rape fantasy, 128
sadomasochistic fantasies, 122-123
seduction scene, 127-128
stranger fantasy, 130
Masturbation methods, 117-121
clitoral stimulation, 106, 120
in infancy, 117
insertion of objects into anus, 118-119
insertion of objects into vagina, 120
mounting behavior, 118
rubbing, 117-118
threat to use of hands and, 118
two zone stimulation, 120
use of books, movies or pictures, 120-121
use of water, 119
vibrators, 116, 120
Maternal abandonment
case report, 228
wish for baby in adolescent girl and, 269-276
Maternal invasiveness and anorexia nervosa, 263-269
Maternal loss
castration anxiety and fear of, 70-73

death of mother, 92-94, 232-238
penis envy and fear of, 73-77
Maternal transference, case report, 232
Maternalization of father, fantasy of, 65-70
Men's fear and hate of women, 11
Menometrorrhagia, 141
Menopause, 156-158
Menstruation, 136-142
in adolescence, 112-113
amenorrhea, 142
ambivalent attitudes to, 139
castration and, 141-142
dysmenorrhea, 141
early development, 138
femininity and, 141-142
first exposure to, 136-137
irregular, 141
learning about, 138
menometrorrhagia, 141
premenstrual irritability, 139-141
Metapsychological considerations in theory of female sexuality, 45-52
Karme on, 49-50
Schafer on, 45-49
summary and conclusions, 50-52
Mind, Freud's model of, 4
Minimal brain damage, case report, 212-223
Morality
Freud on, 45-47
men and women compared, 45-46
Mother
death of, see Death of mother
good enough mother, 148-149, 282
preoedipal, longing for, 253
separation from, 88-94; see also Separation-individuation
working, 149-150
Mother-child relationship
handling, 18, 53
Mahler on, 22-23
practicing subphase proper, 23
phase one/autistic, 22-23
rapprochement subphase, 23
separation-individuation phase, 23
third year of life, 24

Mother-daughter-in-law relationship, 160
Mother-infant symbiosis and transsexualism, 34
Motherhood, 147-152
case report, 260
Kestenberg on, 21-22
Mothering
daughter as narcissistic extension of self, 148
good enough, 148-149, 282
Mutilating experiences, 161-169
hysterectomy, 165-169; see also Hysterectomy
mastectomy, 161-165; see also Mastectomy

Narcissism, 177-178, 284
father's personality and daughter's, 177
Thompson on, 13
Nature versus nurture argument, 15
Nursing/breastfeeding, 164-165

Object relations, 284
Obsession, 284
Obsessional features, 46
Oedipal considerations, 79-107, 284-285; see also Separation-individuation and oedipal conflict
in boy, 2-3
female genitalia, vagueness of, 80-81
in girls, 3, 4
Greenacre on, 16-17
masturbation fantasies and, 125-126
pathways to conflict, 32, 33
penis envy and, 104-105
physical disability and, 94-96
physical illness and, 94-96
separation from mother and, 88-94
severe trauma and, 82-88
summary and conclusions, 103-107
wish for baby and, 96-103
Oral phase, 285
Orgasm
clitoral vs vaginal, 9, 28, 29, 106
female's capacity for, 28, 29

masochism and, 176
Masters and Johnson on, 28
multiple, 105
simulation of, 133-136
stimulation to achieve, 28
surrender to loss of control in, 134
type of/ clitoral vs vaginal, 9, 28, 29, 106

Parameter, 189, 285
Paranoia, case report, 186-196
Parental intercourse, repeated witnessing of, 238-250
Passivity, Thompson on, 13, 14
Paternal seduction, wish for baby in adolescence and, 269-276
Penis envy, 104-106, 285
Blum on, 41
case report of, 186-196, 208-209
fear of maternal loss and, 73-77
femininity and, 41
Freud on, 104-105
Horney on, 11, 12
Karme on, 49-50
Kestenberg on, 19-22
meanings of, 49-50
oedipal complex and, 104-105
pathological, 195-196
separation-individuation and, 106
universality of, 49
Personality of father, 177
Phallic mother, fantasy of, 55-56
Phallocentric, word, 77
Phallus, fantasy of illusory, 57-62, 103-104, 283
Phobia, 285
Physical disability, case report, 212-223
Physical illness, oedipal considerations, 94-96
Postoedipal considerations, 109-142
adolescence, 111-116; see also Adolescence
masturbation, 116-136; see also Masturbation
menstruation, 136-142; see also Menstruation
simulation of orgasm, 133-136
special issues, 116-141

Pregnancy, 143-147; *see also* Baby, wish for
countertransference and, 146-147
Freud on wish for, 7-8
as integrating force, 21-22
Kestenberg on, 20-21
oedipal guilt and separation-individuation worked through in, 145-146
physical complaints in, 144-145
Premenstrual irritability, 139-141
Preoedipal considerations, 53-77
castration anxiety related to fear of maternal loss, 70-73
penis envy and fear of maternal loss, 73-77
Preoedipal mother, longing for, 253
Preoedipal reparative fantasies, 55-70
illusory phallus, 57-62, 103-104, 283
maternalization of father, 65-70
phallic mother, 55-56
vagina dentata, 62-64
Prephallic development, 47-48
Primary process, 285-286
Projection, 286
Projective identification, 286
Promiscuity, case report, 238-250, 258
Prostitution fantasy, 128-130
Psychic structure of women, 171-179
ego, 178
ego ideal, 173-175
masochism, 175-177
narcissism, 177-178
superego, 171-173
Psychoanalysis, *see also* Historical review of female psychology
Freud's contribution, 1-8
Freud's female contemporaries, 5-15; *see also* Freud's contemporaries
late contribution from, 15-25
Greenacre, 16-18
Jacobson, 24-25
Kestenberg, 19-22
Mahler, 21, 22-24, 25
rules as condition for, 189-190
Psychosis, 286

Rape fantasy, 128
Rapprochement, 286-287
Rationalization, 287
Reaction formation, 287
Reconstruction, 287
Regression in the service of the ego, 287
Reparative fantasy
oedipal, illusory penis, 103-104
preoedipal, *see* Preoedipal reparative fantasies
Repression, 228
Research and direct observation, 27-43
adult studies, 27-29
child studies, 28-39
Galenson and Roiphe, 30-32
Kinsey, 27
Kleeman, 36-39
on latency, 39-41
Masters and Johnson, 27-29
Money and Erhardt, 34-36
Parens, 32-33
Sherfey, 28, 29
Stoller, 33-34, 37, 38
Resistance, 288
Romance fantasy, 110, 126-127

Sadism, 175, 288
Sadomasochistic fantasies, 122-123
Screen memory
case report, 245-246
definition of, 288
Seduction fantasies, 127-128
Seductive fathers, 177
Seductive parent, 177, 269-276
Self, 288
Self-representation, 288
Separation anxiety, 288-289
Separation from mother, 88-94; *see also* Separation-individuation
Separation-individuation, 23, 79-80, 88-94, 289; *see also* Separation-individuation and oedipal conflict
adolescent problem with, 115-116
Deutsch on, 8
masochism and, 176-177
penis envy and, 106
Separation-individuation and oedipal

conflict, 143-160
abortion and, 152-155
grandmotherhood and, 158-160
menopause and, 156-158
motherhood and, 147-152
pregnancy and, 143-147
stillbirth and, 155-156
Sex of object choice, 3
Sex reassignment, 35-36
Sex roles, Klein on, 14, 15
Sexual desirability after mastectomy,
    162-163
Sexual function after mastectomy, 162
Sexual identity, early, 31; see also
    Core gender identity; Gender
    identity
Sexual organs, female, 9
Sexual urge/drive
Bonaparte on, 10-11
strength of, 28
Sexual promiscuity, case report, 238-
    250, 258
Sexuality, female
active vs passive, 27
Freud on, 6-7
Horney on, 11
metapsychological considerations in,
    see Metapsychological consid-
    erations in theory of female
    sexuality
nature versus nurture argument on,
    15
Socioeconomic inferiority of women,
    13-14
Somatic symptoms, 289
Splitting, 289
Stillbirth, 155-156
Sublimation, 289
Successful woman, symptom-free, 179
Suicide, case report of, 204-212, 267
Superego (conscience), 4, 109, 289-
    290
of boys, 172
father-daughter relationship and,
    171-172
introjection of harsh, 109
in latency, formation of, 40-41

morality and, 46-47
of women, 171, 173
Symbiotic phase, 290
Symbolization, 290
Symptom, 290
Symptom-free successful woman, 179

Taboos, 12
Therapeutic alliance, 290-291
Therapist's gender, 181-186
Transference, 5, 291
Transference neurosis, 291
Transitional objects, 291
Transsexualism
female, 34
male, 34
Trauma
body image and, 82-88
case of early severe, 223-234
Treatment of women by women, 181-
    276; see also Case reports
longing for preoedipal mother and,
    253
therapist's gender, 181-186

Unconscious, 291
Undoing, 291-292
Urinary awareness, 30-31

Vagina
awareness of, 2, 16; see also Gen-
    ital awareness
orgasms and clitoris and, 9, 28, 29,
    106
Vagina dentata, fantasy of, 62-64
Vibrators, 116, 120

Wish
incestuous, 126
to have baby, see Baby, wish for
Women psychiatrists, 183-186
collaboration of, 151-152
treatment by, see Treatment of
    women by women
Working mothers, 149-150
Working through, 292